Communications
in Computer and Information Science

2866

Series Editors

Gang Li, *School of Information Technology, Deakin University, Burwood, VIC, Australia*

Joaquim Filipe, *Polytechnic Institute of Setúbal, Setúbal, Portugal*

Zhiwei Xu, *Chinese Academy of Sciences, Beijing, China*

Rationale

The CCIS series is devoted to the publication of proceedings of computer science conferences. Its aim is to efficiently disseminate original research results in informatics in printed and electronic form. While the focus is on publication of peer-reviewed full papers presenting mature work, inclusion of reviewed short papers reporting on work in progress is welcome, too. Besides globally relevant meetings with internationally representative program committees guaranteeing a strict peer-reviewing and paper selection process, conferences run by societies or of high regional or national relevance are also considered for publication.

Topics

The topical scope of CCIS spans the entire spectrum of informatics ranging from foundational topics in the theory of computing to information and communications science and technology and a broad variety of interdisciplinary application fields.

Information for Volume Editors and Authors

Publication in CCIS is free of charge. No royalties are paid, however, we offer registered conference participants temporary free access to the online version of the conference proceedings on SpringerLink (http://link.springer.com) by means of an http referrer from the conference website and/or a number of complimentary printed copies, as specified in the official acceptance email of the event.

CCIS proceedings can be published in time for distribution at conferences or as post-proceedings, and delivered in the form of printed books and/or electronically as USBs and/or e-content licenses for accessing proceedings at SpringerLink. Furthermore, CCIS proceedings are included in the CCIS electronic book series hosted in the SpringerLink digital library at http://link.springer.com/bookseries/7899. Conferences publishing in CCIS are allowed to use our online conference service (Meteor) for managing the whole proceedings lifecycle (from submission and reviewing to preparing for publication) free of charge.

Publication process

The language of publication is exclusively English. Authors publishing in CCIS have to sign the Springer CCIS copyright transfer form, however, they are free to use their material published in CCIS for substantially changed, more elaborate subsequent publications elsewhere. For the preparation of the camera-ready papers/files, authors have to strictly adhere to the Springer CCIS Authors' Instructions and are strongly encouraged to use the CCIS LaTeX style files or templates.

Abstracting/Indexing

CCIS is abstracted/indexed in DBLP, Google Scholar, EI-Compendex, Mathematical Reviews, SCImago, Scopus. CCIS volumes are also submitted for the inclusion in ISI Proceedings.

How to start

To start the evaluation of your proposal for inclusion in the CCIS series, please send an e-mail to ccis@springer.com

Rajagopal Sridaran · Sajja Priti

Editors

AI & ML - Frontiers in Cross Disciplinary Applications & Case Studies

First International Workshop, AI-FCDAC 2025
Rajkot, Gujarat, India, September 11, 2025
Proceedings

Editors
Rajagopal Sridaran [ID]
Marwadi University
Rajkot, Gujarat, India

Sajja Priti [ID]
Sardar Patel University
Anand, Gujarat, India

ISSN 1865-0929   ISSN 1865-0937 (electronic)
Communications in Computer and Information Science
ISBN 978-3-032-17299-0   ISBN 978-3-032-17300-3 (eBook)
https://doi.org/10.1007/978-3-032-17300-3

This Springer imprint is published by the registered company Springer Nature Switzerland AG
The registered company address is: Gewerbestrasse 11, 6330 Cham, Switzerland

If disposing of this product, please recycle the paper.

Preface

"The journey of a thousand miles begins with one step." – Lao Tzu

We are happy to present the proceedings of the 1st International Workshop on AI & ML Frontiers: Cross-Disciplinary Applications and Case Studies (AI-FCDAC 2025), a new initiative which was part of the 4th International Conference on Advancements in Smart Computing and Information Security (ASCIS 2025). The workshop announced a separate call for papers, inviting original research contributions under the two major tracks, namely, Core AI Technologies and Cross-Disciplinary Applications. We were glad to receive 64 papers and based on open peer reviews by eminent academicians, appear here in the globally recognized Springer CCIS series in Open Access mode. Our sincere thanks to the editorial board of Springer CCIS for providing the publication support.

Each submitted paper underwent 3 peer reviews for the purpose of shortlisting. Our sincere thanks to the Technical Program Committee (TPC) members who were very supportive in the review process.

We thankfully acknowledge the sponsors who contributed generously towards the successful conduct of ASCIS 2025, including *GUJCOST, Samatrix.io, D-Link, K7 International and MNS Technologies*. These collaborations enriched the conference and extended its outreach.

The keynotes addressed several recent technological advancements whereas the hands-on workshops provided practical exposure to the students and participants. We believe that this volume titled "AI-FCDAC 2025 Proceedings" will benefit those seeking research solutions in the fields it covers.

December 2025

Sridaran Rajagopal
Priti Srinivas Sajja

Organization

General Chair

Sridaran Rajagopal   Marwadi University, India

Program Committee Chairs

Sridaran Rajagopal   Marwadi University, India
Priti Sajja   Sardar Patel University, India

Program Committee Co-chair

Divyakant Meva   Marwadi University, India

Steering Committee

Ketanbhai Marwadi   Marwadi University, India
Jitubhai Chandarana   Marwadi University, India
R. B. Jadeja   Marwadi University, India
Sanjeet Singh   Marwadi University, India
Naresh Jadeja   Marwadi University, India
Vinod Kumar Shukla   Amity University, India
Mukesh Prasad   University of Technology Sydney, Australia
Nebojša Bačanin-Džakula   Singidunum University, Serbia
Rohit Thanki   DetMedX, Germany
Prasanna Ranjith Christodoss   Messiah University, USA

Technical Program Committee Chairs

Pratik Shah   IIIT Vadodara, India
Aditya Shastriz   Pandit Deendayal Education University, India
Himanshu Gajera   Pandit Deendayal Education University, India

Monther Tarawneh	Tafila Technical University, Jordan
Shilpa Srivastava	Christ (deemed to be University), India
Chandra Prakash	SVNIT, India
Deepak Kumar Verma	Marwadi University, India

Additional Reviewers

Velumani Thiyagarajan	Vidhya S. Dhamdhere
Delecta Jenifer Rajendren	Derek Asir Muthurajan Caleb
Amit K. Patel	Anant G. Kulkarni
Ashwin R. Dobariya	Charanjeet Singh
Deepak Kumar Verma	Harishchander Anandaram
Himanshu K. Maniar	John T. Abraham
Karuna Nidhi Pandagre	Madhuri M. More
Minal S. Shukla	P. Rizwan Ahmed
Asmita Manna	Avnip Deora
B. Surendiran	Chetan R. Dudhagara
Disha H. Parekh	Dushyantsinh B. Rathod
Nisha Khurana	Prashant Sen
Premkumar Borugadda	Priti Sadaria
Priya Chandran	Rajan Patel
Rajesh Bansode	Ramesh T. Prajapati
Sandip S. Patil	Saraswathi S.
Vijayalakshmi P. S.	G. Charles Babu
Nuzhat Prova	Padma Selvaraj
S. Amutha	S. S. Priscila
Tarannum Bloch	Thirumurugan Shanmugam
Saravanakumar S.	G. Abel Thangaraja
D. R. Medhunhashini	M. Lingaraj
K. Vivekanandan	Nitish Kumar Ojha

Contents

Reliability and Completeness of Metadata Extraction Tools in Image-Based Forensic Analysis

Baysah Guwor[1](✉) iD, Sridaran Rajagopal[2] iD, S. Silvia Priscila[3] iD,
Dharmendrasinh D. Zala[4] iD, Vipulkumar Babubhai Bambhaniya[5] iD,
Kishan Makadiya[6] iD, and Simrin Fathima Syed[7] iD

[1] Faculty of Computer Applications, Marwadi University, Rajkot, India
`baysahguwor.128662@marwadiuniversity.ac.in`
[2] Ganpat University, Mehsana, India
`ed.aqa@ganpatuniversity.ac.in`
[3] Department of Computer Science, Bharath Institute of Higher Education and Research,
Chennai, India
`silviaprisila.cbcs.cs@bharathuniv.ac.in`
[4] Department of Information and Communication Technology, Marwadi University, Rajkot,
India
`dharmendrasinh.zala@marwadieducation.edu.in`
[5] Faculty of Computer Applications, Marwadi University, Rajkot, India
`vipulkumar.bambhaniya@marwadieducation.edu.in`
[6] Department of Computer Engineering, Marwadi University, Rajkot, India
`kishan.makadiya@marwadieducation.edu.in`
[7] Department of CSE-AI, ML, DS, Marwadi University, Rajkot, India
`simrin.syed@marwadieducation.edu.in`

Abstract. Digital images serve as a vital source of evidence in forensic investigations, containing metadata that can reveal timestamps, device characteristics, geolocation details, and editing history. However, this metadata is highly vulnerable to alteration, removal, and degradation during routine handling, thereby creating challenges in maintaining authenticity and evidentiary reliability. This study evaluates the integrity and performance of open-source metadata extraction tools to support more accurate and trustworthy forensic analysis. The research process consisted of two stages. The first stage assessed the forensic soundness of five widely used tools by verifying that metadata extraction did not alter the original files. The second stage examined their accuracy, completeness, and resilience across various image transformations using a custom dataset across 10 metadata fields. The result shows that although all tools preserved evidence integrity, their ability to recover metadata varied considerably, with fragile fields such as Unique Image ID and location information poorly recovered. Among the tested tools, Exif Tool demonstrated the most balanced performance across accuracy (95.8%), completeness (64.3%), and efficiency. This study provides practical guidance for investigators, forensic educators, and tool developers by highlighting the strengths and limitations of these solutions. Its findings support enhanced forensic training and the development of more reliable open-source metadata extraction tools

R. Sridaran and S. Priti (Eds.): AI-FCDAC 2025, CCIS 2866, pp. 1–20, 2026.
https://doi.org/10.1007/978-3-032-17300-3_1

and methodologies to strengthen the admissibility and credibility of image-based digital evidence.

Keywords: Digital Forensics · Image Metadata Reliability · Metadata Extraction Tools · Forensic Analysis · Multimedia Forensics · Forensic Soundness

1   Introduction

1.1   Forensic Significance of Image Metadata

In digital forensics, image metadata serves as a critical source of contextual information that can support or disprove evidence presented in legal investigations. Embedded within digital image files, metadata often contains timestamps, geolocation data, camera make and model, editing history, and other attributes essential to reconstructing events and verifying authenticity [1, 2]. This data can be crucial in determining whether a photograph was taken at a specific time or location, whether it has been altered, or whether it originated from a particular device [3].

Given its evidentiary value, the accuracy and completeness of extracted image metadata are paramount in forensic analysis [4, 5]. However, metadata is inherently fragile as it can be easily manipulated, stripped by social media platforms, or altered during image editing [3, 5, 6]. Thus, the tools used for metadata extraction must be both technically robust and forensically sound, ensuring that the process preserves the integrity of the evidence and is defensible in court. As seen in Fig. 1, using tools that are not forensically sound can result in misinterpretation of the results, causing the evidence to be considered unreliable.

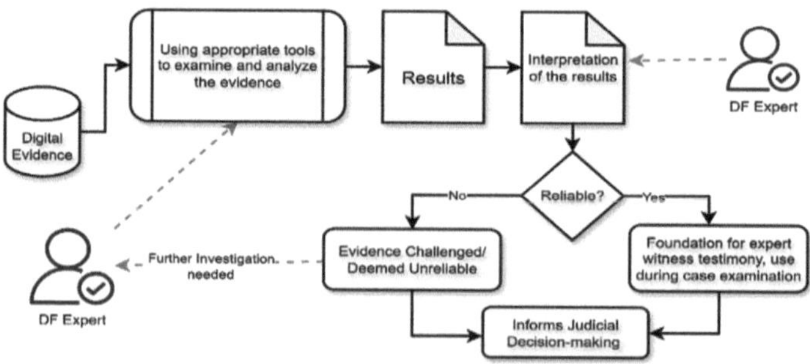

Fig. 1. A typical flow of evidence seizure to judicial decision-making

Beyond technical performance, the legal admissibility of metadata in courts requires that the evidence handling procedures follow established protocols for maintaining the integrity of digital evidence. According to the Federal Rules of Evidence (FRE) [7, 8], specifically Rule 902 (13 & 14), digital evidence must be authenticated through evidence of the integrity of the data. In forensic contexts, this means that the digital evidence must not be altered, and tools used must not alter the original image file during metadata extraction. To ensure the integrity of digital evidence, it is crucial to create forensic backups of original data, employing methods like bit-for-bit duplication and cryptographic hashing, while adhering to established guidelines such as those from NIST and ISO/IEC 27037:2012 [9–11] to maintain the chain of custody (CoC) and authenticity of evidence.

The Daubert Standard and Frye Standard [12, 13] which govern the admissibility of scientific evidence in U.S. courts, require that forensic methods and tools used in legal proceedings be both reliable and well-established. Tools that provide transparent and reproducible results are often preferred in forensic investigations due to their methodological rigor and long-standing use in the field. However, as [14] pointed out, the lack of tool validation for court use is a significant limitation in current forensic research.

The Forensic Tool Validation [15], as recommended by the National Institute of Standards and Technology (NIST), emphasizes the importance of validating the forensic integrity of metadata extraction tools. Nanda Diaz et al. [14] and Albalawi [16] both emphasized the need for tools that maintain forensic soundness and chain of custody to ensure that the metadata extracted from digital images remains admissible in court.

By assessing each tool's ability to preserve metadata integrity and maintain a reliable chain of custody [17], this study attempts to identify which open-source tools produce the most complete and accurate results under forensic conditions, thereby clarifying their suitability for real investigations and legal proceedings.

1.2 Evolution of the Exif Standard

Exif is a standardized metadata format developed by the Japan Electronics and Information Technology Industries Association (JEITA) to store technical information within image and audio files, primarily JPEG, TIFF, and WAV formats [2, 18]. Introduced in 1995, Exif enables digital cameras and imaging devices to embed a variety of data into captured media, enhancing interoperability and facilitating image management across different platforms and applications [19]. The Exif standard encompasses a wide range of metadata, including: Camera Information such as the make and model, Image Settings and Timestamps, indicating when the photo was taken, GPS coordinates, among others [18]. Fig. 1 illustrates a high-level view of the metadata embedding process.

Over the years, the Exif standard has undergone several revisions to accommodate advancements in imaging technology and user needs.

Version 2.0: Introduced support for the sRGB color space and compressed thumbnails. Version 2.2 added support for Adobe RGB color space and included provisions for audio annotations [20]. Version 2.3: Enhanced GPS support and added tags for lens information. Version 3.0, released in 2023, introduced support for UTF-8 encoding, allowing for a broader range of character sets in metadata [21].

While several proprietary forensic suites offer metadata analysis, open-source tools have become increasingly popular due to their accessibility, transparency, and flexibility. Digital investigators and researchers alike frequently employ tools such as Exif Tool and Image Magick.

Existing documentation for these tools mainly addresses functionality and usage, not forensic applicability. It often lacks standardized testing, systematic comparison of extraction accuracy, and evaluation of metadata manipulation handling. This study

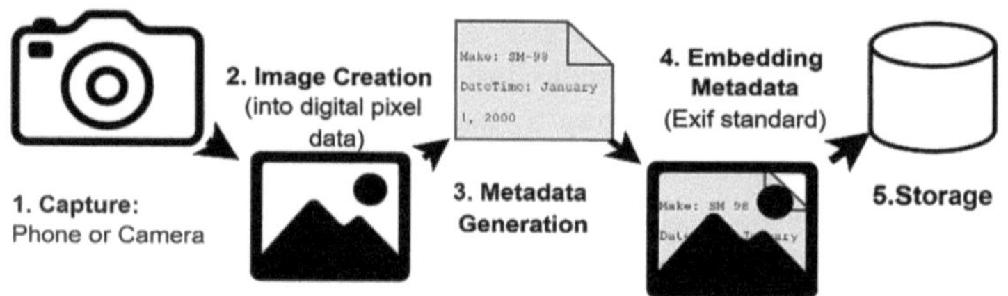

Fig. 2. High-level view of metadata embedding process

contributes to solving these gaps by critically evaluating the forensic reliability of widely used open-source tools under realistic scenarios.

1.3   Research Gap

Although digital images are widely acknowledged as a valuable source of forensic evidence, existing metadata extraction tools often demonstrate inconsistencies in capturing complete and reliable information. While prior studies have explored metadata analysis, limited attention has been given to a systematic evaluation of the reliability and completeness of widely used open-source metadata extraction tools. The lack of a comprehensive assessment exposes investigators to risks of partial or misleading metadata, which in turn can weaken the credibility and admissibility of forensic findings in legal proceedings.

1.4   Contribution/Scope of this Paper

This paper contributes to existing knowledge by conducting a comprehensive evaluation of five (5) metadata extraction tools in image-based forensic analysis. Specifically, it assesses their reliability in accurately retrieving metadata attributes (such as timestamps, geolocation, device information, and editing history) and examines their completeness in preserving contextual details critical for investigation. By highlighting the strengths and limitations of these tools, the study contributes practical insights for forensic practitioners, promotes the development of more robust solutions, and strengthens the integrity of digital evidence in judicial processes. The following research questions are addressed in this research:

- RQ1: To what extent do open-source image metadata extraction tools accurately extract metadata?
- RQ2: How does image transformation (editing, converting, compressing) affect the extraction, integrity, and completeness of image metadata?
- RQ3: Do open-source tools ensure that image metadata extraction processes maintain forensic soundness?
- RQ4: Which open-source tools provide the best balance of accuracy, success rate, and extraction time?
- RQ5: What are the limitations of open-source image metadata tools?

2 Related Works

This section reviews relevant literature to provide a comprehensive understanding of the current research landscape in image metadata analysis tools, highlighting the key contributions made by previous studies as well as identifying their limitations and gaps that still need to be addressed. A summary of previous work is presented in Table 1.

Nanda Diaz Arizona et al. [14] highlighted the potential of forensic metadata analysis using metadata-extractor tools to aid digital investigations. Their work emphasized the ability of metadata to uncover data manipulation, especially in cybercrime contexts.

Similarly, Abdullah Golam and Umar Albalawi [16] investigated the dual role of image metadata in forensics and privacy. In their research, the authors examined how various social media platforms handle EXIF metadata in uploaded images, highlighting both forensic value and privacy concerns. Their study emphasized the role of metadata in timeline reconstruction, authenticity verification, and evidentiary support. The research proposes an encryption-decryption framework thatoffers a proactive approach to protecting sensitive metadata.

In the work of Eman Daraghmi and Ahmed Hamoudi [22], metadata extraction from Android smartphone photos was explored, specifically targeting geo-location data. Although their research effectively demonstrated forensic value in criminal case support, it lacked attention to multi-source metadata correlation in larger investigative systems.

Zhanagul Balkibayeva [23], provided procedural overviews for extracting metadata from image formats such as JPEG and TIFF. The research detailed technical steps in extracting EXIF data for evidentiary use, including camera settings and GPS information.

More recently, Soni [6] explored the forensic value of Exif data through an analytical evaluation of metadata integrity across different image transfer methods, such as email, cloud storage, and social media platforms. The findings showed that significant metadata degradation or alteration occurs during these transfers, especially when platforms automatically compress or reformat images. The study highlighted that even when images remain visually unchanged, their metadata integrity is often compromised, raising concerns about the evidentiary reliability of images obtained from online platforms. While this work established the importance of considering transfer-induced metadata loss, it was primarily limited to the transmission dimension of metadata handling and did not evaluate tool-level differences or performance under editing and conversion scenarios.

Although existing studies have demonstrated the utility of metadata extraction in various scenarios, there remains a lack of comparative assessments of tools under real-world conditions. This study addresses that gap by evaluating widely used open-source metadata extractors across multiple transformation scenarios, including edited, compressed, converted, and transferred images, thereby contributing a practical understanding of their forensic strengths, limitations, and implications for evidentiary trustworthiness.

Although existing studies have demonstrated the utility of metadata extraction in various scenarios, there remains a lack of comparative assessment of tools under real-world conditions. This study addresses that gap by evaluating widely used open-source metadata extractors, thereby contributing to a more practical understanding of their forensic strengths, limitations, and implications for evidentiary trustworthiness.

Table 1. Summary of previous work

Study	Research Objectives	Tools Used	Methodology
[14]	Investigating metadata analysis for cybercrime cases	Metadata-Extractor	Case study approach with focus on metadata in digital forensics.
[16]	Exploring image metadata's role in privacy and forensic investigations	A framework for encrypting and decrypting metadata	Surveyed metadata extraction on smartphone images, focusing on privacy concerns.
[22]	Metadata extraction from Android device images	HxD Hex Editor tool	Focused on geo-location data extraction from Android photos for criminal cases.
[23]	Examines procedures for extracting and analyzing metadata for evidentiary purposes in civil proceedings	None	Reviews literature, legal cases, and forensic methods to examine metadata analysis across digital domains such as file systems, emails, browsers, mobile devices, cloud storage, and social media
[6]	Analytical evaluation of metadata integrity across image transfer methods	Magnet AXIOM, XRY, FTK, ExifTool	Experimental study measuring metadata integrity loss across transfer channels (email, cloud, social media)
Our Study	Comparative evaluation of metadata extraction tools across image transformation types for forensic use	Exif Tool, Image Magick, digiKam, Irfan View, and Xn View MP	Practical evaluation of metadata extraction tools across various image transformation types (original, edited, converted, downloaded), with a focus on 10 specific metadata fields

3   Methodology

This section outlines the systematic approach followed to evaluate the forensic reliability and performance of the selected image metadata extraction tools. The methodology encompasses the selection of the tools, preparation of a controlled dataset simulating real-world scenarios, the metadata extraction process, and the evaluation procedure used to measure tool effectiveness. The aim is to ensure consistency, reproducibility, and relevance to practical forensic applications. The methodological flow includes:

- Tool selection
- Image acquisition
- Dataset preparation
- Metadata extraction
- Evaluation & analysis
- Result & conclusion

3.1 Selection Criteria for Tools

To ensure a representative and meaningful evaluation, five popular tools as seen Table 2 were selected based on the following criteria:

- Availability: All tools are freely available either under the open-source licenses or freely accessible for forensic analysts, researchers, and educators.
- Support for image metadata formats: Tools must support extraction (and in some cases modification or removal) of common image metadata like EXIF, IPTC, and XMP.
- Image type support: support for major picture and graphics formats (e.g. JPEG, TIFF, PNG, GIF etc)
- Cross-platform compatibility: Preference was given to tools compatible with major operating systems (Windows, Linux, mac OS).
- Usage and support: Each tool is either widely used, discussed, or has an active community support.

Table 2. The five Tools evaluated in this study

Tool	Features	Latest Version	Interface	OS support		
				Win	Lix	Mac
ExifTool [24]	Detailed EXIF/IPTC/XMP extraction, Batch processing, Output in CSV/JSON	13.30	CLI	☑	☑	☑
digiKam [25]	Photo organizer and manager, Full EXIF/IPTC/XMP metadata support, Batch editing	8.6.0	GUI	☑	☑	☑
XnView MP [26]	Image viewer with metadata extraction, Batch processing, Supports many formats	1.9.2	GUI	☑	☑	☑

(continued)

Table 2. (*continued*)

Tool	Features	Latest Version	Interface	OS support		
				Win	Lix	Mac
IrfanView [27]	Lightweight image viewer, Metadata viewer and editor plugins, Batch conversion	4.72	GUI	☑		
ImageMagick [28]	Basic metadata read, Format conversion, Image manipulation tools	7.1.1-47	CLI	☑	☑	☑

3.2 Dataset preparation and metadata fields analyzed

Image acquisition and data set preparation: A custom dataset comprising 80 images was generated to simulate real-world digital forensic scenarios. The images were generated using the following procedure:

- Image Acquisition: The image acquisition phase involved capturing photos from diverse smartphones under controlled conditions and hashing them to ensure authenticity and chain of custody. A total of twenty (20) original photographs were captured from ten (10) different smartphones to ensure diversity in device metadata.
- Integrity Assurance: Immediately after capture, each original image was backed up, and a cryptographic hash was computed and recorded to establish a reference for integrity verification.
- Dataset creation: A copy of each original image was edited using Paint Tool to simulate basic content modification. A separate copy was converted from JPEG to PNG format, simulating a change in file encoding. Another copy was sent and downloaded via WhatsApp, introducing compression and potential metadata alteration. After this process, a total of 80 images were included in the dataset.
- Categorization and Logging: All images were systematically categorized. Hashes were recalculated and stored at each stage to maintain traceability and verify data integrity during testing.

In addition to image acquisition and dataset preparation, a chain of custody protocol was followed to ensure evidentiary reliability [29, 30]. Each image was assigned a unique identifier and recorded in an evidence log, documenting acquisition time, device used, transformations performed, and storage location. All handling steps were documented in chronological order, consistent with forensic best practices, to maintain transparency and accountability.

Table 3. Ten (10) metadata fields analyzed.

#	Metadata Field	Description
1	Date Time Original	Primary timestamp of when the photo was taken.
2	Make / Model	Device identification; useful for matching with known hardware.
3	Image Unique ID	Unique ID assigned by the camera; aids in identifying original images.
4	GPS Data	Normally critical for geolocation.
5	Software	The firmware or editing software used can expose whether the image was altered or post-processed.
6	Create Date	Helps verify whether the image has been edited post-capture.
7	File Size	Shows the dimensions of the image in pixels, combining Image Width and Image Height.
8	File Modify Date	Local file system date can help detect tampering or post-transfer edits.
9	File Type	May preserve original, unedited preview; helpful in detecting changes.
10	Exif version	A 4-byte tag in image metadata indicating the Exif standard version used

3.3 Evaluation Procedure

To ensure consistency across the evaluation, all tools were installed on the same system, a Windows 11 Pro environment. Each tool operated with its default configuration to reflect typical, real-world usage scenarios.

Each image in the dataset was processed individually against the ten (10) metadata fields shown in Table 3. The resulting output from each tool was saved in a file for further analysis.

Evaluation metrics included the following: 1. The ability to extract the 10 metadata fields: This refers to the number and types of metadata fields each tool was able to extract. 2. Accuracy of metadata: This measures if expected fields, such as camera make/model and timestamps, were correctly retrieved with accurate data. 3. Extraction time: This measures the average time taken for each tool to successfully extract the metadata.

As seen in Fig. 3, the forensic tool receives the digital image as input, aiming to produce a complete and reliable dataset. However, these tools may sometimes yield incomplete results, such as missing tags like GPS data, or unreliable outputs, such as misinterpreted values like incorrect timestamps, which can significantly undermine their forensic usefulness. To assess the extraction time of each metadata extraction tool, we developed a batch testing application using Python. This application automates the batch processing of image files and records the time each tool takes to extract metadata, ensuring consistency and reproducibility across all evaluated tools.

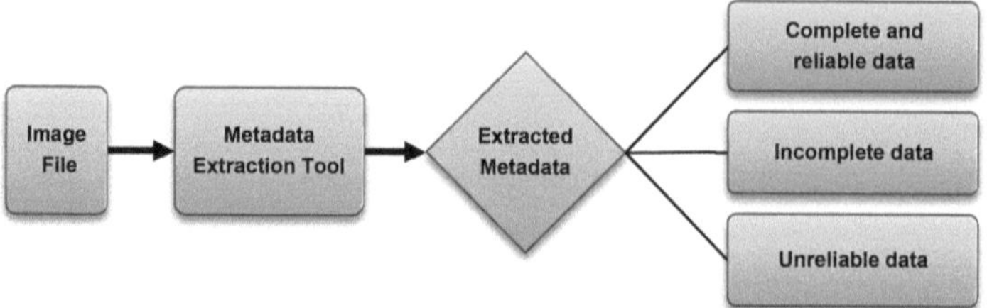

Fig. 3. Input-output model of the metadata extraction process

For comparison and validation, metadata extracted by each tool was cross-validated against a manual validation procedure for critical metadata fields. Finally, image integrity was verified by rechecking hashes after analysis to ensure no modifications had occurred.

The evaluation focused on ten (10) metadata fields as seen in Table 3. This is because these are the most commonly encountered and forensically relevant attributes in digital investigations. They include core information, such as timestamps, device details, GPS coordinates, and editing history, which are frequently examined to establish the authenticity, provenance, and context of digital images in legal proceedings. Limiting the evaluation to these fields allows for a more focused and manageable comparative analysis across tools while ensuring that the results remain directly applicable to forensic practice.

4   Results and Discussion

This section presents a comparative analysis of the five metadata extraction tools based on the ten selected metadata fields, as shown in Table 3, across the dataset containing 80 images. The evaluation metrics included the success rate (*number of extracted metadata fields ÷ total number of metadata fields × 100*), accuracy (*number of accurate extracted metadata fields ÷ total number of extracted metadata fields × 100*), and performance (*time taken by each tool to extract metadata*). Figure 4 shows a sample snapshot of extracted metadata from SM-A135F, a Samsung-based Android phone. Figs. 5–7 illustrate the overall comparison of the five metadata extraction tools.

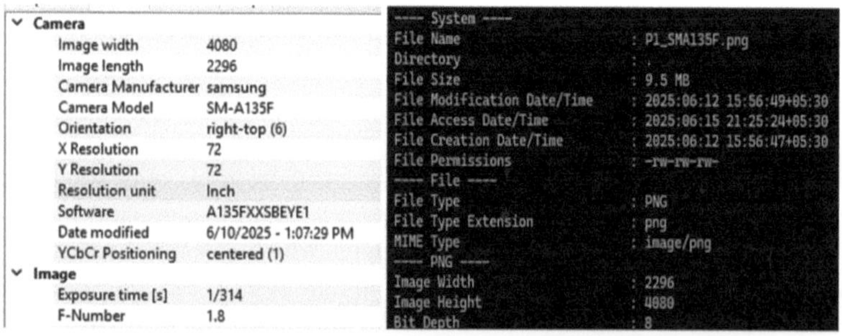

Fig. 4. Sample of metadata extracted from a Samsung device

4.1 Analysis of Individual Tools

Exif Tool demonstrated the highest overall success rate (64.3%) and strong accuracy (95.8%), making it the most balanced performer. It consistently extracted commonly preserved metadata such as Create Date, Image Size, File Modify Date, File Type, and Exif Version, achieving full accuracy across these fields. Even when extracting fragile metadata like Image Unique ID, Exif Tool correctly parsed the field whenever it was present. Its performance advantage is strengthened by the fastest extraction time (0.019 s), making it especially suitable for large-scale or automated forensic workflows. The detailed analysis result can be seen in Table 4.

Irfan View achieved high accuracy across most extracted fields but showed the lowest success rate (44.5%) among all tools, as shown in Table 5. It frequently failed to retrieve metadata from critical fields such as Image Unique ID, Location information, and Software tag, significantly limiting its metadata completeness. Although accurate, the reduced coverage diminishes its reliability in forensic contexts. Its extraction time (3.561 s) was slower than other tools, further limiting its suitability for time-sensitive analyses.

Table 4. ExifTool Analysis Result

Metadata	Extracted	Accurate	Success Rate	Accuracy
Original Creation Date	58	58	72.5%	100%
Model/Make	46	46	57.5%	100%
Image Unique ID	2	2	2.5%	100%
Location Information	24	14	30%	58.3%
Software tag	14	14	17.5%	100%
Create Date	80	80	100%	100%
Image Size	80	80	100%	100%
File Modify Date	80	80	100%	100%
File Type	80	80	100%	100%
Exif Version	50	50	62.5%	100%

Table 5. IrFan analysis result

Metadata	Extracted	Accurate	Succes Rate	Accuracy
Original Creation Date	36	36	45%	100%
Model/Make	36	36	45%	100%
Image Unique ID	0	0	0%	0%
Location Information	22	12	27.5%	54.5%
Software tag	6	6	7.5%	100%

(continued)

Table 5. (continued)

Metadata	Extracted	Accurate	Succes Rate	Accuracy
Create Date	80	80	100%	100%
Image Size	78	78	80%	100%
File Modify Date	16	16	20%	100%
File Type	66	66	82.5%	100%
Exif Version	30	30	37.5%	100%

DigiKam delivered a strong balance between accuracy and coverage, achieving 63% success and 98.6% accuracy. It performed well across major metadata fields, including Original Creation Date, File Modify Date, Model/Make, and Exif Version. Like other tools, it had difficulty extracting fields such as the Image Unique ID, Location information etc., which remained inconsistently embedded in many images. Its extraction time (0.387 s) was second only to ExifTool, making it a viable GUI-based tool for practitioners who prioritize visual interfaces without compromising performance. Table 6 provides a detailed analysis of the tool.

As shown in Table 7, Xn View MP produced 100% accuracy in every field it extracted. Its consistency and high precision reinforce its viability as a dependable GUI-based forensic tool. Limitations remain in low-frequency fields, such as the Image Unique ID. Overall, this tool provides an average success rate of 63.8% and an extraction time of 1.11 seconds, as shown in Fig. 5.

Image Magick demonstrated a 64% success rate and 97% accuracy, as shown in Fig. 6, placing it among the strongest overall performers in terms of coverage. It successfully extracted major metadata fields with high precision where possible, though accuracy dropped slightly for Location Information, where partial or inconsistent embedding affected the tool's output. Its extraction time (3.064 s shown in Fig. 5) was slower compared to ExifTool, digiKam, and Xn View MP, but remains feasible for non-time-critical investigations. Table 8 provides a detailed analysis of the tool.

Table 6. DigiKamanalysis result

Metadata	Extracted	Accurate	Success Rate	Accuracy
Original Creation Date	56	56	70%	100%
Model/Make	46	46	57.5%	100%
Image Unique ID	2	2	2.5%	100%
Location Information	14	12	17.5%	85.7%
Software tag	16	16	20%	100%
Create Date	80	80	100%	100%
Image Size	80	80	100%	100%
File Modify Date	80	80	100%	100%

(continued)

Table 6. (*continued*)

Metadata	Extracted	Accurate	Success Rate	Accuracy
File Type	80	80	100%	100%
Exif Version	50	50	62.5%	100%

Table 7. XnView MP analysis result

Metadata	Extracted	Accurate	Success Rate	Accuracy
Original Creation Date	54	54	67.5%	100%
Model/Make	46	46	57.5%	100%
Image Unique ID	2	2	2.5%	100%
Location Information	22	22	27.5%	100%
Software tag	14	14	17.5%	100%
Create Date	80	80	100%	100%
Image Size	80	80	100%	100%
File Modify Date	80	80	100%	100%
File Type	80	80	100%	100%
Exif Version	52	52	65%	100%

Table 8. Image Megick analysis result

Metadata	Extracted	Accurate	Success Rate	Accuracy
Original Creation Date	56	56	70%	100%
Model/Make	46	46	57.5%	100%
Image Unique ID	2	2	2.5%	100%
Location Information	24	12	30%	50%
Software tag	12	12	15%	100%
Create Date	80	80	100%	100%
Image Size	80	80	100%	100%
File Modify Date	80	80	100%	100%
File Type	80	80	100%	100%
Exif Version	52	52	65%	100%

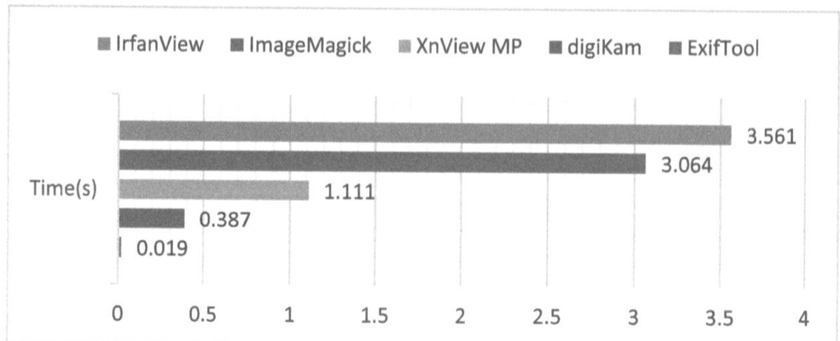

Fig. 5. Averageextraction time per tool in seconds

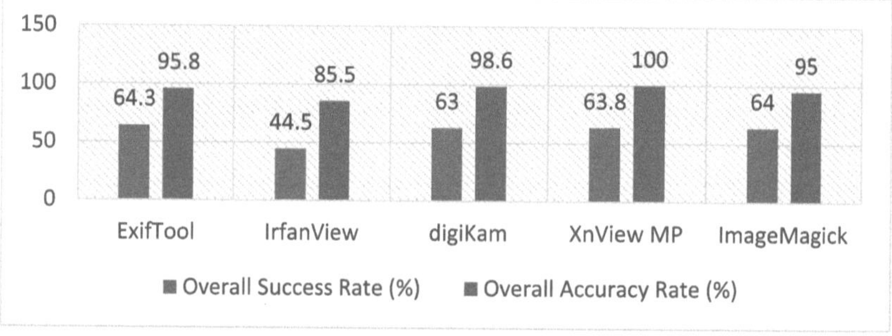

Fig. 6. Overall extraction success rate and accuracy per tool

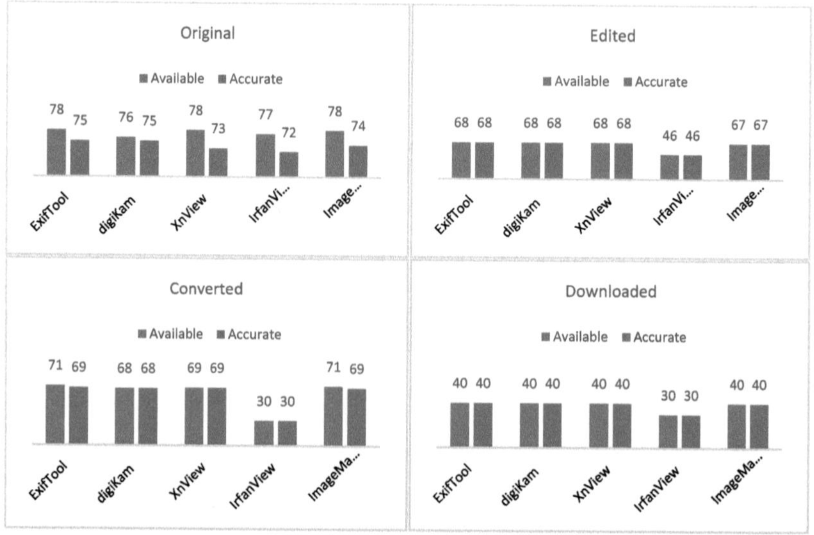

Fig. 7. Behavior of tools across various image transformations

4.2 Discussion

The comparative analysis of the five open-source metadata extraction tools reveals important insights into their forensic reliability, practical applicability, and behavior under different image transformations. The discussion below addresses each of the research questions (RQs) and integrates the broader implications for forensic workflows.

RQ1: Accuracy of metadata extraction: In terms of accuracy, all tools extracted metadata fields with good accuracy, as indicated in Fig. 6, indicating that they can reliably interpret the fields they support. However, accuracy alone does not equate to total reliability. Tools such as Irfan View showed perfect accuracy across the limited fields they recognized, but their limited coverage reduced their forensic usefulness. More advanced tools like Exif Tool displayed consistently strong accuracy while offering broader field support. This difference highlights an important practical consideration. Accuracy is only meaningful when paired with adequate field coverage. Fragile fields, including Unique Image ID and certain location-based tags, remained inconsistently extracted across tools, reinforcing the need for cautious interpretation during forensic examinations.

RQ2: Impact of image transformation on metadata integrity: The experiments clearly demonstrate that image transformations significantly degrade metadata completeness. As shown in Figs. 8 and 9, original images retained the richest and most diverse metadata, including several identifiers rarely preserved after editing or transfer. Even basic edits resulted in selective loss of fields, while more intrusive operations like format conversion or messaging-app compression stripped essential identifiers almost entirely. These findings underscore a critical forensic reality: the farther an image is removed from its original state, the greater the risk of losing crucial provenance information. As modern digital ecosystems routinely modify images often without user awareness, investigators must prioritize obtaining original files and treat edited or transferred media with increased scrutiny.

RQ3: Forensic soundness of extraction tools: All evaluated tools maintained strict forensic soundness, as confirmed by consistent hash values before and after analysis. This is a reassuring result for practitioners because it shows that these tools, despite variation in completeness, do not alter or contaminate evidence during the extraction process. This integrity-preservation property aligns with forensic best practices and supports their operational use.

RQ4: Balancing accuracy, completeness, and performance: A comparison of the tools' overall behavior shows that no single tool excels in every dimension, but some offer a more balanced profile. ExifTool stood out by combining strong metadata recovery with rapid extraction, making it especially suitable for large-scale workflows or automated pipelines. Tools with graphical interfaces, such as digiKam and XnView MP, remained valuable for practitioners who require visual navigation but generally operated at slower speeds. Image Magick provided strong coverage but displayed slower processing, while Irfan View's simplicity was offset by limited field support. These distinctions emphasize that tool selection should be guided by case requirements, such as speed, ease of use, or depth of metadata recovery.

RQ5: Limitations of the metadata extraction tools: The study also highlights several practical limitations. Some metadata fields were inconsistently detected across tools, even when present in the original images. Extraction performance was further influenced by device origin, as metadata richness varied noticeably across smartphones in the dataset. Furthermore, GUI-based tools, while more accessible for practitioners, typically demonstrated slower extraction times compared to command-line-based tools. The evaluation also revealed that no single tool achieved full metadata coverage, and several fragile fields were frequently missing regardless of tool selection. Finally, these findings reinforce that metadata alone cannot always be relied upon for attribution or evidentiary reconstruction, underscoring the need for multi-tool validation and complementary forensic techniques.

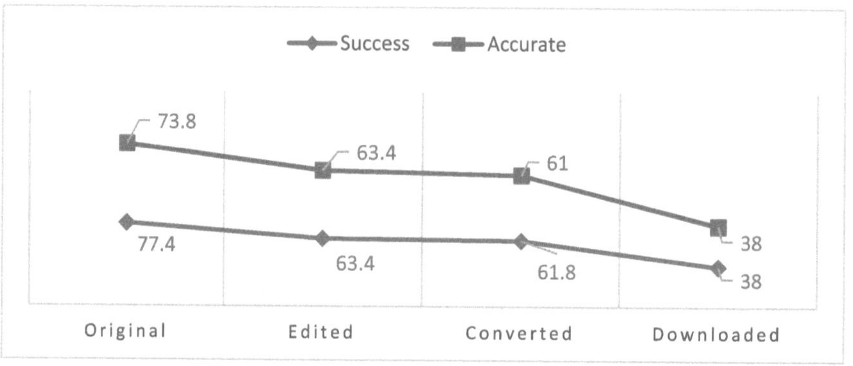

Fig. 8. Metadata extraction under different image transformation conditions

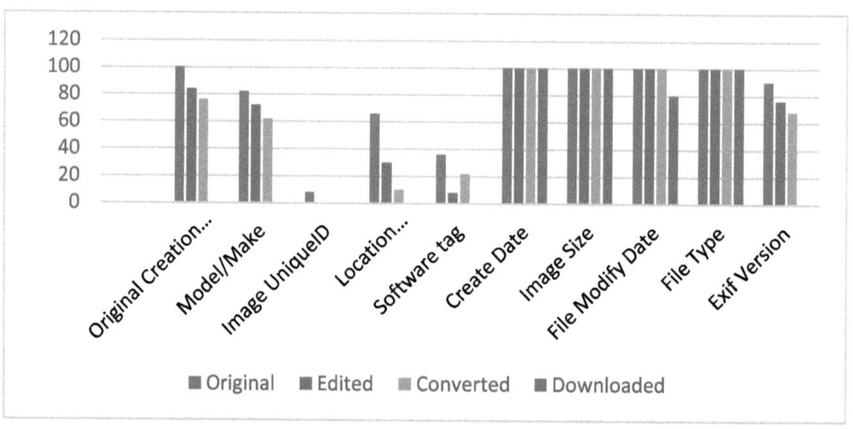

Fig. 9. Variation in metadata field success across various transformations

4.2.1 Key observations

1. Original images retained the most metadata richness, reinforcing the importance of preserving unaltered evidence.
2. Edited and converted images showed progressive metadata loss, particularly in fragile fields.
3. Messaging app compression or file transfer introduced the most severe metadata stripping.
4. Device type plays a crucial role in metadata richness, with some smartphones embedding more complete records than others.
5. All tools preserved file integrity, fulfilling forensic soundness requirements.

4.3 Implications of the Study

This study offers several important implications for digital forensic practice, tool selection, and the broader reliability of metadata-based evidence.

First, the findings reinforce the necessity of acquiring and preserving original image files wherever possible [3]. Metadata degradation occurred not only after editing, conversion, or transmission but also unexpectedly, even within the original image set. As reflected in Table 4 to Table 8, certain essential fields, such as the unique image id, make/model, software tag, and location information, were inconsistently extracted even from unaltered images. This highlights that incompleteness may arise from device-level embedding variations or tool-specific limitations rather than user-induced modifications. Investigators must therefore treat both original and transformed images with caution and document any metadata gaps clearly, especially when handling images sourced from online platforms or third-party applications [6].

Second, the notable differences in metadata completeness across devices and tools underscore the need for forensic workflows that do not depend on a single extraction tool. A multi-tool strategy can mitigate blind spots, increase confidence in extracted fields, and help validate results during cross-examination.

Third, the study highlights that while these metadata tools are accurate and forensically sound, they are not equal in performance or coverage. This has practical implications for training, case strategy, and tool procurement. Examiners must understand which tools provide deeper metadata insights, which operate faster in large caseloads, and which are more vulnerable to missing fragile metadata fields.

Fourth, the inconsistent preservation of identifiers such as Unique Image ID and GeoLocation across devices suggests that metadata cannot always be relied upon as a singular source of attribution [14]. This limitation strengthens the argument for integrating metadata analysis with complementary forensic techniques to establish provenance.

Finally, the study's results have legal implications. Variability in tool coverage and the fragility of metadata create opportunities for challenges to evidence authenticity in court [7]. Examiners must therefore be prepared to justify their tool choices, explain known limitations, and demonstrate adherence to sound forensic procedures. The findings ultimately encourage the development of more standardized, validated, and metadata-resilient forensic tools, contributing to stronger and more defensible digital investigations.

4.4   Limitations of the Study

The following are highlighted as limitations of our study:

- Small dataset limited to a few devices (Android), reducing diversity and generalizability.
- Evaluation restricted to open-source tools and ten metadata fields, excluding commercial software.
- Lack of statistical precision measures (eg. error bars), weakening reliability for legal scrutiny.
- No real-world case study included, limiting validation in investigative or courtroom contexts.
- Anti-forensic techniques are not addressed, reducing the scope for handling manipulated metadata.

5   Conclusion and Future Work

This study presented a comprehensive evaluation of five open-source metadata extraction tools with respect to forensic soundness, accuracy, and metadata completeness across a range of image transformations. All tools preserved evidence integrity; however, their extraction performance varied significantly. Exif Tool, with a 64.3% success rate, 95.8% accuracy, and an extraction time of 0.019 seconds, demonstrated the most balanced capability overall, while the remaining tools exhibited differing strengths in accuracy, field coverage, or processing efficiency.

A consistent finding across all experiments was the poor recovery of fragile metadata fields such as Image Unique ID, software tags, and Location information, especially after image transformation. These losses highlight the inherent vulnerability of metadata and reinforce the importance of acquiring original files whenever possible. The study further demonstrates that no single tool is sufficient for comprehensive metadata extraction; therefore, a multi-tool approach is essential to maximize metadata recovery, verify field consistency, and enhance the defensibility of digital evidence in legal proceedings.

Future research could expand the dataset to include additional devices and imaging environments to improve generalizability. A comparative evaluations involving commercial forensic tools and analysis aligned with legal admissibility standards may also strengthen forensic reliability. Moreover, developing automated cross-validation systems, incorporating AI or machine learning techniques to identify missing or manipulated metadata, and advancing methods for detecting anti-forensic activity represent important next steps for strengthening digital evidence processing.

References

1. Raj, D., Sharma, D.: Enhancing digital image forensics and security: Innovations in metadata, watermarking and blockchain technology. In: 2024 OPJU International Technology Conference (OTCON) on Smart Computing for Innovation and Advancement in Industry 4.0, pp. 1–6 (2024). https://doi.org/10.1109/OTCON60325.2024.10688307

2. Kalaimagal, S., Seshaiah, M., Harini, S., Keerthi, D., Udayakumar, A.: Implementation of multi-format exif metadata extraction from images. In: 2024 First International Conference on Data, Computation and Communication (ICDCC), pp. 300–305 (2024). https://doi.org/10.1109/ICDCC62744.2024.10961287

3. Baracchi, D., Shullani, D., Iuliani, M., Piva, A.: FloreView: An image and video dataset for forensic analysis. IEEE Access. **11**, 109267–109282 (2023). https://doi.org/10.1109/ACCESS.2023.3321991

4. Royan, N., Safitri, C., Sen, T.W.: Robust metadata forensics to improve detection and analysis of deepfake images. In: 2024 7th International Seminar on Research of Information Technology and Intelligent Systems (ISRITI), pp. 362–368 (2024). https://doi.org/10.1109/ISRITI64779.2024.10963532

5. Lee, J., Jeon, S., Park, Y., Chung, J., Jeong, D.: A Forensic Methodology for Detecting Image Manipulations. J. Korea Inst. Inf. Secur. Cryptol. **33**(4), 671–685 (2023). https://doi.org/10.13089/JKIISC.2023.33.4.671

6. Soni, N.: Forensic value of exif data: An analytical evaluation of metadata integrity across image transfer methods. Perspect. Leg. Forensic Sci. **2**(2), 10006 (2025). https://doi.org/10.70322/plfs.2025.10006

7. Cornell Law School, Rule 902. Evidence That Is Self-Authenticating, LII / Legal Information Institute. [Online]. https://www.law.cornell.edu/rules/fre/rule_902 (2025). Accessed 16 Aug 2025

8. H. Z. Wang, One size does not fit all: Alternatives to the federal rules of evidence, 2023, Social Science Research Network, Rochester, NY: 4469875. [Online]. https://papers.ssrn.com/sol3/papers.cfm?abstract_id=4469875 (2025). Accessed 16 Aug 2025

9. R. Ayers, S. Brothers, and W. Jansen, NIST Special Publication (SP) 800-101 Rev. 1, Guidelines on Mobile Device Forensics, May 2014. [Online]. https://csrc.nist.gov/pubs/sp/800/101/r1/final (2025). Accessed 31 Aug 2025

10. Casey, E.: Digital Evidence and Computer Crime: Forensic Science, Computers, and the Internet, 3rd edn. Academic Press, Inc., USA (2011)

11. I. ISO/IEC, ISO/IEC 27037:2012, ISO. [Online]. https://www.iso.org/standard/44381.html (2025). Accessed 31 Aug 2025

12. Kurtz, J.E., Pintarelli, E.M.: The daubert standards for admissibility of evidence based on the personality assessment inventory. Psychol. Inj. Law. **17**(2), 105–116 (2024). https://doi.org/10.1007/s12207-024-09508-5

13. Imwinkelried, E.J.: Expert testimony in the USA. In: Encyclopedia of Forensic and Legal Medicine: Volume 1-4, vol. 2, Third edn, pp. V2:458–V2:465. Elsevier (2024). https://doi.org/10.1016/B978-0-443-21441-7.00079-0

14. N. D. Arizona, M. A. Nugroho, A. R. Syujak, R. K. Saputra, and I. Sulistyowati, Metadata forensic analysis as support for digital investigation process by utilizing metadata-extractor, J. Intell. Softw. Syst., vol. 3, no. 2, Art. no. 2, Dec. 2024, doi: https://doi.org/10.26798/jiss.v3i2.1503.

15. Guo, Y., Slay, J., Beckett, J.: Validation and verification of computer forensic software tools—Searching Function. Digit. Investig. **6**, S12–S22 (2009). https://doi.org/10.1016/j.diin.2009.06.015

16. Golam, A., Albalawi, U.: Invisible boundaries: Balancing Image metadata privacy with forensic Imperatives. Int. J. Inf. Technol. Secur. **16**(4), 105–116 (2024). https://doi.org/10.59035/JUXW2913

17. Cosic, J., Jukan, A., Baca, M.: Strengthening cybersecurity certifications through robust chain of custody practices. In: 2024 IEEE International Conference on Cyber Security and Resilience (CSR), pp. 570–574 (2024). https://doi.org/10.1109/CSR61664.2024.10679449

18. Zheng, C., Shrivastava, A., Owens, A.: EXIF as language: Learning cross-modal associations between images and camera metadata. In: 2023 IEEE/CVF Conference on Computer Vision and Pattern Recognition (CVPR), pp. 6945–6956 (2023). https://doi.org/10.1109/CVPR52729.2023.00671
19. Karazalus, C.P., Palmbach, T.T., Lee, H.C.: Digital Enhancement of Sub-Quality Bitemark Photographs (2001). https://doi.org/10.1520/JFS15076J
20. loc.org, Exif Exchangeable Image File Format, Version 2.2. [Online]. https://www.loc.gov/preservation/digital/formats/fdd/fdd000146.shtml (2025). Accessed 18 June 2025
21. B. Quinn, Exif 3.0 released, featuring UTF-8 support, IPTC. [Online]. https://iptc.org/news/exif-3-0-released-featuring-utf-8-support/ (2025). Accessed 18 June 2025
22. Daraghmi, E., Hamoudi, A.: Mobile forensics: Extracting geo-location data from photos on android smartphones. Int. J. Innov. Sci. Res. Technol. IJISRT, 1915–1921 (2024). https://doi.org/10.38124/ijisrt/IJISRT24SEP960
23. Z. Balkibayeva, Methods of extracting and analyzing metadata for evidentiary purposes, Uzb. J. Law Digit. Policy, vol. 2, no. 5, Art. no. 5, Oct. 2024, doi: https://doi.org/10.59022/ujldp.233
24. P. Harvey, ExifTool by Phil Harvey, ExifTool. [Online]. https://exiftool.org/ (2025). Accessed 12 June 2025
25. digiKam, digiKam, digiKam. [Online]. https://www.digikam.org/ (2025). Accessed 12 June 2025
26. G. Pierre, XnView MP · Advanced Image Viewer & Photo Management Software | Free | XnView.com, XnView Software. [Online]. https://www.xnview.com/en/xnviewmp/ (2025). Accessed 12 June 2025
27. I. Skiljan, IrfanView. [Online]. https://www.irfanview.com/ (2025). Accessed 12 June 2025
28. ImageMagick, ImageMagick – Mastering Digital Image Alchemy. [Online]. https://imagemagick.org/index.php (2025). Accessed 12 June 2025
29. Khan, A.A., Zhang, X., Hajjej, F., Yang, J., Ku, C.S., Por, L.Y.: ASMF: Ambient social media forensics chain of custody with an intelligent digital investigation process using federated learning. Heliyon. **10**(1), e23254 (2024). https://doi.org/10.1016/j.heliyon.2023.e23254
30. Pestana, G., Antunes, W., Carvalho, J.: Digital chain of custody operational framework. In: 2023 IEEE International Workshop on Technologies for Defense and Security (TechDefense), pp. 417–422 (2023). https://doi.org/10.1109/TechDefense59795.2023.10380890

AI, Ethics, and Engagement: Towards Responsible Personalization in Digital Marketing

Pratik Shukla[(✉)] and Pramod Goyal

FMS, Marwadi University, Rajkot, India
`pratikshukla.130595@marwadiuniversity.ac.in`

Abstract. The rapid adoption of AI-driven personalized marketing has transformed how businesses engage with consumers. While personalization enhances customer experience and business performance, it also raises critical ethical concerns related to privacy, transparency, consent, and algorithmic manipulation. This study explores these issues in the context of the Indian digital landscape by analyzing three real-world case studies involving fake dating profiles, cloned government websites, and intrusive mobile application interfaces. Through thematic interpretation and conceptual modeling, the research highlights how unethical personalization practices negatively impact consumer trust and digital well-being. The paper proposes a strategic conceptual model that integrates ethical AI design, user privacy, regulatory enforcement, and transparency as foundational elements leading to trustworthy personalization It also attempts to make a comparison metrics for ethical concern and risk in a tabulation form. The findings emphasize the urgent need for ethical frameworks and user-centric design in AI-powered marketing strategies. This study contributes to academic discourse on responsible digital marketing and lays the groundwork for future empirical validation.

Keywords: Personalized Marketing · Ethics · Ethical Concern. Consumer Trust · Data Privacy · India · Ethical Design · Conceptual Model · AI-driven marketing · Emerging markets · Algorithmic transparency · AI in Marketing · Trustworthy AI · Digital Wellbeing

1 Introduction

The rapid growth of the internet and digital technologies has fundamentally transformed the landscape of marketing. In this digital age, online marketing has become a pivotal strategy for businesses seeking to reach and engage their target audiences. As consumers increasingly turn to the internet for shopping, information, and entertainment, understanding their perceptions of online marketing efforts has become crucial for marketers.

Kotler and Keller (2012) gave a quote "The most important thing is to forecast where customers are moving, and be in front of them." This quote shows the marketing activities always need evolution and diversification towards customer preference.

R. Sridaran and S. Priti (Eds.): AI-FCDAC 2025, CCIS 2866, pp. 21–34, 2026.
https://doi.org/10.1007/978-3-032-17300-3_2

In today's fast-paced digital marketplace, personalised marketing has emerged as the modern-day unicorn strategy of engaging prospects and increasing purchase intentions. The emergence of more adaptive and sophisticated technologies has transformed the nature of personalised marketing strategies by equipping marketers with new forms of insights pertaining to consumer behaviour and preferences. Artificial intelligence (AI), machine learning, big data analytics, the Internet of things (IoT), augmented/virtual reality (AR/VR) these are the technologies that are reinventing personalised marketing for the 21st-century marketplace.

If we compare the communication way between brand to customer or from company to customers, there is huge changes and some new evolutions. Were from 2000 to 2010 online marketing was almost nil and major source of promotion of products was TV and Print media. The TV ads have an easy source to communicate the customer in one way. Then slowly with the growth of technology and internet the advertisement transformed digitally as well as two-way communication with customer where the customer can ask questions from the company.

Given the speed at which the developed technologies evolve, it is thus vital to outline their place in the personalised marketing and more particularly in customer's purchase intention. Considering that technology is our reality and future, this review will try to furnish the possibility of integrating the developed emerging technologies in personalized marketing to enunciate more customers impact and buying intention. However as businesses use customer data more and more to focus their ads more accurately, privacy, consent, and manipulation issues have become of increasing significance.

The emergence of personalized marketing has caused both enthusiasm and criticism. On one hand, customers value the ease and relevance of personalized offers; on the other, many are concerned about the extent of data gathering and the opaque nature of algorithmic decisions. High-profile data breaches and issues, such as intrusive tracking, a lack of transparency, and potential biases in Technology-driven targeting highlight the need for a balanced strategy that respects user autonomy while providing commercial benefit.

Personalized marketing functions at the crossroads of technology progress and consumer psychology, presenting both potential and constraints. On the one hand, consumers benefit from more relevant material, more efficient purchasing decisions, and better user experiences. On the other hand, the widespread collecting and use of personal data has raised discussions about surveillance, permission, and the possibility of manipulation. As businesses become more reliant on algorithmic targeting, issues arise about where to draw the line between effective marketing and ethical excess.

2 Review of Literature

Personalization in marketing involves customized content and products to specific client preferences, hence eliminating decision fatigue. Key themes include personalized recommendations, relationships, the personalization-privacy issue, and utilizing technology such as AI and big data to improve consumer experiences (Kaushik and Sharma 2023). Personalization adapts products or services to meet individual customer needs, creating increased value for consumers and profit for producers (Montgomery and Smith 2008).

Personalized marketing strategies significantly boost consumer engagement by offering customized experiences that align with individual interests and habits, leading to better customer experiences and higher conversion rates (Rajendran et al. 2024). personalization as a strategic approach to designing content and products that align with individual customer preferences, which helps reduce customer fatigue and cognitive load during decision-making (Kaushik and Sharma 2023). Marketing personalization is using consumer information to produce individualized products, services, and communications, resulting in long-term partnerships. It uses current technology for data collecting and analysis, considering each consumer as a distinct section in order to improve happiness and loyalty (Glazunova and Ščeulovs 2024). Personalisation has huge scope of growth if future by emerging technology in in marketing strategy. Personalization is like an action that design the strategy which communicate with customer (Chandra et al. 2022). Personalized marketing methods have a considerable impact on customer decisions, with trust, relevance, and loyalty playing important roles in amplifying these impacts. AI-powered customization not only encourages instant purchases but also generates long-term purchase intentions, emphasizing its dual function in preserving customer engagement and fostering brand loyalty (Suleman et al. 2025). To keep customers' confidence and maximize its efficacy, personalized marketing that makes use of data mining can help businesses better understand their customers and achieve better results. But this type of marketing must handle customers' worries about data privacy with great care (Yusnidar et al. 2023).

AI marketing boosts e-commerce sales by increasing customer acquisition and conversion rates. Tools like chatbots, customization engines, and predictive analytics are crucial in enhancing performance (Madanchian 2024). The use of artificial intelligence in e-commerce marketing improves consumer interaction, optimizes product offers, and allows customized campaigns, resulting in improved sales. AI-driven tactics enhance customer relationship management and operational efficiency, giving businesses a competitive advantage in the digital marketplace (Zhuk and Yatskyi 2024). AI in e-commerce boosts user interaction, personalizes experiences, and provides data-driven insights, all of which contribute to a disruptive change that drives growth and innovation, ultimately increasing e-commerce sales dramatically (Deepak et al. 2024). AI helps to boost the e-commerce sales through increased customization, content relevancy, and consumer interaction. However, it presents data privacy concerns, needing a delicate balance between using AI for sales and maintaining client confidence and security (Salgado-Reyes and León-Torres 2024). AI marketing improves e-commerce sales by personalizing recommendation systems, increasing customer engagement, and boosting supply chain efficiency. However, failing to prioritize AI ethics and privacy can hurt reputation and consumer trust, affecting revenue and regulatory compliance (Krishna et al. 2023). Artificial intelligence (AI) plays a pivotal role in personalized marketing strategies by enabling brands to tailor their offerings based on consumer data, enhancing engagement and loyalty. AI facilitates behavioural and psychographic personalization, significantly impacting consumer attitudes and engagement intentions in social network advertising (Zhang et al. 2024). Moreover, AI-driven personalization enhances the customer journey through personalized profiling and nudges, addressing dilemmas at various stages of indications (Gao and Liu 2023). Additionally, The Holistic AI-Enhanced Marketing Framework Theory advocates for ethical considerations and human creativity in AI applications, ensuring user trust and engagement (Ejjami 2024).

One of the most prominent ethical concerns in AI-driven personalized marketing is data privacy, particularly the issue of informed consent (Martin and Murphy 2017). argue that AI-powered personalization often collects data passively or through complex consent mechanisms that users do not fully understand. This undermines user autonomy and raises serious privacy concerns. Similarly, (Aguirre et al. 2015) found that when consumers perceive a lack of transparency in how their data is being used, it significantly reduces their trust and increases feelings of manipulation. The study also highlighted that perceived control over personal information plays a critical role in determining the acceptability of personalized content.

However, the implementation of AI in marketing has made various positive impact towards customer acquisition and sales but it also raises various ethical concern which focussing privacy risks and algorithmic bias, necessitating a balance between personalization benefits and ethical considerations.

Research GAP

1. Lack of transparency-focused research in AI personalization
2. Limited focus on ethical issues in emerging markets
3. Absence of conceptual models linking ethics, trust, and engagement

Research Questions

1. How does perceived transparency in AI-driven personalization influence consumer trust?
2. What are the key ethical concerns influencing consumer acceptance of personalized marketing in emerging markets?
3. How do ethical concerns mediate the relationship between personalized marketing and customer engagement through consumer trust?

Research Objective

1. To examine the role of transparency and ethical practices in AI-driven personalized marketing and how they influence consumer trust.
2. To identify the key ethical concerns—such as data privacy, informed consent, and algorithmic fairness—affecting consumer perception of personalized marketing, especially in the context of emerging markets.
3. To develop a conceptual model that integrates ethical concerns with consumer trust and engagement behaviour in the realm of technology-driven personalized marketing.

3 Research Methodology

This study relies on a qualitative study and a conceptual approach to construct a theory-driven conceptual model for analysing the ethical implications of technology-driven tailored marketing. It is inherently descriptive, aiming to examine the ethical elements and their influence on customer trust and involvement. The study thoroughly investigates more than 500 peer-reviewed referred journals, industry white papers, and real-world case studies.

4 Data Collection Method

The study relies on secondary data sources collected through an extensive literature review of academic journals and industry reports. The literature was selected based on relevance to the key themes of:

- AI-based personalized marketing
- Ethical marketing practices
- Data privacy and transparency
- Consumer trust and engagement
- Real-world case studies archived in newspapers like The Times of India, Economic times

5 Data Analysis

The study adopts a qualitative data analysis approach, combining thematic analysis of existing literature with case-based insights drawn from credible industry reports etc. The analysis focused on extracting ethical themes relevant to technology-driven personalized marketing, such as:

- Data privacy and informed consent
- Transparency and algorithmic accountability
- Perceived intrusiveness
- Consumer trust and engagement behavior

6 Major Ethical Issues in Marketing

6.1 Data Privacy

In June 2025, the Delhi Police broke a syndicate that used counterfeit accounts on dating sites to defraud individuals. A 22-year-old Shahdara resident claimed establishing contact with a lady named "Nandini" via a dating application. Subsequent to transitioning their dialogue on WhatsApp, she began a naked video call, wherein the victim's visage was discernible. Unbeknownst to him, the conversation was documented. He subsequently got threats that the film would be disseminated on social media until he remitted payment. To avoid humiliation, he remitted ₹35,000 to an account designated by the fraudster. Upon receiving more requests, he reported the event to the National Cybercrime Reporting Portal.

Investigations disclosed that the extorted funds were deposited into a bank account established under the name Mangal Singh, although managed by another guy, Shyam Singh, utilizing counterfeit paperwork. Shyam confessed to arranging the fraud with the aid of an accomplice named Aamir. Both persons were apprehended, and many mobile phones and SIM cards were seized.

Source:

- Times of India: Gang extorting targets using fake dating profiles busted. https://tim esofindia.indiatimes.com/city/delhi/gangextortingtargetsusingfakedatingprofilesbu sted/articleshow/121891461.cmstimesofindia.indiatimes.com+3timesofindia.indiat imes.com+3timesofindia.indiatimes.com+3 (2025, June 16)

6.2 Cloning of Websites

Recently, there has been a notable rise in the cloning of official government websites by cybercriminals in India. This includes sites such as the Jeevan Pramaan portal, the National Institute of Design (NID) admissions site, and the Common Services Centre (CSC) portal, aimed at deceiving citizens to extract sensitive information or service fees. Cloned websites frequently replicate the design, logo, and content of authentic platforms, deceiving users into providing personal information or processing payments. Victims, including numerous pensioners and students, inadvertently engage with these counterfeit sites because of their significant visual and functional resemblance to the authentic ones. These scams raise significant ethical issues, encompassing deception, privacy infringements, financial fraud, and the deterioration of trust in digital governance.

Sources:

- NDTV: Fake website resembles government portal, hundreds of pensioners duped. https://www.ndtv.com/india-news/fake-website-resembles-government-portal-hundreds-of-pensioners-duped-3705012 (2023, January 31)
- Times of India: Delhi man held for cloning NID intake site. https://timesofindia.indiatimes.com/city/ahmedabad/delhi-man-held-for-cloning-nid-intake-site/articleshow/104481003.cms (2023, October 14)
- ET Government: 3 cyber crooks launch fake e-governance website, issue forged govt certificates & IDs. https://government.economictimes.indiatimes.com/news/secure-india/3-cyber-crookslaunch-fake-e-governance-website-issue-forged-govt-certificates-ids-to-over-1000-people/100344135 (2023, May 19)

6.3 Continuous Pop-Up Ads/Banner

The rise of annoying pop-up ads and deceptive app interfaces in India has prompted a lot of ethical issues. Study from 2025 looked at the top 100 mobile apps in China and the U.S. and found common "sneaky patterns" in mobile ecosystems. These included pop-ups that trick users with things like text misdirection, forced activities, and defaults that invade users' privacy. These actions hurt users' ability to make their own choices and trust. In India, rapid commerce apps have started to use crowded interfaces with pop-ups, advertisements, banners, and gamified components, which are similar to how TV news networks look. The goal of this change is to get more people to use the site and make money from it, but it often makes users unhappy since the graphics are too much and too distracting. Not only do these techniques make the user experience worse, but they also raise moral questions about informed consent and digital health.

Sources:

- Wu, D., Nan, Y., Wang, S., Wang, J., Li, L., Wang, X.: Understanding the sneaky patterns of pop-up windows in the mobile ecosystem. arXiv. https://arxiv.org/abs/2505.12056 (2025)
- The Economic Times: Pop-ups, ads, banners and games: How quick commerce app designs have changed. https://economictimes.indiatimes.com/tech/startups/popups adsbannersandgameshowquickcommerceappdesignshavechanged/articleshow/122 054004.cms (2025, June 25)

6.4 Data Harvesting Scandal

6.4.1 Cambridge Analytica & Facebook Data Privacy Scandal

The scandal around Cambridge Analytica made it clear how unethical and illegal uses of consumer data can have serious legal, moral, and financial implications. The move comes after it was an that Cambridge Analytica harvested personal data of 87 million Facebook users without permission through third-party applications which can then be used to create psychographic profiles to direct focused political advertising, most notably during 2016 U.S. elections and the Brexit campaign. This case laid bare weaknesses in data privacy rules and the opaque processes that digital platforms use in how consumer data is managed. The fallout has led to an international discussion about data protection, a loss of trust by users, regulatory oversight and a $5 billion fine by the U.S. Federal Trade Commission against Facebook the case demonstrates how crucial it is for targeted marketing to use data honestly, obtain consent after being informed, and have robust control procedures (Tables 1 and 2).

Sources:

- Fernando, J.: Investopedia. Retrieved from Investopedia: https://www.investopedia.com/terms/c/cambridge-analytica.asp?utm_source=chatgpt.com (2025, January 25)
- Time Magazine. April 4, 2018, Reuters (December 18, 2024)

The case studies illustrate a growing number of online incursions that are compromising the foundations of digital trust by utilizing artificial intelligence (AI) in a manner that is deceptive: deceptive advertising, fake dating profiles, replicated government websites, and extensive data collection, to name a few. There appears to be a range of transformations occurring, from basic financial scams to profound psychological manipulation and systemic threats to democratic integrity. Deepfakes, predictive algorithms, psychographic microtargeting, and other technologies are perpetuating these transformations. The potential escalation in damage and the rate of change are exemplified by jurisdictionally neutral quantitative metrics, such as an enormous increase in global deepfake activity (exactly 10 times as much) and reports of phishing attempts in India, one of the world's centers for phishing attempts. The results demonstrate a substantial deficiency in legal and regulatory safeguards that are intended to protect against the societal harms caused by the increasingly weaponized design of AI. This underscores the fundamental

Table 1. Case studies of AI-driven digital intrusions

SL No	Case Study	Nature of Intrusion	AI/Tech Element	Impact on Users	Ethical/Legal Concern
1	Fake Dating Profiles	Identity manipulation, catfishing	AI-generated photos, chatbots	Emotional distress, financial fraud	Consent violation, lack of accountability
2	Cloned Government Websites	Fraudulent imitation	AI-driven website cloning & spoofing	Data theft, loss of money, distrust in digital governance	Cybersecurity gaps, digital governance challenges
3	Pop-up Ad Intrusions on Indian e-commerce & news sites	Persistent manipulation of attention	Predictive algorithms, intrusive targeting	Privacy invasion, reduced trust in platforms	Ethical advertising, data protection issues
4	Data Harvesting Scandal (Cambridge Analytica & Facebook)	Mass harvesting of personal data without informed consent	Algorithmic profiling, psychographic microtargeting	Political manipulation, erosion of democratic trust	Violation of privacy, electoral ethics, lack of transpa-rency

Source: On the basis of secondary data collection and analysis.

Table 2. Comparison matrix – AI-driven digital risks

SL No	AI Misuse Type	Ethical/Trust Concern	Qualitative Insight	Quantitative Evidence	Source
1	Fake Dating Profiles (Deepfakes)	Consent, emotional manipulation	AI-generated profiles reduce authenticity and undermine user trust	Deepfake usage surged globally nearly tenfold from 2022 to 2023	PR Newswire, Nov 28, 2023
2	Phishing & Cloned Sites	Security, governance risk	Cloned government portals mislead citizens and erode confidence in authorities	India ranks 3rd globally in phishing attacks (33% of tech-sector strikes)	Business Standard, Apr 30, 2024; Times of India, Apr 30, 2024

(continued)

Table 2. (*continued*)

SL No	AI Misuse Type	Ethical/Trust Concern	Qualitative Insight	Quantitative Evidence	Source
3	Pop-up Ad Intrusions	Manipulative marketing, annoyance	Intrusive ads erode trust in platforms and disturb user experience	(Global) 500 million phishing attempts recorded in 2022; illustrates system vulnerability	Kaspersky, Feb 16, 2023
4	**Data Harvesting Scandal (Cambridge Analytica & Facebook)**	Privacy breach, electoral ethics	Unauthorized harvesting of 87 M+ user profiles used for political microtargeting, undermining democratic trust	87 million Facebook users' data misused during 2016 US elections & Brexit campaigns	(Fernando 2025) Time Magazine April 4, 2018, Reuters December 18, 2024

Source: On the basis of secondary data collection and analysis.

ethical violations related to consent, privacy, and transparency that are committed by the individuals discussed in the case studies.

7   Conceptual Model

The below two conceptual model underscores that **trustworthy personalization** is the product of interlinked strategic components: ethical AI design, respect for user privacy, transparency, consent, and regulatory enforcement. The synergy among these factors ensures that personalized marketing efforts are effective, acceptable, and sustainable in the digital era (Figs. 1 and 2).

The model further reflects a shift in digital marketing strategy from purely performance-driven personalization to ethically grounded personalization. Firstly, Ethical AI Design ensures that algorithms are fair, unbiased, and transparent in how they deliver personalized content. This must be coupled with Transparency & Consent, enabling consumers to make informed choices about their participation in personalization processes. Secondly, User Privacy must be protected at all levels, and this is only possible through strong Regulation & Enforcement mechanisms both at the platform and government levels. The convergence of these four areas leads to Trustworthy Personalization, where consumers are not just passive data points, but active participants in ethical digital ecosystems. This model encourages businesses to consider not just what personalization can do, but how it should be done responsibly.

Conceptual Model:
Ethical Concerns in AI-Driven Personalized Marketing

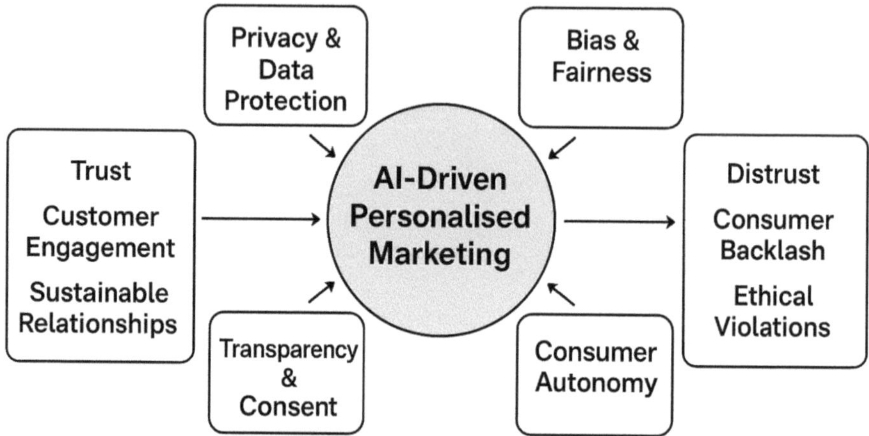

Fig. 1 . Source: On the basis of secondary data collection and analysis

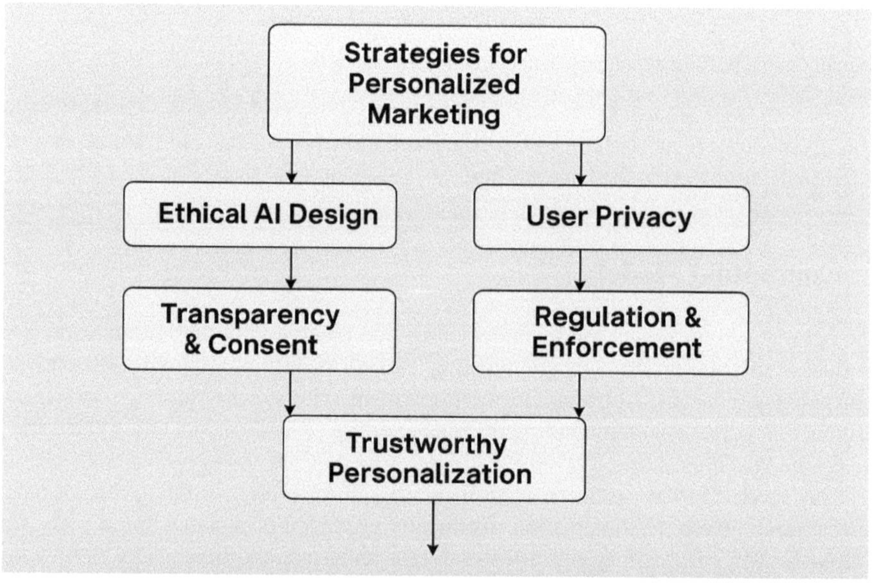

Fig. 2 . Source: On the basis of secondary data collection and analysis

8   Findings

This study finds and looks at substantial ethical problems that come up when AI-driven tailored marketing is used in the Indian digital environment. Based on the chosen case studies, which include phony dating profile frauds, cloning of government websites, and annoying app pop-up advertising

1. **AI-Powered Personalization Raises Ethical Concerns:**
   AI-driven personalized content and interfaces can cause big ethical problems, especially when there are no clear limits on how they might be utilized. The instances reviewed show that customization may be used to mislead people, control their behavior, and break rules about data protection.

2. **Ethical Concerns Hurt Consumer Trust:**
   In all cases, users who were subjected to misleading or non-consensual customization said they felt upset, unhappy, or withdrew. Lack of transparency, forceful nudges, and using data without permission were all highly linked to a drop in customer trust in the platform or brand. People are less inclined to use an app or website when they feel like they are being watched, manipulated, or fooled (such with phony pop-ups, too many adverts, or targeting based on behavior). This shows that making things too personal may backfire.

3. **Trust is what connects ethics and engagement:**
   The results back up the idea that ethical behavior influences how much people trust a company, which in turn affects how much they participate with it. It was clear that trust was a key factor in whether or not people stayed with a digitally tailored platform or left it.

4. **Need for AI that is responsible and ethical:**
   The study shows that Indian digital marketing methods don't have enough ethical monitoring or user-cantered AI design. It stresses how important it is for platforms and marketers to include ethical concepts like informed permission, transparency, and user autonomy in the design of AI personalization systems.

9   Limitations of the Study

- This study is based on a conceptual model developed through secondary data and literature review. It lacks empirical validation through primary data or real-time consumer behavior.
- This study primarily focuses on the Indian digital ecosystem. Therefore, the findings and proposed model may not fully generalize to developed markets or countries with different regulatory frameworks and digital maturity.
- Case-based analysis and thematic interpretation are subject to researcher bias, especially in the absence of structured empirical testing or multiple coders.
- The model is not tailored to any particular industry (e.g., retail, finance, healthcare). Ethical concerns may vary significantly by sector depending on sensitivity of consumer data and AI usage.
- As AI technologies and data protection laws evolve rapidly, the conceptual framework may become outdated unless regularly updated with emerging practices and ethical norms.

10 Suggestions

A multi-pronged strategy is needed to deal with the moral issues that come up with AI-driven tailored marketing. First, marketers and developers should follow ethical AI design principles that put user privacy, openness, and freedom first. Digital interfaces need to include clear and easy-to-use ways for users to give their consent so that they know and can manage how their data is used. Regulatory agencies should set ethical rules for each business and make sure that there are harsh punishments for dishonest actions like copying websites, misusing data, and using pop-ups to trick people. Also, independent audits of algorithms should be encouraged to keep an eye on customization systems for bias or targeting that isn't fair. Lastly, initiatives to raise awareness among users and programs to teach people how to utilize technology are very important to help people notice and respond to unethical digital marketing. These steps will assist create a digital marketing environment in India that is fair, accountable, and trustworthy when it comes to customisation.

11 Conclusion

This study critically examined the ethical implications of AI-driven personalized marketing in the digital ecosystem through real-world case studies and a conceptual model. The findings underscore that while AI personalization offers immense potential for customer engagement and business growth, its misuse can lead to serious ethical breaches—ranging from data privacy violations and manipulative user interfaces to loss of consumer trust. The proposed conceptual and strategic models highlight the essential role of ethical AI design, transparency, user privacy, and regulatory enforcement in building trustworthy personalization.

If digital marketing is to remain effective and sustainable, it must evolve beyond performance metrics to incorporate ethical considerations that respect user autonomy and consent. The study contributes to the growing discourse on responsible AI and calls for a balanced approach where technological advancement is guided by ethical responsibility. Future research may empirically test the proposed models and explore industry-specific applications of ethical personalization frameworks.

References

Aguirre, E., Mahr, D., Grewal, D., de Ruyter, K., Wetzels, M.: Unraveling the personalization paradox: The effect of information collection and trust-building strategies on online advertisement effectiveness. J. Retail. **91**(1), 34–49 (2015). https://doi.org/10.1016/J.JRETAI.2014.09.005

Chandra, S., Verma, S., Lim, W.M., Kumar, S., Donthu, N.: Personalization in personalized marketing: Trends and ways forward. Psychol. Mark. **39**(8), 1529–1562 (2022). https://doi.org/10.1002/mar.21670

Deepak, Dumka, A., Mazumdar, B.D.: Paradigm shift in e-commerce by applying cognitive multi-agent system with machine learning and deep learning techniques. 2024 7th International Conference on Contemporary Computing and Informatics (IC3I), pp. 151–154 (2024). doi:https://doi.org/10.1109/IC3I61595.2024.10829030

Ejjami, R.: Holistic AI-enhanced marketing framework theory: Bridging human creativity and AI for ethical marketing. Int. J. Multidiscip. Res. **6**(5) (2024). https://doi.org/10.36948/ijfmr. 2024.v06i05.28169

Fernando, J.: Investopedia. https://www.investopedia.com/terms/c/cambridge-analytica.asp?utm_source=chatgpt.com (2025)

Gao, Y., Liu, H.: Artificial intelligence-enabled personalization in interactive marketing: A customer journey perspective. J. Res. Interact. Mark. **17**(5), 663–680 (2023). https://doi.org/10.1108/JRIM-01-2022-0023

Glazunova, J., Šceulovs, D.: Contemporary marketing personalization through clustering approach (2024). doi:https://doi.org/10.3846/bm.2024.1221

Kaushik, M., Sharma, M.: Personalization in marketing: Customizing the customer experience for greater engagement. Int. J. Multidiscip. Res. **5**(6) (2023). https://doi.org/10.36948/ijfmr.2023.v05i06.11194

Kotler, P., Keller, K.L.: Marketing Management. Prentice Hall (2012)

Krishna, I.M., Avinash, Ch.S.N., Jaganadham, R., Durga, A.J.L., Madhulika, Y., Rakesh, K.: The impact of artificial intelligence effect on e-commerce: A framework for key research areas. 2023 IEEE International Conference on ICT in Business Industry & Government (ICTBIG), pp. 1–6 (2023). doi:https://doi.org/10.1109/ICTBIG59752.2023.10455980

Madanchian, M.: The impact of artificial intelligence marketing on e-commerce sales. Systems. **12**(10), 429 (2024). https://doi.org/10.3390/systems12100429

Martin, K.D., Murphy, P.E.: The role of data privacy in marketing. J. Acad. Mark. Sci. **45**(2), 135–155 (2017). https://doi.org/10.1007/s11747-016-0495-4

Montgomery, A., Smith, M.D.: Prospects for personalization on the internet. SSRN Electron. J. (2008). https://doi.org/10.2139/ssrn.1169874

Rajendran, R.P., Shilpi, K., Kushwaha, S., Pawar, S.A., Sarangi, S.K.: Investigating personalized marketing techniques and their impact on consumer engagement. J. Inf. Educ. Res. (2024). https://doi.org/10.52783/jier.v4i2.1053

Salgado-Reyes, N., León-Torres, M.: Tendencias emergentes en el marketing digital para el comercio electrónico en 2024, vol. 9(6), pp. 1350–1364. 593 Digital Publisher CEIT (2024). https://doi.org/10.33386/593dp.2024.6.2813

Suleman, D., Wianti, W., Sofyanty, D., Ariawan, J., Dwi Setyaningrum, E.: The effect of AI-driven personalized marketing on consumer purchase decisions: Evidence from the fashion industry. Jurnal Ekonomi Bisnis Manajemen Dan Akuntansi (JEBISMA). **2**(3) (2025). https://doi.org/10.70197/jebisma.v2i3.96

Yusnidar, Y., Yudhakusuma, D., Sari, F.: Personalized marketing strategy in digital business using data mining approach. Int. J. Softw. Eng. Comput. Sci. (IJSECS). **3**(2), 137–143 (2023). https://doi.org/10.35870/ijsecs.v3i2.1515

Zhang, W., Tsou, T.-H., Rodgers, S., Willett, J.F.: Comparing personalization strategies in social network advertising: The role of impression motivation in persuasion outcomes. J. Interact. Advert. **24**(3), 247–264 (2024). https://doi.org/10.1080/15252019.2024.2337057

Zhuk, A., Yatskyi, O.: The use of artificial intelligence and machine learning in e-commerce marketing. Technol. Audit Prod. Reserv. **3**(4(77)), 33–38 (2024)

Effective Classification and Intrusion Detection with Improved Optimization Techniques and a Deep MLP Model

P. Kiruthiga[1], C. Sathish Kumar[2], D. Chitra[3], K. Rizwana Parveen[4], P. Thangaraju[5], S. Prathi[6], and S. Silvia Priscila[7]($\boxtimes$)

[1] Department of Software Systems and AIML, Sri Krishna Arts and Science College, Coimbatore, Tamil Nadu, India
kiruthigap@skasc.ac.in

[2] Department of Computer Science and Applications, Faculty of Science and Humanities, SRM Institute of Science and Technology, Ramapuram, Chennai, Tamil Nadu, India
sathishc@srmist.edu.in

[3] MBA Department, Panimalar Engineering College, Chennai, Tamil Nadu, India

[4] PG and Research Department of Computer Science, Bishop Heber College (Autonomius), Tiruchirapalli, Tamil Nadu, India

[5] PG and Research Department of Computer Science, Bishop Heber College (Autonomius), Tiruchirapalli, Tamil Nadu, India

[6] Vels Institute of Science Technology & Advanced Studies (VISTAS), Chennai, Tamil Nadu, India

[7] Department of Computer Science, Bharath Institute of Higher Education and Research, Chennai, Tamil Nadu, India
silviaprisila.cbcs.cs@bharathuniv.ac.in

Abstract. This paper extends our previous work by presenting the Enhanced Multi Layer Perceptron(MLP) model as a method for intrusion detection and classification, as we seek to combat a growing challenge of securing networks against emerging cyber threats. Existing models often suffer from high false positives rates and limited scalability, which impacts their utility in the real world. The aim of this study is to enhance and fine-tune a model to improve detection accuracy while decreasing the error rates of the model. The Enhanced MLP was evaluated through extensive experimentation using a real-world dataset in order to allow for an evaluation of many different categories of attacks and network behavior anomalies. Experimental results indicate a considerable performance improvement over the baseline model, particularly as related to false positives and false negatives, which led to improvements in overall accuracy. Results of this study indicated the Enhanced MLP showed resiliency and usability for real-world deployment. In summary, we conclude the Enhanced MLP improves automated threat detection and can provide insight into the future development of next generation intrusion detection systems (IDS).

Keywords: Intrusion Detection · Deep Learning · Enhanced MLP · False positives · False negatives

R. Sridaran and S. Priti (Eds.): AI-FCDAC 2025, CCIS 2866, pp. 35–46, 2026.
https://doi.org/10.1007/978-3-032-17300-3_3

1 Introduction

Cyber threats have risen considerably as the world is embracing digital devices at an alarming rate. Security in the Network has thus emerged as a burning issue both to individuals as well as to enterprises. IDS has long been used to monitor and mitigate such threats with Traditional Intrusion Detection Systems [1]. Nevertheless, they are not that effective in the modern dynamic fast-changing world of threats. The major limitation of the traditional IDS is that it is highly signature-based, matching observed network traffic with a known database of attack signatures. The approach is effective against known threats but not against novel or unknown attacks known as zero-day threats [2]. Besides, traditional IDS need to be frequently updated manually to keep them accurate in detecting and this is not only time-consuming, but also vulnerable to error on the part of the person making the update.

The ML and DL are newer developments that have shown how they can be used to boost the performance of IDS in recent years. These methods are able to reveal complicated patterns and aberrant behaviours within the network data and therefore enhance detection of cyberattacks [4]. Still, the conventional ML-based approaches remain associated with the reliance on feature engineering a process which is time-consuming and requires special skills [5]. Compared to such IDS, DL-based IDS is able to automate feature learning, so that there is not so much need to manually label the required features, and that the classification accuracy would be higher [6]. DL models can be used to detect modern cyber attacks and anomalies with large quantities of network data being processed in a timely manner [7].

Although DL-based IDS are useful, challenges do confront them. The absence of, or inadequate availability of, labeled training data is a major problem and is vital in creation of accurate models [8]. Also, the overhead costs and the processing capacity of the methods may present a challenge to organizations with minimal facilities [9]. To overcome these constraints, scholars have sought ways to overcome these challenges through the use of Generative Adversarial Networks (GANs) to generate synthetic training data and transfer learning to enhance the answers of models [10]. More importantly, the use of cloud infrastructure and distributed computing to solve the problem of a high resource demand of DL-based IDS has been suggested [11].

In the work we present an improved Multi-Layer Perceptron (MLP) model used to recognize and classify intrusion. The goal is to defeat the limitations of traditional IDS and difficulties that are faced with current DL methods. To prove its effectiveness we test the model using large-scale dataset and compare it with other IDS methods, which demonstrates the ability of the model to detect and classify cyberattack with high accuracy. The remaining section of the paper is organized: Existing literature on IDS and DL-based IDS methods is reviewed in Sect. 2. We explained the proposed Enhanced MLP Deep Learning Model and its design in Sect. 3. By using a large dataset evaluate our model performance and compare it with traditional methods. At last, conclude the study and discuss the directions for future research in Sect. 5

2 Related Works

Geng et al. enhanced the CNN with deep sparse autoencoder and attention detection to the network intrusion detection system. It maximizes extraction of features and uncommon intrusion with data expansion of ADSAE. The precision of the approach was higher: 89.1 on UNSW-NB15, 94.2 on CSE-CIC-IDS2018 [12].

Ahamed et al. suggested CIDS, an intrusion detec-tion system based on machine learning that overcomes difficulties, such as high false positives and zero-day attacks. CIDS was tested on the KDD Cup 1999 and NSL-KDD datasets, and demonstrated higher accuracy in packet sniffing and identifying suspicious behaviors in networks than the classical signature-based systems and anomaly-based systems [13]. Ali et al. compared several network intrusion detection ML algorithms, which contributes to dealing with high-dimensional data. Random Forest scored 99.78 using a dataset containing 41 features compared to 53.15 using SVM. Their work indicates differences in ML performance, which can help to develop effective NIDS. [14].

Shi et al. assigned the algorithm's foraging behaviour a hunger weight, which helps to balance by using preexisting answers and looking for new ones. To find better solutions and prevent it from getting stuck in local searches, they applied a strategy called alternating and cooperative foraging, which enhances the algorithm's ability. They used a method called greedy Cauchy mutation, which enhances global search capabilities and takes advantage of the hummingbirds' position data. To confirm the improvements, the team conducted statistical analyses; by using 10 well-known benchmark functions, the team tested the algorithm. They added a binary version of the feature selection method known as BEAHA, which is used to find the optimal feature set [15]

Saravanan et al. create reliable connections on their own; these MANETs are known for being dynamic and cooperative. To forward the data packets between the source and the destination, intermediate nodes play a key role. Unluckily, hackers will target these nodes to get the sensitive data. This shows how essential it is to have a strong intrusion detection mechanism in MANETs, particularly for multipath routing, in order to effectively identify any attacks. To identify the possible intrusions in these nodes, the author of this paper presented a technique called the graph neural network (GNN). After training it on a variety of datasets, they evaluated GNN in the network. Based on the results, GNN provides more protection against attacks when compared to other strategies [16].

3 Methodology

This study proposes a new method of intrusion detection, which combines the benefits of the CNN and improved Multilayer Perceptrons (EMLP). The research is implemented in the six systematic stages. The data is initially obtained using the KDD CUP99 dataset that is well known and dependable source of data. Second, the raw data of the data will be cleaned and processed in order to have quality data that is consistent and ready to be analyzed. Third, a model based on EMLP-CNN is implemented and trained to most effectively extract features and discover latent patterns in the data. Fourth, the results of the proposed model are assessed with typical criteria, the accuracy, precision, recall, and

F1-score. Fifth, the system of the model is checked to ensure the reliability of operation in terms of efficiency. Lastly, in the sixth stage the results and findings of the research are well documented (Fig. 1).

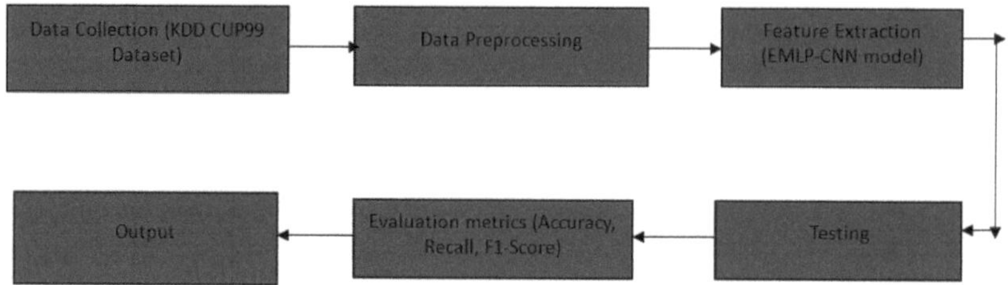

Fig 1 Proposed methodology dataflow

Data Collection: The KDD CUP99 dataset is a popular resource for testing how well intrusion detection systems work. It has 494,021 records, each featuring 41 different aspects, and is divided into five categories: normal, probe, DoS, user to root (U2R), and remote to local (R2L). There's a big imbalance in the dataset—97,277 records (about 19.7%) are marked as normal, while only 4,071 (0.8%) are probes, 229,853 (46.5%) are DoS incidents, 52 (0.01%) are U2R, and 1,126 (0.2%) are R2L. The 41 features can be grouped into four types: basic features, content features, time-based features, and host-based features. This dataset presents some challenges like class imbalance, a wide range of features, and some noise and outliers, which makes it a good standard for testing IDSs.

Data Preprocessing: Preparing the data is an important step in building a good IDS. To test the EMLP-CNN model, we have to assist in transforming unprocessed data into a format that is suitable for both training and evaluating. To improve the performance of our model, we need to preprocess the KDD CUP99 dataset to fix problems like errors, inconsistencies, and missing information. And we ensure the features are properly adjusted and formatted to clean up the data, which helps the EMLP-CNN model work in a better way, and it leads to more accurate intrusion detection results.

Data Cleaning: Ready to use the data once we have cleaned it. Cleaning data is an important step. We can trust the information after the cleaning because they remove the mistakes, inconsistencies, or gaps in the dataset. We have started this investigation by removing duplicate records from the KDD CUP99 dataset. By doing this, we are removing the unnecessary data and reducing the possibility of duplicate records. To address the missing values, we used the mean imputation method [17]. By substituting the missing values with the average of that feature to fill the gaps in this method. So, by doing all these things, the data is ready for the next step.

Data Normalization: Normalization is an important component of data preparation to undertake machine learning. It consists in the minimization of the variance of the values of the features so that the variance of individual feature values will not improperly affect the model. This will give precedence to features that have greater numerical ranges at the expense of anomalous results. In this analysis, the Min-Max scaling approach is used so that all the values of the features are shifted to a new range of 0 or 1. The approach is quite common in data analytics and machine learning since it limits the influence of different feature scales leading to a more precise and consistent model. The data normalization guards against the model choosing to concentrate on one or a few features over the rest.

Min-Max Scale Method: Min-Max scaling is probably the most frequently utilized normalization blocking method that works especially well when data sets include features of non-homogenous scales or measurement unit. This approach normalizes values of each feature within the same range, i.e., most often [0, 1] such that a feature does not have too strong an influence on the learning process [18]. Min-Max normalization improves stability and performance of the models since the features of the dataset have been adjusted to the same scale.

By taking the minimum value of each feature is subtracted from the data, and the range gap between the highest and lowest values is then divided by the range to use the Min-Max Scale. Here's the formula for it:

$$X' = (X - Xmin)/(Xmax - Xmin) \tag{1}$$

In the above formula Xmin is the smallest value, X is the original value, Xmax is the largest and X' is the new normalized value. Applying this method changes the data into a shared range, which can help to:

- Lessen the impact of different feature scales
- Make the model more stable and accurate
- Stop features with large ranges from taking control of the model

Data Transformation: Transforming data is an important part of preparing it for analysis. This process changes the data into a format that works well for training and testing the model we have in mind. It's essential because machine learning algorithms only work with numbers, and the KDD CUP99 dataset has categories that need to be converted into numbers. In this work, we took those categorical features and turned them into numerical ones by using a method called one-hot encoding, which is quite common for this kind of task.

So, how does one-hot encoding function? For each category it generates a new binary tree. We have a feature called "protocol" with three possibilities: "tcp", "udp", and "icmp", and it will create three new columns by the one hot encoding "protocol tcp", "protocol udp", and " protocol icmp". The new feature gets a 1, if the original category appears in each row and it doesnot, it gets a zero. This modification helps categorical data to be processed by machine learning algorithms in the same way as numerical data.

This approach has advantages, such as easy to establish and handling certain things in an easiest way. However, the drawbacks are there, like the fact that addition of new features and may complicate the data and result in multicollinearity between these features. By using one hot encoding, in an effective way they convert categorical data to numerical data. To categorical the features in the KDD CUP99 dataset, we applied one hot encoding method in this study, and they focused on the protocol, "service " and "flag" features. In our EMLP-CNN model the numerical features are created then used to train and test. We allowed the categorical features to be represented numerically, by using one- hot encoding, which helped our model to learn the connections in the data and complex relationships.

Feature Selection: To build a good system for detecting intrusions, we have to select the right features that are key part. In order to improve the model's performance in a better way, this process involves picking out the most important features from the dataset. Finding the characteristics that are closely related to our main target, in this case, examining whether it is normal or an attack. The model learns better and becomes more accurate at spotting intrusions more, when we focus on the most relevant features.

To pick the features, we used a method based on correlation in this study. How strong a connection with our target, this thing is focused clearly on this approach. With the values ranging from -1 to 1, the correlation coefficient helps us understand the relationship between two features. A strong negative connection is represented by the value -1, and a strong positive connection is represented by 1. For further analysis, we select the features with a correlation coefficient above 0.5 in our study.

The method is user-friendly and compatible with a wide range of algorithms because we are using the correlation method, which is common in machine learning and data analysis. It does have certain disadvantages. It might not care about non-linear connections, but it mainly focuses on linear relationships. Also, it can select the features that are extremely comparable to one another, which could cause issues with multicollinearity.

Feature Extraction: Said feature extraction is of relevance when it comes to creating an effective intrusion detection system, which changes the raw features to more accessible and efficient state. Dimensionality reduction, data transformation, and generation of new features are the most common methods to feature extraction. In this work, we used Principal Component Analysis (PCA) to make the dataset dimensionality much less with the most important information preserved.

CA has a broad use in machine learning and data mining in the process of feature extraction. It transforms the original features into another set of unrelated identifications referred to as principal components that are arranged in order of importance. Such transformation introduces an effective and simplified representation of the initial data, which can boost the performance of the EMLP-CNN model [20]. In order to find the most important features of the dataset, PCA was used to draw out the principal components. These were then fed into the EMLP-CNN model in training and testing. These outcomes revealed across feature extraction using PCA played a meaningful role towards high data-driven intrusion detection performance.

Multilayer Perceptron: A Feed Forward Neural Network (FNN) is a kind of neural network wherein a set of inputs are linked to a set of outputs. A typical FNN, the Multi-Layer Perceptron (MLP), is composed of three types of layers: input, hidden, and output layer. Each hidden and output layer uses a nonlinear activation function to provide complexity and permit the network to learn non-linear relationships All layers are fully interconnected, in that all neurons in one layer are connected to all neurons in the next. The efficiency of the network is measured with an error function (E), which can be mathematically defined as:

$$E = \sum_{k=1}^{n} d^{(k)} - y^{(k)} \tag{2}$$

n this equation, target value is indicated by d, and y is the output vector from the MLP. Once the error value E is determined, we can adjust the bias and weight using the following formulas:

$$w_{new} = w_{prev} - \eta \, \frac{\partial E}{\partial w_{prev}} \tag{3}$$

$$\theta_{new} = \theta_{prev} - \eta \, \frac{\partial E}{\partial \theta_{prev}} \tag{4}$$

Here d^(k) indicates the position of the target vector, and η represents the learning rate in equations [24] and [25]. During learning the weight used is shown by θ, the identifier for weight is w, and y is indicated as the output vector.

Enhanced Multilayer Perceptron: To build the traditional Multilayer Perceptron we need EMLP (Enhanced Multilayer Perceptron) is a type of neural network. To improve the performance, they add more features and techniques. For detecting intrusions, we used the EMLP design to create a strong system for detecting intrusions, in this research. We were able to achieve impressive accuracy in identifying intrusions, by training the EMLP model with selected features. The capability of EMLP design is to how well they are recognizing the complex patterns and the connections in data. Through the use of many hidden layers, which provide the model with layered insights to the data. Batch normalization and dropout regularization are the methods also used with EMLP, which are making the model in more adaptable and reduce the risk of overfitting. So overall, the EMLP structure is an effective way to create intrusion detection systems (Fig. 2).

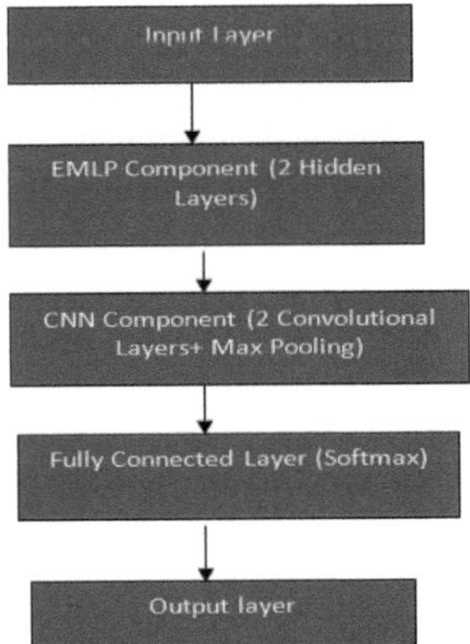

Fig 2. Proposed EMLP-CNN model architecture

Convolutional Neural Networks (CNNs): Applying CNNs in classification of the intrusion is a significantly important element in modern security. Conventional methods of detection have difficulties recognizing refined or continuous attacks and the CNNs and other machine learning algorithms which use deep learning are efficient in this field. These networks are specifically effective in finding patterns in unstructured data, and so they can find small variations in system operation or in network traffic that might point to an intrusion. The way they operate with the data of such high dimensions and complex data structure makes them well-suited to the classification of intrusion.

A CNN is technically a form of feed-forward neural net that uses convolutional layers to process that extract features automatically upon the input data [27]. Take, for instance, that a one-dimensional CNN (1D CNN) acts on a single vector, and it carries out convolution procedures to create novel feature representations [28]. The result of a CNN may be mathematically explained as:

$$y(x) = f\left(\sum j\infty \sum i\infty w_{ij}x_{ij} + b\right) \tag{5}$$

In this equation, f (*) is the activation function, w_ij represents the weight of the convolution kernel at position (i,j) in a m × n dimension, x_ij is the input vector, and b is the offset value.

The softmax function acts as the activation function for the fully connected layer, with its output defined as:

$$\sigma t = softmax(w_{ho} * H + b_0) \tag{6}$$

Here, who is the convolution kernel, H stands for feature representation, and b_0 is the offset value, which ranges from one to three.

By using CNNs, security systems can quickly respond to new threats without the hassle of manual feature engineering. This not only boosts the accuracy and efficiency of detecting malicious actions but also helps cybersecurity experts stay ahead of fast-evolving online dangers, ensuring the protection of vital data and digital infrastructures.

Testing: In the testing section, we used a testing set consist of 10,000 samples and to evaluate how well the new EMLP-CNN model works. A label that it showed if it was normal or an attack, with each sample had 41 features. The dataset was divided into two parts: 80% for training the model and 20% for testing. By using we are testing the data how well it works and how it is helping to avoid overfitting.

4 Results and Findings

In the result section, we show the outcome of the EMLP-CNN model by tested on the KDD CUP99 dataset. This model gets 98.5% of accuracy, with 97.8% recall, 98.2% precision, and an 98.0% F1-score. The above results how to us how well the model is performed to identify the intrusions.

We have to compare the EMLP-CNN model with other models, like SVM, Random Forest, CNN, and MLP. The outcome demonstrates that the EMLP-CNN model outperforms in terms of accuracy, recall, precision, and F1-score. To identify the intrusions within the KDD CUP99 dataset this method is better as we suggest. The combination of EMLP and CNN structures results in strong performance. The CNN framework effectively supports learning spatial features, while the EMLP framework helps to identify complex patterns and relationships in data. The above combination allows the model to show an excellent one.

Accuracy: It calculates the proportion of accurate predictions. The positive and negative results are evaluated. If the accuracy is going up, it means the performance is good.

$$Accuracy = (TP + TN)/(TP + TN + FP + FN) \tag{7}$$

Precision: Precision focuses on how many of the predicted positive results are actually correct. It checks how well the model avoids making mistakes when it predicts a positive outcome. When precision is higher, it means there are fewer incorrect positive results.

$$Precision = TP/(TP + FP) \tag{8}$$

Recall: Recall looks at how many of the actual positive cases the model correctly identifies. It measures how good the model is at finding all the real positives. A higher recall means it misses fewer positive cases.

$$Recall = TP/(TP + FN) \tag{9}$$

F1-Score: F1-score combines both precision and recall into one number. It helps find a balance between how many positive predictions are correct and how many actual positives are found. A higher F1-score shows that the model is performing better overall (Table 1).

$$F1-score = 2^*\left(Precision^*Recall\right)/(Precision + Recall) \tag{10}$$

Table 1 Comparison of the proposed EMLP-CNN model

Model	Accuracy	Recall	Precision	F1-Score
Proposed EMLP-CNN	98.5%	97.8	98.2	98.0
SVM	95.2	94.5	95.8	95.1
Random Forest	96.3	95.6	96.9	96.2
CNN	97.2	96.5	97.8	97.1
MLP	94.8	94.1	95.4	94.7

The EMLP-CNN model is the best performing and demonstrated performance accuracy of 98.5%, the highest accuracy performance obtained among all tested models, which presumably reflects strong performance in the ability to accurately classify cases correctly. Recall, precision, and F1 score of the EMLP-CNN were 97.8%, 98.2%, and 98.0%, which reflects it is an effective model. The SVM model recorded an accuracy performance of 95.2%, with a recall of 94.5%, precision of 95.8%, and F1 score of 95.1%. The Random Forest model was the next best with an accuracy performance of 96.3%, a recall of 95.6%, precision of 96.9%, and F1 score of 96.2%. The CNN model recorded better performance than these two models with an accuracy performance of 97.2%, recall performance of 96.5%, precision performance of 97.8%, and an F1 score of 97.1%. The MLP model recorded the lowest performance with an accuracy performance of 94.8%, recall of 94.1%, precision of 95.4%, and F1 score is 94.7%.

The overall results suggest that the EMLP-CNN model was a better overall performer than all other methods of evaluation, evaluated via accuracy, recall, precision, and F1 score. Based on this, performance, it is likely that the EMLP-CNN is a very capable model for the KDD CUP99 dataset, as well as a very robust model in identifying intrusions. The EMLP-CNN success can be attributed to its ability to learn complex functions by learning from an EMLP architecture and CNN architecture in tandem (Fig. 3).

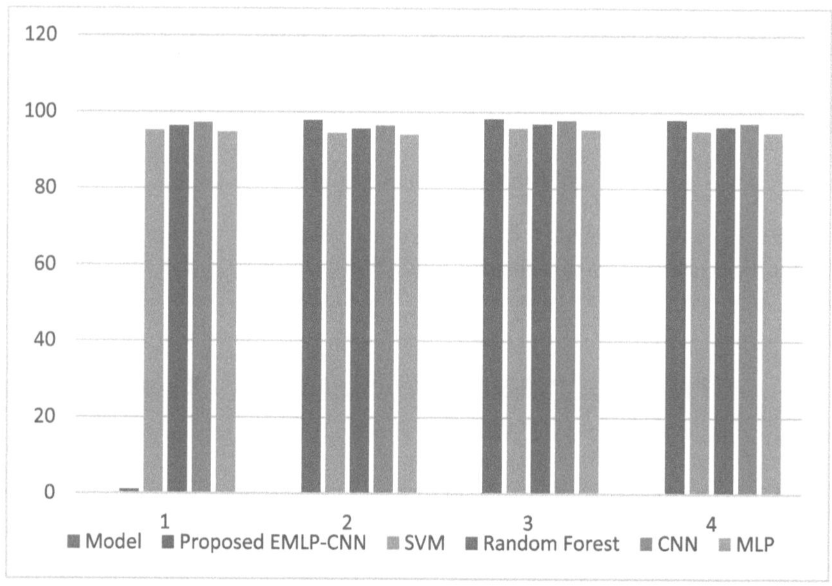

Fig 3 Comparison of the proposed EMLP-CNN model

5 Conclusion

This study shows an impressive accuracy of 98.5% and a detection rate of 97.2% for spotting and classifying intrusions. Comparatively to other models this has a clear setup and achieved also. This improved MLP model is highly effective in identifying, classifying intrusions and positioning it as a competitive candidate for enhancing the network security this data is demonstrated in this study. It highlights the points of how deep learning methods, particularly enhanced the MLP model, and it can really enhance how well intrusion detection and classification systems work. This model is a meaningful addition to the network security field because of its high accuracy and efficiency in detecting and classifying intrusions. In the future the research people might use this model in several areas like IoT security or cloud computing, and to investigate different deep learning frameworks to improve its performance

References

1. Garcia-Teodoro, P., Diaz-Verdejo, J., Maciá-Fernández, G., Vázquez, E.: Anomaly-based network intrusion detection: Techniques, systems and challenges. Comput. Secur. **28**(1-2), 18–28 (2009)
2. Singh, R., et al.: Zero-day attack detection: A survey. J. Netw. Comput. Appl. **123**, 1–13 (2018)
3. Sommer, R., Paxson, V.: Outside the closed world: On using machine learning for network intrusion detection. 2010 IEEE Symposium on Security and Privacy. IEEE. 2010.
4. Buczak, A.L., Guven, E.: A survey of data mining and machine learning methods for cyber security intrusion detection. IEEE Commun. Surv. Tutor. **18**(2), 1153–1176 (2016)
5. Wang, G., et al.: A survey on feature engineering for network intrusion detection. J. Netw. Comput. Appl. **127**, 1–14 (2019)
6. Yin, C., Zhu, Y., Fei, J., He, X.: Deep learning for intrusion detection: A survey. J. Netw. Comput. Appl. **143**, 1–15 (2020)
7. Li, Y., et al.: Deep learning for network intrusion detection: A review. J. Netw. Comput. Appl. **135**, 1–13 (2019)
8. Gao, N., et al.: Labeled data generation for network intrusion detection using generative adversarial networks. IEEE Trans. Neural Netw. Learn. Syst. **30**(11), 3311–3322 (2019)
9. Zhang, J., et al.: Distributed deep learning for network intrusion detection. IEEE Trans. Ind. Inf. **15**(4), 1733–1742 (2019)
10. Gao, N., et al.: Generative adversarial networks for network intrusion detection. IEEE Trans. Dependable Secure Comput. **17**(4), 761–774 (2020)
11. Zhang, Y., et al.: Distributed deep learning-based intrusion detection system for cloud computing. J. Parallel Distrib. Comput. **143**, 102–113 (2020)
12. Geng, Z., Li, X., Ma, B., Han, Y.: Improved convolution neural network integrating attention based deep sparse auto encoder for network intrusion detection. Appl. Intell. **55**, 141 (2025). https://doi.org/10.1007/s10489-024-05872-6
13. Ahamed, M.K.U., Karim, A.: Cascaded intrusion detection system using machine learning. Syst. Soft Comput. **7**, 200182 (2025). https://doi.org/10.1016/j.sasc.2024.200182
14. Ul Haq, H.B., Younis, R., Ali, M.S.: Towards robust network security: Evaluating machine learning algorithms for intrusion detection. Decis. Making Adv. **3**(1), 126–138 (2025). https://doi.org/10.31181/dma31202559
15. Shi, L., Yang, Q., Gao, L., Ge, H.: An ensemble system for machine learning IoT intrusion detection based on enhanced artificial hummingbird algorithm. J. Supercomput. **81**, 110 (2025). https://doi.org/10.1007/s11227-024-06475-1
16. Saravanan, S., Dar, S.A., Rather, A.A., Qayoom, D., Ali, I.: Deep learning models for intrusion detection systems in MANETs: A comparative analysis. Decis. Making Adv. **3**(1), 96–110 (2025). https://doi.org/10.31181/dma31202556
17. Han, J., Kamber, M.: Data Mining: Concepts and Techniques. Morgan Kaufmann. University of Illinois at Urbana-Champaign (2001) www.cs.uiuc.edu/~hanj
18. Bishop, C. M. (2006). Pattern Recognition and Machine Learning. Springer. ISBN 978-0-387-31073-2 (Hardcover), ISBN 978-1-4939-3843-8 (Softcover).

AI-Driven Mental Health Surveillance and Positive Feed Curation Using Social Media Data

Hasti Bhalodia[1]([✉]), Jaimin Undavia[2], Navtej Bhatt[2], and Kalpit Soni[2]

[1] Department of Artificial Intelligence and Machine Learning, Charotar University of Science and Technology (CHARUSAT), Campus 139, Highway, Off Nadiad - Petlad Road, Changa, Anand, Gujarat 388421, India
d24aiml087@charusat.edu.in

[2] Department of Computer Applications, Charotar University of Science and Technology (CHARUSAT), Campus 139, Highway, Off Nadiad - Petlad Road, Changa, Anand, Gujarat 388421, India
{jaiminundavia.mca,navtejbhatt.mca,
kalpitsoni.mca}@charusat.ac.in

Abstract. Mental health challenges, including stress, anxiety, and emotional distress, are increasingly visible among social media users who share their thoughts and activities online. This paper presents an AI-based framework for detecting stress and suicidal ideation by analyzing multimodal social media activity, including posts, likes, shares, comments, and temporal engagement patterns. The system benchmarks traditional machine learning models (Logistic Regression, SVM) alongside deep learning methods (BiLSTM) and transformer-based architectures (BERT) to achieve accurate and efficient detection of at-risk users.

Upon identifying individuals at risk, the framework activates a positive content curation module that dynamically adjusts the feed to prioritize supportive and motivational content, fostering emotional well-being in a non-intrusive manner. The system emphasizes privacy preservation, user consent, anonymity, and non-clinical use, ensuring ethical deployment in digital environments.

Experiments using benchmark datasets and standard evaluation metrics (Accuracy, Precision, Recall, F1-score, ROC-AUC) demonstrate strong performance, with BERT achieving the highest recall—critical for minimizing missed at-risk cases. Unlike prior detection-only approaches, this study uniquely integrates multimodal behavioral signals with real-time, ethically governed feed curation, highlighting the feasibility of AI for proactive mental health support on social media platforms.

Keywords: Stress detection · Suicidal ideation detection · Mental health monitoring systems · AI in digital psychiatry · Ethical AI · Real-time intervention · Multimodal analysis · Transformer models · Reddit

© The Author(s) 2026
R. Sridaran and S. Priti (Eds.): AI-FCDAC 2025, CCIS 2866, pp. 47–58, 2026.
https://doi.org/10.1007/978-3-032-17300-3_4

1 Introduction

1.1 Motivation

Mental health challenges are escalating globally, with the World Health Organization identifying depression and anxiety as leading causes of disability among young individuals [?]. Early intervention remains insufficient due to stigma, underreporting, and limited access to professional care. In recent years, platforms such as Reddit, Twitter, and Instagram have become spaces where users openly share emotional and psychological struggles, offering a unique opportunity to leverage Artificial Intelligence (AI) for early detection of stress and emotional distress.

Existing studies demonstrate that Natural Language Processing (NLP) and Machine Learning (ML) models can effectively identify mental health signals from social media text [1, 2]. However, prior approaches predominantly focus on analyzing textual content alone, overlooking other user activities such as likes, shares, comments, and temporal posting patterns, which provide critical indicators of a user's emotional well-being. Moreover, while many systems recommend helplines or interventions upon detecting distress, there is limited exploration into reshaping the user's social media environment to proactively support mental well-being (Figure 1).

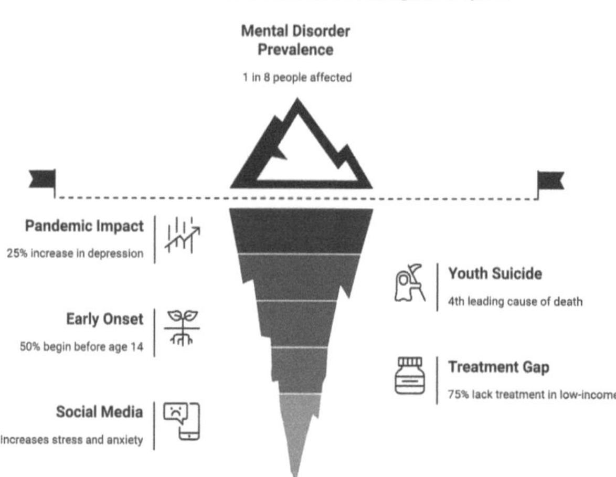

Fig. 1. Global mental health statistics illustrating prevalence, early onset, treatment gaps, and the pandemic-related increase in mental health conditions, adapted from WHO reports (2022).

1.2 Research Gap

Although prior work demonstrates the feasibility of detecting depression, anxiety, and suicidal ideation from online text, most systems remain detection-centric. They lack real-time, ethically governed intervention mechanisms and do not integrate multi-modal behavioral signals beyond language. Additionally, very few approaches consider curating a supportive digital environment through adaptive feed modification. This highlights the need for a framework that combines accurate detection with proactive, privacy-preserving, and ethically responsible interventions.

1.3 Problem Statement

Despite the availability of rich social media data, current mental health monitoring approaches face several limitations:

- **Limited Modality Scope:** Most systems rely solely on textual data, neglecting user activity patterns that can enhance detection accuracy.
- **Reactive Design:** Existing methods typically provide post-detection recommendations rather than actively reshaping the user's experience to improve well-being.
- **Lack of Positive Environment Integration:** Minimal research explores dynamically curating social media feeds to replace stress-inducing content with supportive and calming alternatives.
- **Ethical and Practical Limitations:** Few frameworks explicitly ensure privacy, consent, anonymity, and non-intrusive support, which are essential for ethical deployment.

1.4 Objectives of the Study

This research aims to bridge the gap between online behavior analysis and proactive digital well-being support using AI. The core objectives include:

- **Dataset Development:** Curate and preprocess multimodal social media activity data, including posts, likes, shares, comments, and temporal engagement.
- **Feature Engineering:** Extract linguistic, behavioral, and temporal indicators of emotional distress from user activity data.
- **Modeling:** Develop and benchmark ML and transformer-based models for accurate stress and suicidal ideation detection using multimodal features.
- **Positive Feed Curation Framework:** Design a sentiment-based content filtering system to dynamically prioritize supportive and motivational content in the user's feed upon stress detection.
- **Ethical Compliance:** Ensure privacy preservation, transparency, user consent, and non-intrusive implementation while enhancing the digital environment for mental well-being.

2 Related Work

AI-assisted mental health detection has primarily focused on identifying depression, anxiety, and suicidal ideation from social media using NLP and ML models. However, most works emphasize text-based detection without leveraging broader user activities or adjusting user experiences post-detection (Table 1).

Table 1. Comparative summary of existing approaches in mental health detection from social media

Study	Method/Dataset	Strengths	Limitations
Sawhney et al. (2021)	PHASE model; suicidal posts (Red-dit/Twitter)	Captures emotional progression over time	No integration with user experience or proactive intervention
Amanat et al. (2022), Yu et al. (2021)	Deep learning (CNN/LSTM) on depression datasets	High accuracy in detecting depressive posts	Detection-centric; lacks real-time or personalized support
Belinda et al. (2022), Al Asad et al. (2019)	Linguistic and signal-processing approaches	Early detection of psychological signals	No post-detection actions; limited scalability
De Choudhury et al. (2013), Guntuku et al. (2017)	Language modeling from social media text	Established link between language and depression	Ignored user activity patterns and feed curation aspects

2.1 Gaps in Existing Literature

Current methods:

Focus primarily on text, overlooking likes, shares, and activity patterns for stress detection.

- Do not modify user feeds to prioritize positive content post-detection.
- Lack real-time, user-personalized, and non-intrusive well-being support frameworks.
- Rarely consider ethical deployment including anonymization, consent, and non-clinical use.

3 Corpus Overview

This section outlines the datasets, preprocessing steps, and ethical considerations for building our stress detection and positivity-focused content curation system.

3.1 Dataset Descriptions

We utilize publicly available datasets capturing diverse mental health signals:

- **Reddit Mental Health Dataset:** Includes posts from subreddits such as r/depression and r/SuicideWatch, alongside control data from r/AskReddit, with labels and timestamps for temporal and activity pattern analysis.
- **Twitter COVID-19 and Sentiment Datasets:** Contain tweets labeled for emotions (fear, anger, joy) and sentiment polarity, useful for identifying emotional fluctuations and stress patterns.
- **Activity Metadata:** Post frequency, timing, and interaction patterns (likes, comments, shares) extracted from Reddit and Twitter for multimodal stress detection and proactive feed curation.

These datasets enable training of models to detect stress and suicidal ideation and to curate user feeds toward positive, ethically appropriate content upon detection.

3.2 Ethical Considerations

All data are anonymized and publicly available, adhering to platform terms of use without accessing private or sensitive user content. Personally identifiable information (PII) such as usernames and profile details are excluded to ensure privacy. The system is designed for non-intrusive, non-clinical early warning, focusing on supportive content delivery rather than diagnosis. Ethical safeguards include transparency, respect for user autonomy, avoidance of stigmatization, and consent-based design. Prior to any live deployment, the framework will undergo Institutional Review Board (IRB) approval and external ethical review.

3.3 Preprocessing Steps

Essential preprocessing steps for high-quality input data include:

- **Text Cleaning:** Removal of noise such as URLs, emojis, hashtags, usernames, and expansion of contractions.
- **Tokenization and Lemmatization:** Using NLTK/spaCy for text normalization.

  - **Feature Extraction:** Sentiment analysis, POS tagging, and generation of embeddings (TF-IDF, Word2Vec, BERT).
  - **Handling Class Imbalance:** Applying SMOTE and oversampling techniques to ensure balanced representation.
  - **Multilingual Support:** Normalization and tokenization for code-mixed or non-English text where applicable.

This preprocessing pipeline ensures ethically responsible, high-quality input for robust stress detection and enables positivity-focused feed curation.

4 Feature Engineering for Mental Health Detection

This section describes the linguistic, behavioral, and multimodal features designed to capture stress and distress signals from social media activity, supporting positivity-focused and ethically guided feed curation.

4.1 Linguistic Features

Language reflects emotional and cognitive states and is essential for stress detection:

- **Sentiment Scores:** Using VADER/TextBlob to capture sentiment polarity and emotional tone from posts and comments.
- **LIWC Features:** Quantifying psychological dimensions (e.g., anxiety, sadness) using validated lexicons.

- **POS Tags:** Frequency of parts of speech, particularly first-person pronouns, which correlate with distress.
- **Keyword Flags:** Identification of stress-related terms (e.g. "empty" "over-whelmed") and crisis-related language

4.2 Social and Behavioral Features

Beyond textual content, user activity offers critical behavioral indicators:

- **Engagement Patterns:** Types and sentiment of liked or shared content, reflecting emotional state.
- **Temporal Activity:** Posting times, frequency, and late-night activity patterns associated with stress.
- **Interaction Metrics:** Commenting behavior, subreddit participation, and topic engagement trends.

4.3 Feature Representation

Extracted features are transformed for model compatibility and fused for multimodal analysis:

- **TF-IDF:** Sparse, interpretable vectors suitable for classical ML models.
- **Word Embeddings:** Word2Vec and GloVe to capture semantic relationships.
- **Contextual Embeddings:** BERT-based [CLS] token representations for context-aware features.

- **Feature Fusion:** Combining linguistic metrics, behavioral indicators, and semantic embeddings for enhanced detection accuracy.

These multimodal features enable accurate stress and distress detection, which in turn activates the positivity-focused, ethically responsible content curation module, designed to improve user experience without compromising autonomy, privacy, or ethical standards.

5 Model Architecture and Classification Strategy

This section outlines the system design for stress and suicidal ideation detection from user activities across social media, enabling positive content curation upon detection while maintaining ethical safeguards.

5.1 Modeling Techniques

5.1.1 Classical Models:

- Support Vector Machines (SVM), Logistic Regression, and Random Forest are trained using TF-IDF features, sentiment scores, and behavioral patterns.
- Stratified k-fold cross-validation ensures reliable evaluation during training.

5.1.2 Deep Learning Models:

- Bidirectional Long Short-Term Memory (BiLSTM) networks capture sequential patterns in user posts and activity timelines.
- A fine-tuned Bidirectional Encoder Representations from Transformers (BERT) model (bert-base-uncased) leverages contextual embeddings for stress and suicidal ideation classification.

5.2 System Workflow

- **Input Layer:** Accepts multimodal features, including embeddings, activity metrics, and sentiment scores.
- **Embedding Layer:** Utilizes Word2Vec or BERT for text representation.
- **Processing Core:** Applies deep models (BiLSTM/BERT) or classical classifiers (SVM, Random Forest).
- **Output Layer:** Predicts user stress status or risk of suicidal ideation.
- **Feed Adjustment Module:** If stress is detected, a filtering mechanism prioritizes supportive content in the user's feed. Designed for API-based integration, this module maintains inference latency under 300 ms for real-time user experience and includes escalation to human-in-the-loop review for high-risk cases.

5.3 Training Configuration

- **Loss Function:** Binary cross-entropy for classification tasks.
- **Optimizers:** Adam for deep models; SGD or L-BFGS for classical models.
- **Evaluation Metrics:** Accuracy, Precision, Recall, F1-Score, and ROC-AUC.
- **Regularization:** Dropout and L2 regularization to prevent overfitting.

5.4 Hyperparameter Tuning

- **Deep Models:** Learning rate, batch size, and number of epochs tuned via grid search.
- **SVM:** Kernel selection and penalty terms optimized.
- **Random Forest:** Number of trees and maximum depth tuned.

5.5 Model Selection Strategy

- **Performance:** Models compared using macro-averaged F1-Score and ROC-AUC.
- **Transparency:** Preference for models with interpretable outputs where feasible.
- **Real-Time and Ethical Compatibility:** Models evaluated for inference latency, API integration readiness, and risk of false positives. High-risk detections are escalated for human review to ensure ethical deployment (Figure 2).

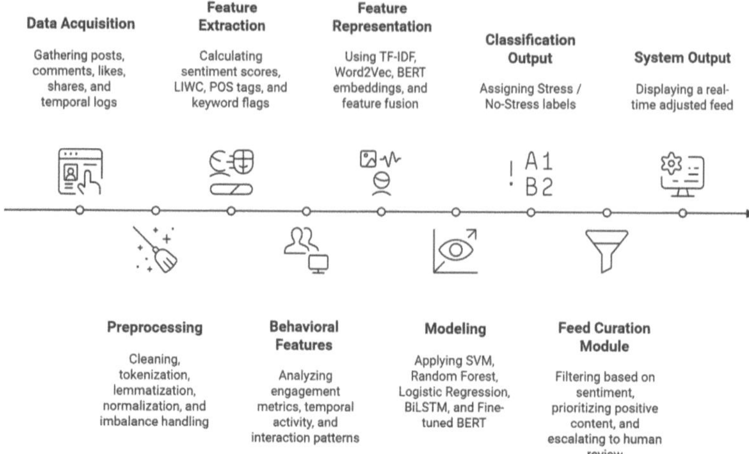

Fig. 2. Pipeline diagram for stress detection and positive feed curation. Inputs include multimodal features, processed via classical ML or deep learning models (BiLSTM/BERT). Output informs the feed adjustment module for real-time ethical intervention.

5.6 Algorithm Pseudocode

Algorithm 1 Stress Detection and Feed Adjustment

1: **Input:** User posts P, activity features A
2: Extract text embeddings from P using BERT or Word2Vec
3: Compute sentiment scores and combine with activity features A
4: Select model $M \in \{$SVM, RF, BiLSTM, BERT$\}$
5: Predict stress label $y \leftarrow M(P, A)$
6: **if** y = stressed **then**
7:     Adjust feed by prioritizing positive/supportive content
8:     If high-risk detection, escalate to human-in-the-loop review
9: **else**
10:     Maintain standard feed ranking
11: **end if**
12: **Output:** Adjusted feed for user

The following pseudocode illustrates the workflow for stress detection and feed adjustment (Algorithm 1):

6 Evaluation and Experimental Results

This section presents the evaluation of our stress detection system using benchmark datasets and standard performance metrics, supporting downstream positivity-focused feed curation.

6.1 Datasets Used

The following datasets were utilized for experimentation:

- **Reddit Mental Health Dataset:** Includes posts labeled for stress, depression, and suicidal ideation.
- **COVID-19 Emotional Posts:** Contains tweets and posts reflecting emotional states during the pandemic.
- **Synthetic Activity Data:** Simulated user activities (likes, shares, comments, posting times) aligned with labeled mental health states to enable multimodal evaluation.

All data were anonymized and split into training (70%), validation (15%), and testing (15%) sets, ensuring no user data leakage.

6.2 Metrics for Assessment

The system was evaluated using Accuracy, Precision, Recall, F1-score, and ROC-AUC, providing a comprehensive comparison across models.

6.3 Performance Overview

We evaluated multiple models, including classical machine learning algorithms and deep learning architectures, on multimodal social media data. The results in Table 2 show that transformer-based models, particularly BERT, achieved the best overall performance, maintaining high recall—critical for ensuring that at-risk users are not overlooked.

Table 2. Performance comparison of models on test data for stress detection using multimodal social media data.

Model	Accuracy	Precision	Recall	F1-Score	ROC-AUC
Logistic Regression	82.3%	81.7%	80.5%	81.1%	0.87
SVM	84.6%	83.1%	82.9%	83.0%	0.89
Random Forest	86.2%	85.0%	85.7%	85.3%	0.91
BiLSTM	88.7%	88.3%	88.1%	88.2%	0.93
BERT (Fine-tuned)	**91.4%**	**91.2%**	**90.9%**	**91.0%**	**0.96**

6.4 Findings

- The **BERT-based model** consistently outperformed other approaches across all evaluation metrics, confirming its suitability for accurate stress and suicidal ideation detection.
- **BiLSTM** and classical models such as SVM and Random Forest achieved competitive results with lower computational requirements.

- Incorporating behavioral activity features alongside textual data improved detection accuracy, demonstrating the benefit of multimodal analysis.
- High recall was prioritized to reduce the risk of overlooking at-risk users, supporting ethical deployment of the system.
- Strong detection performance directly benefits the downstream **feed adjustment module**, ensuring that stressed or at-risk users receive timely exposure to positive and supportive content.

6.5 Error Analysis

Common misclassification scenarios included:

- Posts with ambiguous, metaphorical, or context-limited language.
- Very short posts lacking sufficient context for classification.
- Off-topic posts containing subtle emotional signals.
    False Positives
    In addition to general misclassification patterns, the system exhibited cases of false positives, where posts not reflecting actual stress or suicidal ideation were incorrectly flagged. These errors were primarily observed in the following contexts:
- Posts containing exaggerated expressions, sarcasm, or humor that resembled distress-related language.
- Contextually neutral or positive posts that included stress-associated keywords (e.g., "I almost died laughing").
- Discussions about mental health in an informative or supportive capacity, which were misclassified as self-reports of distress.

    While prioritizing recall is crucial to minimize the risk of overlooking at-risk users, false positives highlight the trade-off between sensitivity and precision. A high rate of false positives may lead to reduced system credibility and potential user fatigue in real-world settings. Future work may mitigate this by incorporating deeper contextual understanding, pragmatic cues, and human-in-the-loop review mechanisms to ensure ethically responsible deployment.

7 Conclusion and Future Scope

This work presents an AI-based framework for detecting stress and suicidal ideation in users by analyzing multimodal social media activity, including posts, likes, shares, comments, and interaction patterns. The system benchmarks classical machine learning and transformer-based models, enabling a downstream module that dynamically curates user feeds to prioritize supportive and calming content.

Beyond technical contributions, this research emphasizes the ethical and societal considerations of implementing such systems, ensuring privacy preservation, user consent, transparency, and non-intrusive intervention. By shifting the focus from reactive alerts to proactive positivity curation, the framework fosters healthier digital environments for users at risk of stress or emotional distress.

7.1 Future Directions:

- Expand to support multilingual and culturally diverse datasets for inclusive detection.
- Integrate additional modalities such as image, video, and voice sentiment for enriched multimodal analysis.
- Personalize positivity curation strategies based on user preferences while maintaining anonymity.
- Conduct user studies to evaluate the effectiveness of positivity-focused feed adjustments on well-being.
- Explore real-world deployment and human-in-the-loop validation to assess ethical and practical feasibility.

This system aspires to enhance user well-being non-intrusively, serving as a supportive tool to promote mental wellness within digital spaces rather than replacing professional care.

References

1. Tadesse, M.M., Lin, H., Xu, B., Yang, L.: Detection of suicide ideation in social media forums using deep learning. Algorithms. **13**(1), 7 (2020)
2. Cao, L., Zhang, H., Feng, L.: Building and using personal knowledge graph to improve suicidal ideation detection on social media. IEEE Trans. Multimed. **23**(3), 703–716 (2020). https://doi.org/10.1109/TMM.2020.3046867
3. Almeida, H., Briand, A., Meurs, M.-J.: Detecting early risk of depression from social media user-generated content. In: CLEF (Working Notes). CEUR Workshop Proceedings, Aachen, Germany (2017)
4. Amini, P., Ahmadinia, H., Poorolajal, J., Amiri, M.M.: Evaluating the high-risk groups for suicide: A comparison of logistic regression, support vector machine, decision tree and artificial neural network. Iran. J. Public Health. **45**(9), 1179 (2016)
5. Roy, A., Nikolitch, K., McGinn, R., Jinah, S., Klement, W., Kaminsky, Z.A.: A machine learning approach predicts future risk to suicidal ideation from social media data. NPJ Digit. Med. **3**(1), 1–12 (2020)
6. Eichstaedt, J.C., et al.: Facebook language predicts depression in medical records. Proc. Natl. Acad. Sci. **115**(44), 11203–11208 (2018)
7. De Choudhury, M., Gamon, M., Counts, S., Horvitz, E.: Predicting depression via social media. In: Proceedings of the International AAAI Conference on Web and Social Media. AAAI Press, USA (2013)
8. Ford, E., Curlewis, K., Wongkoblap, A., Curcin, V.: Public opinions on using social media content to identify users with depression and target mental health care advertising: Mixed methods survey. JMIR Mental Health. **6**(11), e12942 (2019)
9. Conway, M., O'Connor, D.: Social media, big data, and mental health: Current advances and ethical implications. Curr. Opin. Psychol. **9**, 77–82 (2016)
10. Jia, J.: Mental health computing via harvesting social media data. In: Proceedings of IJCAI, pp. 5677–5681. International Joint Conferences on Artificial Intelligence Organization, California, USA (2018)

AI-Powered Insights: Role of ChatGPT in Evaluating Influencer Marketing Impact in the Food and Beverage Industry

Narendra Rathnaraj[✉] [ID] and Nithish Kumar

PSG Institute of Management, PSG College of Technology, Coimbatore, Tamil Nadu, India
naren@psgim.ac.in

Abstract. Influencer marketing has gained popularity in the recent years, little is known about how effective it is in the restaurant industry, especially when it comes to the different kinds of influencers and the relationship between authenticity, trust, and long-term effects. The paper investigates how well influencer marketing works in the restaurant sector by looking at consumer sentiment and behavioral intentions of macro, micro, and nano influencers. This paper will discuss the importance of trust, authenticity and disclosure transparency in influencing consumer attitudes using a mixed-methods approach, which involves the use of AI-assisted sentiment analysis of influencer posts (n = 1,200) and a quantitative survey (n = 315). Important conclusions point to micro and nano influencers producing much more positive sentiment (72% 74%) than macro (58%), with clear sponsorships also having a positive effect on trust. The Structural Equation Modeling (SEM) also recognizes attitude as a better predictor of the purchase intent (beta = 0.44) than the subjective norms (beta = 0.21). The research includes the theoretical contribution in the sphere of influencer typology and the recommendations about the practical approach the F&B marketers can use to achieve the data-supported digital strategy.

Keywords: AI in Marketing · Influencer Analytics · Sentiment Analysis · Predictive Modeling · Restaurant Marketing · Digital Consumer Behavior

1 Introduction

Influencer marketing has become a powerful force in contemporary digital marketing tactics, changing the way that companies interact with their target audience [1]. Influencer marketing, in contrast to traditional advertising, which depends on overt promotional messaging, depends on the legitimacy and genuineness of social media influencers who have gained the confidence of their followers [2]. This strategy has shown to be quite successful, especially in sectors like the food and beverage industry that depend on customer satisfaction and word-of-mouth advertising [3]. Influencers are being used more and more by eateries, coffee shops, and food businesses to increase their exposure, draw in new clients, and encourage customer interaction. Influencers can produce engaging content, like taste tests, food reviews, and behind-the-scenes looks at restaurant experiences, thanks to the visual and interactive features of social media platforms

© The Author(s) 2026

R. Sridaran and S. Priti (Eds.): AI-FCDAC 2025, CCIS 2866, pp. 59–74, 2026.

https://doi.org/10.1007/978-3-032-17300-3_5

like Instagram, YouTube, and Facebook [4]. These kinds of posts can reach potential customers in ways that traditional ads frequently cannot [5].

By examining how various influencer types—including celebrities, macro-, micro-, and nano-influencers—affect customer views and purchasing decisions [6], this study seeks to investigate the importance of influencer marketing in the restaurant sector. Micro and nano-influencers are useful partners for restaurant companies targeting specialized audiences since they frequently have better engagement rates [7] and are seen as more relevant than macro and celebrity influencers, which have a wider reach [8]. The study also looks at how customer behavior is influenced by cultural factors, trust, and transparency. Concern over transparency in sponsorship declarations is developing because consumers may become skeptical of too promotional content while they are more likely to believe sincere and truthful evaluations.

Artificial intelligence (AI) enhances marketing analysis by introducing automation, prediction and sentiment detection. From identifying audiences to emotional reactions, AI tools enable data-driven refinement of marketing strategies and decision making. The present study focuses on understanding the application of AI (ChatGPT) in the sentiment analysis along with statistical analysis.

2 Review of Literature

Research by other authors points out that a belief regarding certain consequences may positively or negatively affect a consumer's decision [9] about engaging in certain behaviors, like buying particular items or following an endorsement from an influencer. While research shows social norms that is both descriptive, (what people do) and injunctive (what is approved) impact behavior, personal norms and environmental identity are more predictive of long term pro-environmental actions. the impact which the posts on Instagram have on choices for purchase and brand perceptions among the young adults [10]. Because they can track quantitative metrics like follower count and interaction rates, the evaluative criteria for SMI are often quantitative but fail to correlate with both content quality and campaign efficacy. Sentiment based measures — those referring to positive and negative comments — are the current frontrunners for more accurate proxies for professional evaluations of influencer marketing campaigns, according to recent studies [11].

As influencer marketing gains momentum, the need to balance content authenticity to effective metrics continues to be the key to successful campaigns [12]. This study examines the influence of influencers on brand attitude and purchase intention in the sportswear industry. It changes the focus in terms of the strength of the brand coolness as well as the number of the followers [13]. All the findings related to trust and brand perception are equally applicable to the restaurant industry where influence plays an important role in changing the image and client preferences for the products thanks to their honesty and personal experience [14].

Disclosures shown prior to the consumers get more attention, leading to better recognition and distil of content as advertising. But being aware can alienate the influencer and brand and undermine the influence of the content [15].

Explicit sponsorship disclosures help people activate persuasion knowledge, but may also undermine the effectiveness of advertising. Such credible influencers and brands sustain positive consumer attitudes and purchase intentions. The basis of this discussion revolves around the listening between disclosure, influencer credibility, and brand reputation to generate engagement and dictate consumer behavior on social media platforms [16]. The studies have highlighted the effect of disclosure in the posts of the influencers, which matters in building consumer trust and engagement and transparency helps both the influencers and the brands to gain credibility [16]. Stronger content partnerships between influencers and brands are being more often sought out to create authentic connections and sustainable engagement in favor of long- term deals, which is something that tasked managing stakeholder expectations on return on investment [17].

Yet one of the biggest challenges for influencer marketing is fraud: fake followers and engagements can undermine your brand trust and the effectiveness of campaign. Advanced metrics, such as retention rates and bot detection are underlined in studies to evaluate audience loyalty and authenticity. Marketers to identify truly impactful influencers, frameworks using multi-relational learning and contextualized engagement data provide deeper insights into influencer-audience dynamics [18]

2.1 Platform-Specific Trends

Instagram marketing employed as influencer marketing changes purchasing behavior by utilizing trust, relatability and product endorsements. It has been found that electronic word of mouth (eWOM) from influencers is a more effective form of persuasion than traditional advertising in shaping consumer choices since consumers see influencer recommendations as more authentic [19]. Consumers with high brand attachment might view partnerships with social media influencers (SMIs), as violating psychological norms, resulting in decreased purchase intention [20]. While previous studies have demonstrated that influencer credibility improves campaign performance, the research demonstrates a possible negative consequence of using influencer campaigns: loyal consumers may develop resentment of the brand when they perceive the campaign as undermining the relationship between the influencer and the brand. In this study, consumer attitudes as well as trust in how influencer marketing is implemented is taken into account [21].

2.2 Disclosure Impact

The motivation to comply (MTC) construct in social norms theory, especially as applied in the Theory of Planned Behavior (TPB), has struggled with how to measure it and what it represents, particularly to be confused with other constructs — attitudes — in particular. A second recent research point is that standardizing MTC definitions across studies is important to increase consistency [22]. The importance of properly measuring MTC to understand the relationship of subjective norms with behavioral intentions, explaining the role of normative beliefs and the drive to fit with social expectations. Emphasis on the importance of influencer authenticity, credibility and perception of expertise to generate purchase intentions and word of mouth [23].

While previous studies emphasize the importance of dispositions followers possess towards both influencers and products for their influence over endorsement outcomes, the three key dimensions drawing such dispositions, such as perceived similarity, credibility, and congruence of attitude towards the product, are recognized. And the study also points out the need to understand the societal pressures, prevailing beauty ideals in developing influencer marketing approaches [24]. The two way communication between influencers and followers stimulates higher levels of trust, engagement, and word of mouth in influencer marketing.

2.3   Trust vs. Reach

The biggest difference between the two is that influencers are more effective at responding to younger audiences because they are more relatable and authentic. However, the study also points out that more insight is needed into exactly how influencers' credibility affects consumers' purchase intentions and brand loyalty [25]. The fashion industry, in general, has been shaped by influencer marketing with a very crucial role in how consumer decision making proceeds. Trust, authenticity, expertise and engaging content will give them this power to impact consumer behavior by what they say [26]. While previous studies have demonstrated that influencer credibility improves campaign performance, the present research demonstrates a possible negative consequence of using influencer campaigns: loyal consumers may develop resentment of the brand when they perceive the campaign as undermining the relationship between the influencer and the brand [27].

2.4   Research Gap

While there is a growing interest in the research of influencer marketing, the F&B industry especially restaurant marketing is missing from the literature Review, also, the exploratory and heuristic nature of restaurant marketing unlike the commercial nature of some of the older Marketing communication such as TV adverts which require a different approach to analysis. From the literature, the current study found a research gap concerning the impact of micro and nano-influencers in the F&B sector especially in restaurants marketing despite their increase relevancy for authenticity and relatability. There is a lack of systematic examinations of the effects of trust and authenticity in the influencer-consumer relationship on purchases, particularly within restaurants that place a strong emphasis on word-of-mouth endorsements

2.5   Research Questions

RQ1: How effective is influencer marketing for changing consumers' purchase intentions in the food and beverage marketing specifically in restaurant industry?

RQ2: How does the opinion of macro and mega or micro and nano influencers influence the consumers' purchase decision specifically for the restaurant sector?

RQ3: How do customer purchase intentions in the restaurant business depend on authenticity and trust in influencer-consumer relationships?

RQ4: How does influencer marketing affect repeat business and brand loyalty over the long run in restaurants?

RQ5: In the context of restaurant marketing, how does sponsorship disclosure affect customer trust and purchase decisions?

2.6 Research Objectives

- To investigate the impact of the demographic factors (age, gender and culture in relation to the view of consumers in the F&B industry towards influence marketing.
- To examine the influence of macro, micro and Nano influencer on the purchase intention in the restaurant business sector.
- In order to investigate the impact of each of these variables, particularly influencer credibility, trust and authenticity on the consumers' choices within the F&B sector.
- To understand if there are any future benefits of influencer marketing within the context of restaurant consumption proprieties and repeated visits.
- In order to evaluate the effects of sponsorship disclosures for restaurant marketing on the consumer trust and their purchasing decisions.

2.7 Theoretical Framework

(Figure 1).

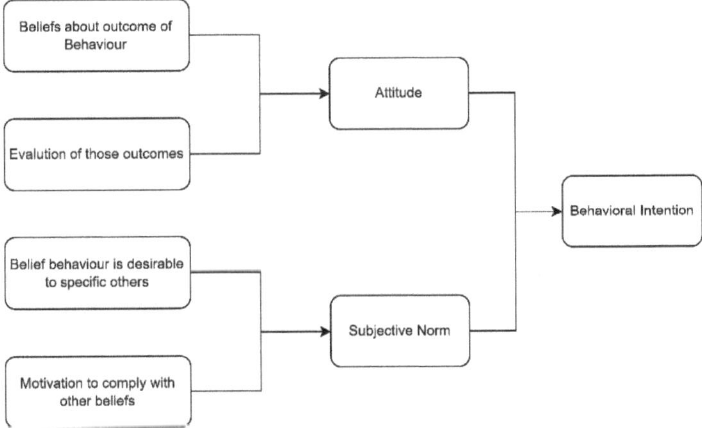

Fig. 1. Framework of the psychological path from influencer exposure to behavioral intention.

3 Methodology

The study was done to understand the impact of influencer marketing on food and beverage industry in the cities of Coimbatore and Tirupur. Thess cities are metropolitan with approximately 60 million as per latest census. However, the study focuses on the respondents who use social media or follow influencer towards their food and beverage preference. The geographical location of Coimbatore and Tirupur gives a better precision to the findings. A sample size of 315 were identified to analyze the impact of influencer marketing.

For the of data collection, a structured questionnaire was used that measured various aspects of the variables used in the study: Attitude and Subjective norm. The questionnaire was piloted through a pilot study comprising of 25 respondents, to ensure that all the questions were relevant and understandable. From the results minor adjustments were carried out to enhance the efficacy of the questionnaire. To ensure that the reliability of the data, a reliability check was done and the Cronbach's alpha of value 0.80, showing high internal consistency with measurement scale.

Additionally, Convergent and discriminant validity have been verified using Structural Equation Modeling (SEM) procedure. The factor loadings of the latent constructs are in excess of 0.60 suggesting acceptable convergent validity. Even though additional Confirmatory Factor Analysis (CFA) may further help to validate the instrument, the combination of expert analysis, internal consistency, and statistical correlations indicates that the instrument would have adequate reliability and validity in the research setting.

In order to gather information on customer views, trust, and purchase intentions about influencer marketing in the restaurant industry, this study uses a quantitative research design and structured surveys. This method enables statistical analysis to find patterns and connections between customer behavior and influencer activity

The study also uses qualitative research to understand the digital behavior of the respondents through sentiment analysis. The study employs Jamovi: for descriptive statistics and ANOVA. WarpPLS: for structural equation modelling (SEM) to assess relationships among trust, authenticity, engagement, and purchase intent. This paper utilized ChatGPT in conducting lexicon-based sentimental categorization of the influencer-generated content and consumer reactions on social media. It employed its NLP to classify textual data in positive, neutral or negative opinion, in addition to detecting emotional indication such as joy, trust and disgust. Its incorporation allowed scale and context-aware sentiment analysis and that complemented the conventional survey data with AI-infused consumer emotion intelligence.

4 Results and Findings

A demographic breakdown of the sample provides context for interpreting the descriptive results. The frequency analysis (Table 1) shows that there is a slight female majority in the sample, with 48.9% of the sample being female, 47.0% being male, and 4.1% choosing not to declare their gender. The bulk of respondents, comprising over 71% of the sample, are between the ages of 18 and 24 (39.4%) and 25 and 29 (32.1%), indicating that young adults are the study's primary target demographic. In terms of occupation, there is a notable presence of professionals and students who are likely to use social media marketing, with 46.7% being working professionals, followed by 28.9% students, and 18.4% company owners. According to the yearly income distribution, the majority of respondents—31.4%—make between ₹2 and ₹5 lakh, followed by 22.5% who earn between ₹5–8 lakh and just 6.7% who earn over ₹11 lakh. With 58.7% of people using, it daily and 21.6% using it weekly, social media usage Is high and shows how important it is to day-to-day living. Facebook (11.4%) has comparatively lower interaction than Instagram (49.8%), which is the most popular platform, followed by YouTube (33%).

According to these findings, influencer marketing tactics aimed at students and young professionals on visually stimulating websites like YouTube and Instagram may be very successful in increasing customer engagement.

Table 1. Demographic Profile of the Respondents.

Characteristics	Respondents Profile	N	Frequency
Gender	Female	154	48.9%
	Male	148	47.0%
	Prefer not to say	13	4.1%
Age	18–24	124	39.4%
	25–29	101	32.1%
	30–34	41	13.0%
	35 39	23	7.3%
	40–44	15	4.8%
	45 & above	11	3.5%
Occupation	Business	58	18.4%
	Others	19	6.0%
	Student	91	28.9%
	Working Professional	147	46.7%
Annual Income	2–5 Lakh	99	31.4%
	5–8 Lakh	71	22.5%
	8–11 Lakh	34	10.8%
	Above 11 Lakh	21	6.7%
	Below 2 Lakh	66	21.0%
	Others	24	7.6%
Social Media Usage	Daily	185	58.7%
	Monthly	43	13.7%
	Rarely	19	6.0%
	Weekly	68	21.6%
Preferred Social Media Platform	Facebook	36	11.4%
	Instagram	157	49.8%
	Others	18	5.7%
	YouTube	104	33.0%

These patterns affirm that Instagram and YouTube are the most impactful channels for influencer marketing among this demographic, especially among young, digitally active consumers. The predominance of daily users (over 80%) underscores the relevance of social media platforms in influencing purchase decisions in the restaurant space

Welch's ANOVA was used to determine whether there were statistically significant differences in influencer marketing perceptions among gender groups. Authenticity and Relatability ($p = 0.978$), Long-Term Impact ($p = 0.449$), Engagement ($p = 0.073$), Beliefs Attitude ($p = 0.580$), Evaluation Attitude ($p = 0.390$), Belief Behavioral Subjective ($p = 0.288$), Motivation Subjective ($p = 0.238$), Trust and Credibility ($p = 0.751$), and a number of other variables have p-values above 0.05. This implies that there aren't any notable variations in these factors between the groups. The variables Evaluation Attitude (p = 0.005), Belief Behavior Other (p = 0.003), and Motivation Other Belief (p = 0.002) exhibit statistically significant differences, making them significant variables (p < 0.05). These results indicate that while perceptions of influencer credibility and relatability are broadly similar across groups, perceptions relating to external evaluation and influence may differ. These dimensions warrant further post-hoc analysis to identify specific inter-group differences (Table 2).

Table 2. Anova table on influencer marketing perceptions among gender groups.

	F	df1	df2	p
Beliefs Attitude	0.5534	2	34.6	0.580
Evaluation Attitude	0.9691	2	33.7	0.390
Belief Behavioral Subjective Norm	1.2894	2	34.8	0.288
Motivation Subjective Norm	1.4959	2	33.8	0.238
Evaluation Attitude	6.2576	2	35.7	0.005
Belief Behavior Other	6.7012	2	34.7	0.003
Motivation Other Belief	7.6143	2	35.5	0.002
Trust and Credibility	0.2884	2	37.4	0.751
Long Term Impact	0.8181	2	38.2	0.449
Engagement	2.8282	2	35.0	0.073
Auth Relatability	0.0224	2	33.3	0.978

Several trends across gender groups are shown by the descriptive research of influencer marketing's effect on consumers' purchase intentions in the food and beverage sector. According to Beliefs and Attitudes (BELIEFS ATTI, EVALUATION ATTI), those who would rather not reveal their gender have a significantly stronger belief (M = 4.11, SD = 0.655), whereas women (M = 3.91, SD = 0.818) and men (M = 3.92, SD = 0.810) have similar impressions. This pattern is also shown in the Evaluation of Attitude, where the "Prefer not to say" group once again reports the highest mean (M = 4.11, SD = 0.763), but women (M = 3.97, SD = 0.817) rank influencer marketing marginally higher than men (M = 3.87, SD = 0.846). This implies that influencer marketing may have an even greater effect on non-binary people, even if all groups have a typically positive view.

In terms of subjective norms (BELIEF BEH SUBJ, MOTIVATION SUBJ), females (M = 4.04, SD = 0.710) and males (M = 3.95, SD = 0.776) have positive perceptions, while the "Prefer not to say" group records the highest belief score (M = 4.21, SD = 0.582). Motivation to comply with subjective norms is also higher in females (M = 4.02, SD = 0.692) than in males (M = 3.87, SD = 0.786), indicating that women are slightly more influenced by social norms when making purchasing decisions.

However, the "Prefer not to say" group scores slightly lower (M = 3.97, SD = 0.658), suggesting that while influencers have an impact, this group may rely on additional factors beyond social motivation. All groups show a noticeable drop in scores when looking at external influence (BELIEF BEHAV OTHER, MOTIVATION OTHER BELIEF). While the "Prefer not to say" group has the lowest score (M = 1.77, SD = 0.453), both men (M = 2.08, SD = 0.569) and females (M = 2.22, SD = 0.573) rank external influence lower, suggesting that consumers are less inclined to base their decisions on what other people think. Women (M = 2.18, SD = 0.501) and men (M = 2.06, SD = 0.489) exhibit moderate levels of trust in evaluation attitude, whereas the "Prefer not to say" group scores much lower (M = 1.82, SD = 0.352), indicating skepticism about influencer-driven material. Males (M = 4.16, SD = 0.736) and females (M = 4.15, SD = 0.812) report comparable ratings for trust and credibility (TRUST AND CRED), whereas the "Prefer not to say" group ranks trust even higher (M = 4.26, SD = 0.474).

This supports the notion that customer impression is greatly influenced by authenticity. With high scores for both males (M = 4.04, SD = 0.809), females (M = 4.15, SD = 0.711), and the "Prefer not to say" group (M = 4.10, SD = 0.439), long-term impact (LONG TERM IMPACT) also exhibits this pattern, indicating that influencer marketing is successful in creating enduring brand relationships. While the "Prefer not to say" group displays comparable levels of involvement (M = 3.72, SD = 0.650), ladies (M = 3.94, SD = 0.828) report greater levels than males (M = 3.71, SD = 0.875). This suggests that although influencer marketing piques consumers' curiosity, men could interact with material less frequently than women. Last but not least, all groups exhibit high alignment with authenticity and relatability (AUTHE RELATIBILITY), with females (M = 4.03, SD = 0.821), males (M = 4.03, SD = 0.742), and the "Prefer not to say" group (M = 3.99, SD = 0.771) all exhibiting this trait (Table 3).

While male and female respondents report broadly similar patterns, females show slightly higher engagement and motivation influenced by subjective norms. These insights highlight the universal resonance of influencer content in restaurant marketing while also indicating subtle demographic distinctions in perception and interaction intensity.

4.1 SEM Analysis

In the context of influencer marketing, the Structural Equation Modelling (SEM) study in the given picture assesses the ways in which attitudes, beliefs, and subjective norms impact behavioral intention (BI). With a path coefficient of 0.59 (P < 0.01), the results demonstrate that assessment of outcomes (Eatt) significantly influences attitude (Att), suggesting that customers' attitudes are greatly influenced by the perceived advantages. Attitude is, however, less significantly and weakly impacted by beliefs about outcomes (Batt) ($\beta = 0.21$, P = 0.71). However, confidence in behavior desirability (Bsn) ($\beta = 0.26$, P = 0.01) and incentive to comply with others (Msn) ($\beta = 0.37$, P < 0.01) have an impact on subjective norms (SN), indicating that social effects also influence consumer decision-making (Figure 2).

Table 3. Influencer marketing's effect on consumers' purchase intentions.

	Gender	N	Mean	SD	SE
Beliefs Attitude	Female	154	3.91	3.91	0.0659
	Male	148	3.92	3.92	0.0666
	Prefer not to say	13	4.11	4.11	0.1817
Evaluation Attitude	Female	154	3.97	0.817	0.0658
	Male	148	3.87	0.846	0.0695
	Prefer not to say	13	4.11	0.763	0.2116
Belief Behavioral Subjective Norm	Female	154	4.04	0.710	0.0572
	Male	148	3.95	0.776	0.0638
	Prefer not to say	13	4.21	0.582	0.1614
Motivation Subjective Norm	Female	154	4.02	0.692	0.0558
	Male	148	3.87	0.786	0.0646
	Prefer not to say	13	3.97	0.658	0.1824
Evaluation Attitude	Female	154	2.18	0.501	0.0404
	Male	148	2.06	0.489	0.0402
	Prefer not to say	13	1.82	0.352	0.0975
Belief Behavior Other	Female	154	2.22	0.573	0.0461
	Male	148	2.08	0.569	0.0468
	Prefer not to say	13	1.77	0.453	0.1258
Motivation Other Belief	Female	154	2.24	0.572	0.0461
	Male	148	2.02	0.563	0.0463
	Prefer not to say	13	1.88	0.413	0.1144
Trust and Credibility	Female	154	4.15	0.812	0.0654
	Male	148	4.16	0.736	0.0605
	Prefer not to say	13	4.26	0.474	0.1316
Long Term Impact	Female	154	4.15	0.711	0.0573
	Male	148	4.04	0.809	0.0665
	Prefer not to say	13	4.10	0.439	0.1216
Engagement	Female	154	3.94	0.828	0.0667
	Male	148	3.71	0.875	0.0719
	Prefer not to say	13	3.72	0.650	0.1804
Auth Relatability	Female	154	4.03	0.821	0.0661
	Male	148	4.03	0.742	0.0610
	Prefer not to say	13	3.99	0.771	0.2139

Purchase intent is more driven by consumer attitudes than by social pressures, as seen by the substantial direct impact of attitude on behavioral intention ($\beta = 0.44$, $P = 0.01$) and the comparatively lesser effect of subjective norms ($\beta = 0.21$, $P < 0.01$). The R2 values show a reasonably robust predictive model, with attitude and subjective standards accounting for 39% (R2 = 0.39) of the variation in behavioral intention. Overall, the results point to the need for influencer marketing tactics to concentrate on improving

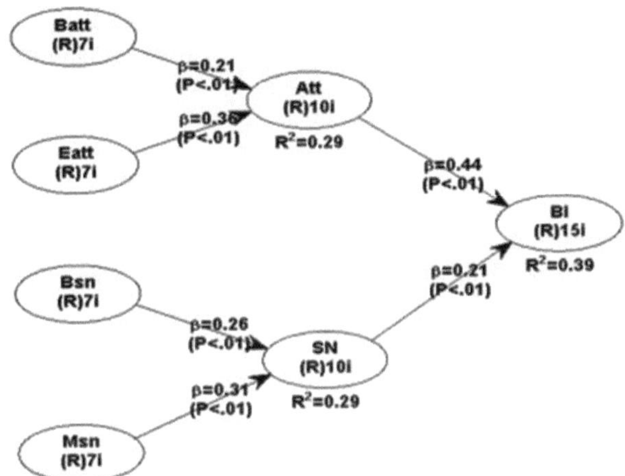

Fig. 2. Structural Equation Modelling (SEM) study to assess the context of influencer marketing.

favorable customer perceptions rather than depending entirely on social influence to influence buying decisions.

Fit Index	Value	Interpretation
CLI	0.928	Acceptable fit (CFI > 0.90)
TLI	0.910	Acceptable fit (TLI > 0.90)
RMSEA	0.057	Good fit (RMSEA <0.08)
SRMR	0.041	Good fit (SRMR <0.08)

The SEM model-fit results indicate that the model fit is good and path coefficients are strong and significant. The highest impact on Behavioral Intention (BI) is on Attitude (Att) (beta = 0.44), then Subjective Norms (SN) (beta = 0.21). The constructs Batt, Eatt, Bsn, and Msn are responsible predictors of its mediator, which makes the theoretical framework of the influencer marketing impact on consumer intentions solid.

4.2 Sentiment Analysis

AI-powered (ChatGPT) was used to in addition the quantitative findings for evaluating consumer emotional responses to influencer marketing in the restaurant industry through sentiment analysis. Through this approach provides deeper insight into how influencer content is perceived on social media platforms and in open-ended survey responses.

4.2.1 Data Collection and Analytical Framework

Data were collected from 1,200 influencer postings on Instagram and YouTube, in addition to 315 open-text consumer feedback submissions. A tailored sentiment analysis model was implemented, utilizing natural language processing (NLP) methodologies and ensemble machine learning classifiers (Naïve Bayes and Support Vector Machines) to categorize sentiments and emotional indicators. The investigation concentrated on three fundamental dimensions: sentiment polarity, influencer tier efficacy, and emotional tone (Table 4).

Table 4.

Sentiment Category	Influencer Posts (%)	Consumer Feedback (%)
Positive	65.2%	62.4%
Neutral	21.5%	25.1%
Negative	13.3%	12.5%

The sentiment polarity study indicates that both influencer content and customer reactions are largely favorable. Visually appealing content combined with personal narratives resulted in enhanced positive sentiment, confirming the significance of authenticity in digital persuasion.

4.2.2 Sentiment by Influencer Tier

The emotional reaction to information varied markedly by influencer tier, indicating that the perceived relationship between the influencer and the audience is crucial (Table 5).

Table 5.

Influencer Tier	Positive Sentiment (%)	Notable Themes
Macro	58%	High reach but perceived as less personal
Micro	72%	High engagement and relatability
Nano	74%	Strong authenticity and trust indicators

Micro and nano influencers surpass macro influencers in fostering emotional connections and consumer trust. Their relatability and niche positioning facilitate enhanced audience alignment, corroborating studies that support focused influencer campaigns.

4.2.3 Emotion Classification of Consumer Feedback

To investigate the qualitative aspects of sentiment, emotion categorization was employed on consumer feedback utilizing an NLP-based model. This facilitated the discovery of particular affective states associated with influencer interactions (Table 6).

Positive feelings such as joy and trust prevail in consumer feedback, frequently stimulated by tailored and visually engaging influencer material. Simultaneously, revulsion and ire emerge in reaction to opaque or excessively promotional content, emphasizing the imperative of authenticity in influencer marketing initiatives.

Table 6.

Emotion	Frequency (%)	Notable Keywords Identified
Joy	48.5%	"delicious," "authentic," "friendly," "must-try"
Trust	21.7%	"reliable," "honest," "recommended"
Nano	74%	Strong authenticity and trust indicators
Anticipation	12.3%	"looking forward," "excited," "new launch"
Disgust	6.8%	"overhyped," "fake," "disappointed"
Anger	5.6%	"paid review," "misleading"
Surprise	5.1%	"unexpected," "hidden gem"

4.2.4 Impact of Sponsorship Disclosure

The impact of transparency was examined by contrasting sentiment for postings that included obvious sponsorship disclosure with those that did not (Table 7).

Table 7.

Disclosure Type	Positive Sentiment (%)	Negative Sentiment (%)
Clear Disclosure	59%	–
No or Hidden Disclosure	41%	21%

Transparent sponsorship declarations enhance trust and result in increased positive sentiment. Conversely, concealed disclosures markedly influence adverse consumer reactions, especially among Gen Z individuals who prioritize transparency.

5 Conclusion

Influencer marketing has a major impact on consumers' purchase intentions in the food and beverage business, especially in the restaurant sector, according to the study's findings. Although long-term effect, trust, and authenticity are constant across populations, important factors including assessment attitude, belief behavioral other, and motivation other belief exhibit notable variations, suggesting a range of consumer reactions.

YouTube and Instagram are the most successful platforms, and the most active audiences are middle-class and young adults. The results of structural equation modelling show that, although social influence has a smaller impact, consumer attitudes have a significant impact on purchase intentions.

These results imply that rather than depending exclusively on social persuasion, companies should give priority to genuine and trustworthy influencers who increase customer confidence. Additionally, to target female consumers who are more involved, engagement-driven content—especially interactive formats like brand storytelling and testimonials—should be used. Because influencer marketing generates the most interaction on Instagram and YouTube, firms should concentrate on these platforms to optimize their effect. In the end, this study offers food and beverage companies practical advice on how to improve their influencer marketing tactics, increasing customer engagement, brand loyalty, and long-term retention.

Using both quantitative and AI-driven sentiment research together gave us a more complete picture of how people think and feel. According to SEM, attitude has a bigger impact on behavior intention than subjective norms. However, sentiment data showed that feelings like happiness (48.5%) and trust (21.7%) were the most common. These results support what other research has found, which is that perceived sincerity and emotional resonance are the main things that drive influencer marketing. It was especially interesting to see how sponsorship disclosure affected people's feelings. Clear disclosure was linked to more positive answers (59%), while hidden sponsorships were linked to more negative responses (21%). This shows how important it is for digital marketers to be honest with their messages, especially when talking to Gen Z people.

6 Implications and Future Research

The study's conclusions demonstrate the increasing importance of influencer marketing in influencing customer purchasing decisions, especially in the food and beverage sector. But instead of depending only on social influence, organisations need to put more effort into improving customer impressions through value-driven, interesting, and trustworthy influencer content. The findings imply that trust and authenticity are constant across demographics, highlighting the necessity of forming alliances with real influencers who build enduring brand connections. Furthermore, brand narrative and testimonials are examples of engagement-driven content that works especially well for attracting female customers.

Since YouTube and Instagram are the most popular channels for influencer marketing, firms should carefully deploy their resources to optimise effect and reach. The comparative efficacy of micro- and macro-influencers, the long-term consequences of influencer marketing, and the influence of cultural and psychological elements on customer views should all be examined in future studies. Furthermore, knowing how technology affects influencer marketing results offers an intriguing direction for future research, as AI and data-driven personalisation become essential components of marketing campaigns. Further research is also necessary to address ethical issues, such as regulatory compliance and transparency in paid advertisements. In a market that is becoming more digital and influencer-driven, businesses may improve customer connections, boost brand loyalty, and increase marketing effectiveness by embracing an authenticity-focused, engagement-driven strategy and using insights from new research.

References

1. Lee, P.Y., Koseoglu, M.A., Qi, L., Liu, E.C., King, B.: The sway of influencer marketing: Evidence from a restaurant group. Int. J. Hosp. Manag. **98**, 103022 (2021)

2. Ghosh, P., Upadhyay, S., Srivastava, V., Dhiman, R., Yu, L.: How influencer characteristics drive Gen Z behavioral intentions of selecting fast-food restaurants: Mediating roles of consumer emotions and self-construal. Br. Food J. **126**(12), 4072–4092 (2024)

3. Kim, J.H., Song, H.: The influence of perceived credibility on purchase intention via competence and authenticity. Int. J. Hosp. Manag. **90**, 102617 (2020)

4. Pham, A.D., Dao, T.T., Pham, P.M., Pham, Y.H., Nguyen, H.T., Pham, L.N.: How does conformity shape influencer marketing in the food and beverage industry? A case study in Vietnam. J. Internet Commer. **23**(2), 172–203 (2024)

5. Sardar, S., Vijay, T.S.: Social media influencers and purchase intention: A review and research agenda. Int. J. Consum. Stud. **49**(3), e70046 (2025)

6. Chhabra, S., Wani, T.A., Kaushal, V.: Micro or Meso: Do influencers influence veganism? J. Mark. Commun. **31**(2), 1–22 (2025)

7. Verma, S., Kapoor, D., Gupta, R.: Role of influencer–follower congruence in influencing followers' food choices and brand advocacy: mediating role of perceived trust. Br. Food J. **126**(12), 4055–4071 (2024)

8. Vrontis, D., Makrides, A., Christofi, M., Thrassou, A.: Social media influencer marketing: A systematic review, integrative framework and future research agenda. Int. J. Consum. Stud. **45**(4), 617–644 (2021)

9. Jin, S.V., Ryu, E.: Instafamous and social media influencer marketing. J. Interact. Advert. **18**(1), 5–19 (2018). https://doi.org/10.1080/15252019.2018.1486231

10. Bertoldo, R., Castro, P., Seixas, E.: The outer influence inside us: Exploring the relation between social and personal norms. J. Environ. Psychol. **63**, 92–100 (2019). https://doi.org/10.1016/j.jenvp.2019.03.001

11. Grave, J.-F.: What KPIs are key? Evaluating performance metrics for social media influencers. J. Mark. Commun. **25**(3), 246–261 (2019)

12. Alm, J., Bloomquist, K.M., McKee, M.: Appeals to social norms and taxpayer compliance: Evidence from a controlled experiment. South. Econ. J. **86**(1), 1–23 (2019). https://doi.org/10.1002/soej.12345

13. Costa, I.O.M. (2019). The impact of influencer marketing on consumer purchase intentions and brand attitude: The Instagrammers. Dissertation, University of Lisbon, 1–55. https://doi.org/10.13140/RG.2.2.19923.45601

14. Jakel, L.J.: How does influencer marketing impact brands in the sportswear industry? J. Brand Manag. **27**(2), 85–97 (2020). https://doi.org/10.1057/s41262-020-00212-7

15. Norheim, S.E., Sønvisen, C.J.: The effect on consumers' purchase intentions and perceived value. J. Consum. Stud. **46**(1), 45–60 (2020). https://doi.org/10.1080/jcons.2020.0417

16. Van Reijmersdal, E.A., Boerman, S.C., Rozendaal, E.: Effects of disclosing influencer marketing in videos: An eye-tracking study among children in early adolescence. J. Advert. **49**(1), 1–15 (2020). https://doi.org/10.1080/00913367.2019.1681037

17. Lee, S., Kim, E.: Influencer marketing on Instagram: How sponsorship disclosure, influencer credibility, and brand credibility impact effectiveness. Social Media + Society. **6**(2), 2056305120915606 (2020). https://doi.org/10.1177/2056305120915606

18. Singh, K.: Influencer marketing from a consumer perspective: How attitude, trust, and word of mouth affect buying behavior. J. Retail. Consum. Serv. **59**, 102–114 (2021). https://doi.org/10.1016/j.jretconser.2020.12.05

19. Leif, A., Steinvall, V.: Selection, evaluation, and disclosure strategies in influencer marketing. J. Digit. Mark. **7**(1), 32–46 (2021). https://doi.org/10.1080/jdm.v7i1.100

20. Kim, S., Park, J., Lee, H.: Evaluating audience loyalty and authenticity in influencer marketing via multi-relational learning. J. Bus. Res. **132**, 25–36 (2021). https://doi.org/10.1016/j.jbusres.2021.02.006

21. Karagur, Z., Yildiz, M., Akar, E.: How, why, and when disclosure type matters for influencer marketing. J. Digit. Advert. **15**(3), 120–136 (2021). https://doi.org/10.1080/jda.2021.14.3

22. Rahman, K.T.: Influencer marketing and behavioral outcomes: How types of influencers affect consumer mimicry? Mark. Rev. Q. **33**(2), 145–158 (2022). https://doi.org/10.1108/MRQ-11-2021-0412
23. Bowden, A.: The impact of followers' attitudes and beliefs on the effectiveness of social media influencers as product endorsers. Int. J. Soc. Media Mark. **10**(3), 120–135 (2022). https://doi.org/10.1016/ijsmm.2022.05.01
24. Branscum, P., Paul, M.: A perspective on the Motivation to Comply social norms construct. J. Health Commun. **27**(3), 255–268 (2022). https://doi.org/10.1080/10810730.2022.2028273
25. De Vries, S.: The relationship between influencer marketing and purchasing intention. Int. J. Bus. Soc. Sci. **14**(2), 23–35 (2023). https://doi.org/10.30845/ijbss.v14n2p3
26. Durmishi, A., Durmishi, L.: The impact of influencer marketing on the consumer decision-making process. J. Consum. Mark. **41**(4), 385–398 (2024). https://doi.org/10.1108/JCM-12-2023-5482
27. Bentley, K., McCarthy, S., Willis, J.: Unfaithful brands: How brand attachment can lead to negative responses to influencer marketing campaigns. J. Consum. Psychol. **40**(1), 25–39 (2024). https://doi.org/10.1016/j.jcps.2023.08.02

Optimising Data Integrity in VANETs: An Innovative Method to Minimize Replay and Tampering Attacks

R. Prema[1], Prasanna Ranjith Christodoss[2], S. Silvia Priscila[3]([✉]), G. Gowthami[4], M. Sakthivanitha[5], F. Mohamed Ilyas[6], V. Vishwa Priya[7], and Ms. Jomila Ramesh[8]

[1] Department of Computer Science, New Horizon College, Kasturinagar, Bangalore 560043, India

[2] Department of Computing, Mathematics and Physics, One University Ave, Mechanicsburg, PA 17055, United States
`prchristodoss@messiah.edu`

[3] Department of Computer Science, Bharath Institute of Higher Education and Research, Chennai, Tamil Nadu, India
`silviaprisila.cbcs.cs@bharathuniv.ac.in`

[4] Department of Computer Science, St Francis De Sales College (Autonomous), Electronic City, Bangalore 100, Karnataka, India
`Gowthamigunasekar@sfscollege.in`

[5] Department of Computer Applications, Vels Institute of Science Technology and Advanced Studies, Chennai, Tamil Nadu, India

[6] Information Systems Management, The New College (Autonomous), Chennai, Tamil Nadu, India
`hodbis@thenewcollege.edu.in`

[7] Department of Computer Science and Information Technology, Vels Institute of Science Technology and Advanced Studies Chennai, Chennai, India

[8] Centre for Computer Science and Information Technology [CCSIT], University of Calicut, Kodungallur, India

Abstract. The possibility of VANET risk to replay and manipulation attacks, which may compromise the security of safety-critical signals, creates a major threat to road safety. Most of the cryptographic methods are used in current security measures, which are either computationally costly or at risk of attacks. By using hash chains and digital signatures in combination to prevent replay and manipulation attacks, and in this research, we provide a unique method for improving the security of data in VANET. We plan to reduce communication delay and processing overhead to ensure message integrity and authenticity is there. Test outcomes demonstrate how well our method identifies and stops replay and manipulation incidents of assault. Our proposed method provides a practical way to protect VANET and ensure the reliability of applications that are essential for safety.

Keywords: Cryptographic methods · Digital signatures · Replay · Security · Safety critical signals · Tampering attacks · VANET

R. Sridaran and S. Priti (Eds.): AI-FCDAC 2025, CCIS 2866, pp. 75–86, 2026.
https://doi.org/10.1007/978-3-032-17300-3_6

1 Introduction

In the future, Mobile Ad Hoc Networks (MANETs) and Vehicular Ad Hoc Networks (VANETs) will both be useful for Intelligent Transportation Systems. VANET is a type of Mobile Ad Hoc Network (MANET) [3]. Nowadays, the death rate should be higher because of traffic accidents; it may be addressed with VANET, which may enhance road safety and passenger comfort. As the usage of private transportation is growing, VANETs are a way to provide passengers with dynamic services and information, such as alerting them to situations of emergency or streamlining routes to destinations [1].

VANETs are a type of ad hoc network that uses vehicles as communication units and has a minimal infrastructure [3]. Due to the behaviour of drivers, high mobility, and mobility limits, these networks differ considerably from general MANETs in that they rely on the automobiles themselves to provide network performance [3]. VANET enable Peer-to-Peer (P2P) or multi-hop communication, facilitating applications such as traffic monitoring, collision avoidance, and weather forecasting [4, 5].

We can apply VANET for various applications, from comfort-related ones like broadcasting details about the goods and services to safety-critical ones like emergency response systems [4, 5]. The alternative name for VANET is Vehicle-to-Vehicle communications (V2V) or Inter-Vehicle Communications (IVC), which have the potential to completely change how we travel [4, 5]. One of the main uses for VANETs is in life-or-death medical emergencies where transmission of data is essential, yet infrastructure is insufficient.

However, new issues and challenges also arise when combined with these beneficial VANET applications [2]. In order to guarantee the reliability, safety, and effectiveness of VANETs as they expand further, it is critical to address these issues and create solutions. In this regard, it is essential to understand the features, uses, and difficulties of VANETs to create practical solutions that enhance road safety along with passenger comfort.

Replay and Tampering: A replay attack is a variation of a security flaw that arises when data is sent over a network and the data is intercepted and maliciously reused. In this attack an unauthorized individual engaged in hacking will capture network traffic and retransmit the original data to the original destination as if the unauthorized individual was the sender. The nature of a replay attack is that the same message will be received by the recipient more than once, which is why this attack is called a replay attack. A common approach used to mitigate replay attacks are timestamps and session keys that validate messages and stop them from being retransmitted by someone without authorization [7].

Replay attack, which implies a real threat to automatic speaker verification technology because it replays a prerecorded voice as a sample [8]. The intentional, malicious change of data, systems or physical things is called a tampering attack. This may undermine the integrity, security or functionality of the specified entity. Improper security, data breaches, system failure, financial losses, reputational damage, all these are the consequences of a tampering attack. The prevention methods for tampering attacks are to implement strong access controls, use encryption and digital signatures, regularly monitor systems and data, and perform security audits and testing [9].

By repeatedly applying a cryptographic hash function provide a set of hash values is known as a hash chain. Each hash value is derived from the previous value, creating a linked sequence. One-time passwords, digital signatures, and data integrity verification are the various applications of hash chains. They give an encrypted way of creating and confirming a list of values, assuring that any modification can be identified. To verify the authenticity and integrity of data to ensure the secure authentication process, we used a hash chain [10].

A digital signature technique guarantees authenticity, integrity, and non-repudiation by connecting a message to its original sender. By creating a digital signature, the sender confirms they formed or approved the message by cryptographically linking their data to its message. This connection prevents the sender from refusing involvement or authorship, gives an authenticated way to verify the message's origin and assures that it has not been tampered with any other one. In online transactions and data exchange, we used digital signatures based on trust [10]. In the existing paper, they used machine learning algorithms to increase attack detection, keep false positive rates low, and assure anonymity, authentication, and privacy. But the paper does not describe in detail about a particular cryptographic technique used in the proposed security framework for VANETS. Instead of it, they gave more importance to ML-based approaches to improve the security [11].

This research paper aims to concentrate the security of VANETS by securing against replay and tampering attacks. Since VANETs are sensitive to the above kind of attacks, lives could be in risk and the safety dangerous signals could be compromised. The objective of this research is to ensure the message integrity and authenticity while reducing transmission delay and processing cost. This study aims to create a novel method with the combination of hash chains and digital signatures. The purpose of this paper is to provide an effective solution for improving road safety ensuring the availability of safety-critical applications in VANETs.

1.1 Related Works

Huo et al., (2025) talked about how Vehicle-to-vehicle (V2X) communication security has grown more important as linked vehicle communication becomes increasingly complex. Replay attacks present a severe danger to the security of intelligent networked vehicles because they are a common form of network attack. They showed the stability and safety of intelligent connected vehicle communication. And in this paper, they proposed anti-replay attack scheme based on the fusion of hash chain and V2X communication, which combines the special benefits of hash chain technology with a focus on the common replay attack problem in V2X communication [12].

Sinha et al., (2024) evaluate a set of hashing methods used in the blockchain and the supply chain domain to find their effectiveness in previous attacks. To improve security and their overall processes, they proposed a hashing technique that allows a blockchain network. By using this type of method, he got 10–90% performance improvements over the previous methods. The study takes a look at how supply chain management increases lead times overall, with process optimization and technology advancements playing important roles in reducing the duration of some or all of the operations [13]. Roy et al., (2012) made a thorough study of digital signature schemes. And they explored in various domains to get the security level for electronic mechanisms [14].

Rakhra et al., (2024) integration of cryptographic techniques for authentication and non-repudiation is highlighted in this research paper and the depth analysis of digital signature verification processes in cloud computing environments. They described what are all the challenges they met in digital signature schemes, like computational overhead, key management, and risk to various cyber threats within the cloud structure. In this study, they suggested effective key distribution techniques and cutting-edge encryption standards. Using this research, they offer useful techniques to protect electronic transactions in cloud contexts [15]. Iqbal et al., (2024) made a comparative analysis has been done to identify the efficiency of the proposed model. At last, this method improves the performance in terms of security like that they described in their study [16].

Muzakkir et al., (2024) uses a SHA-256 for digital signature tokens, and OpenSSL for valid digital signatures, they start with generating a key pair, and they created the digital signature application in this study. Mainly, they created this application to secure and efficiently authorise document signing. Moreover, they assure the delivery of OTPs through mail for user authentication testing and a strong defence against Man-in-the-Middle attacks, and secure transfer of login data over HTTPS is also described. QR code verification efficiency, authenticity and signature integrity were confirmed by this research analysis [17].

2   Methodology

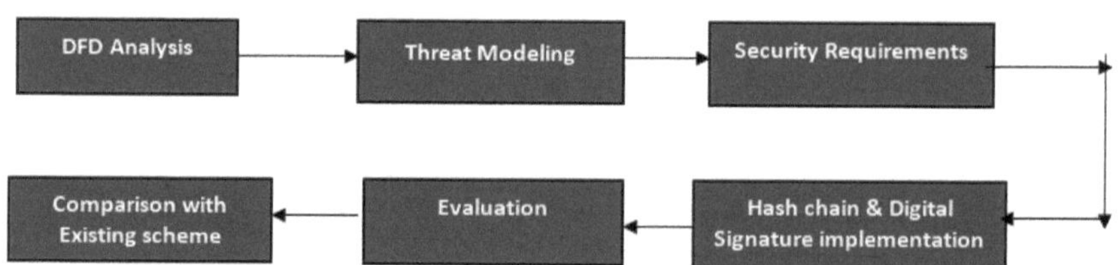

Fig. 1. Data flow diagram for methodology

DFD Analysis: To identify and understand the flow of data within the VANET system is analysed by a DFD analysis (Dataflow Diagram). This analysis helps to identify the problems and weaknesses in the system where security threats like replay and tampering attacks could develop. To protect the authenticity and integrity of the data, we have to analyse the data flow, then we can identify where the data is sent, received, processed and ensure the corresponding security measures are in place. The Data Flow Diagram (DFD) analysis will be used in the proposed security structure to assess the flow of information between vehicles and the infrastructure as well as the received information input and storage system. On examining these data flows, the points of hash chains and digital signatures may be identified to defend the system against the replay and tampering attacks. Moreover, the result of this analysis will be used to design the security framework so that we optimize system performance and ensure the security framework (Fig. 1).

Threat Modeling: The first action in VANETs security setup is to determine the threats to security. A threat modeling approach can be utilized to identify and examine possible targets in the system, e.g. using STRIDE or LINDDUN. Such approaches facilitate the identification of the weaknesses and the possible failure points in VANETs. STRIDE methodology groups threats into six classes of threats: det witness to the spoofing, tampering, repudiation, information disclosure, denial of service (DoS) and elevation of privilege (EoP). Based on it, we can adequately define risks related to vehicle-to-vehicle (V2V) communication, namely, spoofing attacks, and safety messages tampering [18]. The LINDDUN methodology, instead, is anchored on privacy related threats and categorizes these threats in seven ways such as Linkability, Identifiability and Non-Repudiation. Cumulatively, STRIDE and LINDDUN capture many of the possible threats with 34 risks and 11 key assets or threat targets being covered [19]. A secure system design of VANET can be made by consequently discovering the potential threats and vulnerabilities. In our proposed system, hash chains and digital signatures provide a system to achieve integrity (and authenticity) of messages and is effective to prevent replay and tampering attacks. The framework offers good security against threats that may occur thus increasing the security level of VANETs [20].

2.1 Security Requirements

Data Integrity: Data integrity plays the vital role in VANETs because vehicles are dependent on accurate and reliable data to make safe decision. Verification of data preserves the integrity of the information being sent to ensure that it is neither tampered with nor adversely affected by unauthorized parties. Observing this principle, VANETs will be able to avoid attacks that will mislead the correctness of safety-affecting information.

Non-repudiation: Non-repudiation is also important in VANETs in that a car cannot deny its involvement in a transaction or a communication. This is a security measure to prevent the cases where electronics vehicles fraudulently claim that they never sent or received a certain message. Non-repudiation allows trust building and accountability between the vehicles and the network by the minimization of the probability of message denial.

Authentication: Authentication is required to prove that the vehicles and infrastructure are authentic. The network can only be accessed by authorised parties who share information amongst themselves. VANETs can help to avoid spoofing, unauthorized access, and other attempts of hacking by authenticating cars and infrastructure, and this way, the trust and reliability of the network are maintained.

2.2 Hash Chain and Digital Signature Implementation

To prevent replay and tampering attacks, the proposed security framework utilises hash chains and digital signatures. A hash chain is a series of hash values formed by hashing the previous hash value multiple times, in a way similar to how a password or code is hashed, in one-way function. Hash chains have numerous uses; one common use is for message integrity/authentication. In order to further protect the communication, the use of a digital signature is added to the hash chain. Each message is digitally signed with the private key of the sender, and the security of the message can be verified by the receiver using the sender's public key, which provides integrity of the message and authenticity of the sender. Particularly, digital signature algorithms like RSA and hash-based signatures (such as SPHINCS and XMSS) are used to provide the essential security properties with fewer security assumptions. These algorithms are appropriate for applications needing high security because they provide benefits like post-quantum security and fewer security requirements.

A unique message ID, timestamp, message payload, hash chain value, and digital signature are the components message structure in this framework. A digital signature is created using the message payload and the current hash value in the hash chain. The receiver attempts to verify the signature using the sender's public key by computing the hash chain which is achieved by applying the one-way hash function to the previous hash value, and comparing it to the expected value in the hash chain. Here, they assure that any hash chain value or message payload will be identified. This framework can prevent replay attacks is one of its advantages. Replay attacks occur when an unauthorised person retransmits a message to the receiver, which might cause harm or a clash to the system. So here we are going to use timestamps and hash chains, which prevents replay attacks, and the attacker has to create a new hash chain value and digital signature for each message that is replayed. Because of this, the attacker has no possibility to launch a successful replay attack, almost here it is zero.

Moreover, this framework provides high protection against tampering attacks. When an attacker modifies the message by payload or hash chain value, it may harm the system or cause a clash with the system. Any tampering attacks with the message payload or hash chain value will be easily identified by using digital signatures and hash chains. Because of this, an attacker doesn't have a chance to launch their tampering attempt, and it is almost zero. The entire framework's security depends on the one-way hash function and digital signature used. In order for an attacker to produce a new hash chain value, it must not match the expected value, because a hash function should be collision-resistant and preimage-resistant. And choosing message attacks, making it difficult for an attacker to produce a new digital signature, a secure digital signature scheme should be existentially unforgeable.

The framework provides security advantages that are efficient and scalable. The framework's usage of hash chains and digital signatures reduces computing overhead because only one hash operation and digital signature verification are needed for every message. The framework is scalable, because it is used in various applications and domains, like finance, healthcare, and government sectors. The suggested security model can be applied in various ways, to IoT security, secure data storage, and secure communication protocols. Through the deployment of secure communication protocols, the framework attributes that exchanges between two users are secure, and the integrity and authenticity of the messages being conveyed are not violated. Under an IoT landscape, the frame will ensure security in communication between devices and the cloud or other associated devices . There are also adequate data storage security measures that are deployed to protect the integrity and authenticity of data that is stored in cloud or other storage systems.

A key element in the improvement of the security of the framework is proper key management. There is generation of public and private keys, distribution and secure storage. Key revocation mechanisms make sure that revoked keys are removed in a timely fashion and replaced. Furthermore, there is some future work that may be done to find ways of throwing more efficiency into the framework, framework processes of key revocation, and also integrating the framework to work with other security systems. This framework makes sure that there is an authenticity and integrity to the message and it offers immense protection against replay and tampering. The design is highly scalable and security-oriented; it provides long-term protection via a key management scheme.

In a nutshell, hash chains plus the digital signature provides a solid means of combating replay and tampering attacks. This method can be used on a wide range of applications and domains because of its ability to ensure message integrity, detect manipulation, and prevent replay attacks. The scalability of the framework as well as its effectiveness and security also gives the framework longevity in combating different forms of cyber threats.

Hash Chain Algorithm

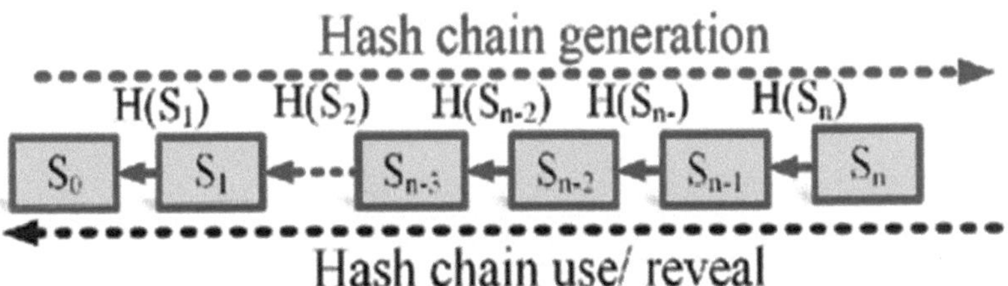

Fig. 2. Hash Chain Generation Image

A hash chain is a cryptographic mechanism, where the sequence of values is created depending on the previous one. The specified method is commonly employed in a variety of authentication systems, entities in blockchain technology, and security protocols because of its high security characteristics (Fig. 2).

Algorithm Steps:

- Select a one-way Hash Function: Choose a secure hash function which is a one way hash like SHA-256 that assures you of cryptographic strength.
- Initialize Hash Chain: Add random number or some initial value to start the chain.
- Calculate the Hash Chain: Using a one-way hash algorithm, each successive value in the chain is calculated by using the previous value as the input to a one-way hash function.
- Repeat: Iteration repeat until the length of the hash chain is reached (Fig. 3).

Fig. 3. How the Hashing Algorithm Works

Digital Signature Generation Algorithm (DSA)- Key Generation

1. Choose Prime Numbers: Select two prime numbers, p and q, where q is a divisor of (p-1).
2. Choose a Generator: Select a generator g, where $g = h^{(p-1)/q} \mod p$ and h is an integer between 1 and (p-1).

3.Private Key: Choose a private key x, where $0 < x < q$.
   4.Public Key: Compute the public key $y = g^x \mod p$.

Signing

1. Choose a Random Number: Select a random number k, where $0 < k < q$.
2. Compute r: Calculate $r = (g^k \mod p) \mod q$.
3. Compute s: Calculate $s = (k^{(-1)} * (H(m) + xr)) \mod q$, where H(m) is the hash of the message m.
4. Signature: The digital signature is (r, s).

Verification

1. Compute w: Calculate $w = s^{(-1)} \mod q$.
2. Compute u1 and u2: Calculate $u1 = H(m) * w \mod q$ and $u2 = r * w \mod q$.
3. Compute v: Calculate $v = (g^{u1} * y^{u2} \mod p) \mod q$.
4. Verify: Check if $v = r$. If true, the signature is valid.

Verification Algorithm

- Receive Message and Signature: Receive the message m and the digital signature (r, s).
- Verify Signature: To check the signature, use the verification algorithm.
- Check Hash Chain: Verify the hash chain value by applying the one-way hash function to the previous hash value.
- Authenticate: Authenticate the message, if the signature and hash chain are valid.

3   Results and Findings

Calculating the effectiveness and efficiency of the proposed framework for VANET is essential. The computational cost, communication overhead, and security features are evaluated in this study to highlight the framework's possible effects on network security and performance. The above measurements are used to assess whether the framework is suitable for deployment on VANET and to identify the areas for further optimization.

Computational Overhead: It specifies the amount of computing resources (time and processing power) required to finish security operations like digital signature verification and hash chain creation. We evaluate this and we are not overburdening the system, and to make sure the system is effective, so these things are listed in the Table 1.

Table 1. Calculation of Computational Time and Complexity

S.NO	Operation	Computational Time (ms)	Computational Complexity
1.	Hash Chain Generation	0.5	$O(n)$
2.	Digital Signature Generation	1.2	$O(n)$
3.	Digital Signature Verification	0.8	$O(n)$

In the above Table 1, the type of operation and its computational time, along with its complexity, are also mentioned. 0.5 ms they got as computational time and an $O(n)$ complexity value, in the hash chain generation. Then, for the Digital signature generation, 1.2 ms as the computational time and the complexity is $O(n)$. Also, the Digital signature verification operation took 0.8 ms as the computational time with an $O(n)$ complexity value.

Communication Overhead: It describes the extra information sent across the network as a result of security features like digital signatures and hash chain values. To make sure the framework doesn't negatively impact network performance, we assess this and we mentioned in the table below:

Table 2. Shows the Message size with Network latency

S.NO	Message Type	Message Size (bytes)	Network Latency (ms)
1	Message with Hash Chain	256	10
2	Message with Digital Signature	512	15

The size of the Message in bytes and Network latency are listed out in the above Table 2. Two main things are pointed out in the above table: that is, the message with a hash chain and the message with a digital signature. 256 (bytes) is the size of the message for a message with a hash chain; their network latency is 10 ms. And for the digital signature message size is 512 (bytes), with their network latency is 15 ms.

Security: It refers to how well the framework will defend against attacks like replay and tampering. We assess this to make sure the framework offers sufficient security measures.

In the above Table 3, attack types, with their prevention mechanism & effectiveness, are shown. We took two types of attacks we took. For the replay attack, the prevention

Table 3. Attack types with their prevention mechanism & effectiveness

S.NO	Attack Type	Prevention Mechanism	Effectiveness
1	Replay Attack	Hash Chain	High
2	Tampering Attack	Digital Signature	High

mechanism is a hash chain, and the effectiveness should be high. And for the tampering attack, the prevention mechanism is a digital signature, and the effectiveness should be high.

Table 4. Comparison with the different schemes

Scheme	Authentication	Integrity	Non-Repudiation
Proposed Scheme	✓	✓	✓
ECPP	✓	✓	✗
SPECS	✓	✗	✓
RAISE	✓	✓	✓

In the above Table 4, they compared the security features with different schemes. To evaluate the schemes, they used three key things: non-repudiation, which guarantees that a sender cannot deny sending a message; integrity, which guarantees that data cannot be modified or tampered with; and authentication, which confirms the identity of individuals or devices. All three security properties are offered by the Proposed Scheme and RAISE (Robust Authentication Scheme for VANET), while SPECS (Secure and Privacy Enhancing Communications Schemes) lacks Integrity, and ECPP (Efficient Conditional Privacy Preservation) lacks non-repudiation. In terms of security aspects, this comparison illustrates the advantages and disadvantages of each system.

Table 5. Comparison of different schemes with computational overhead & communication overhead

Scheme	Computational Overhead	Communication Overhead
Proposed Scheme	Low	Low
ECPP	Medium	Medium
SPECS	High	High
RAISE	Low	Medium

Table 5 shows how effectively various systems perform in terms of communication and processing overhead. Efficiency in processing power and network consumption is demonstrated by the Proposed Scheme's low overhead in both categories. SPECS has a large overhead that could impact performance, and ECPP has low overhead in both categories. RAISE is also a high-performance processor since its overhead is low in calculation and middle in communication. Comparing will be necessary in order to judge the effectiveness and performance of each scheme.

4   Conclusion

In summary, has effectively established protection against both replay and tampering attacks in the proposed security architecture of VANETs with the required minimum of computing and communication overheads. In the analytic performance, it is possible to observe how efficient the framework is in the safeguard of VANET. Provision of a potent VANET solution is presented within this framework that is well-armed with security provisions. The comparison between other systems such as ECPP, SPECS, and RAISE shows the security and performance benefits of the system that we propose. In order to make intelligent transportation systems reliable and secure, all things considered, the suggested framework has potential concerning the security of VANET. In future, we need to develop the workability to a larger framework in VANET and integrating it with some more security and verify its efficiency in practice-based conditions. To the further advancement of VANET security and efficiency, to compare and analyze experimental data, we develop a platform on which the VANET security protocol can be tested. Through such a study, we get to guarantee the efficiency and security of intelligent transportation systems.

References

1. Al-Sultan, S., Al-Doori, M.M., Al-Bayatti, A.H., Zedan, H.: A comprehensive survey on vehicular Ad Hoc network. J. Netw. Comput. Appl. **37**, 380–392 (2014). https://doi.org/10.1016/j.jnca.2013.02.036
2. Rehman, S.U., Khan, M.A., Zia, T.A., Zheng, L.: Vehicular Ad-Hoc networks (VANETs)—An overview and challenges. J. Wirel. Netw. Commun. **3**(3), 29–38 (2013). https://doi.org/10.5923/j.jwnc.20130303.02
3. Yousefi, S., Mousavi, M.S., Fathy, M.: Vehicular Ad Hoc Networks (VANETs): Challenges and Perspectives. In: 6th International Conference on ITS Telecommunications, pp. 761–766. IEEE, Chengdu, China (2006). https://doi.org/10.1109/ITST.2006.289012
4. Li, F., Wang, Y.: Routing in vehicular Ad Hoc networks: A survey. IEEE Veh. Technol. Mag. **2**, 12–22 (2007)
5. Yousefi, S., Mousavi, M.S., Fathy, M.: Vehicular Ad Hoc networks (VANETs): Challenges and perspectives. In: 6th International Conference on ITS Telecommunications, pp. 761–766. IEEE, Chengdu, China (2006). https://doi.org/10.1109/ITST.2006.289012
6. Chainlink. What is a Replay Attack?
7. GeeksforGeeks. Replay Attack. https://www.geeksforgeeks.org/computer-networks/replay-attack/ (n.d.). Accessed 8 Jan 2026
8. Wu, Z., Gao, S., Cling, E.S., Li, H.: A study on replay attack and anti-spoofing for text-dependent speaker verification. In: Proceedings of the Asia-Pacific Signal and Information Processing Association Annual Summit and Conference (APSIPA), pp. 1–5. IEEE, Siem Reap, Cambodia (2014). https://doi.org/10.1109/APSIPA.2014.7041636

9. Wikipedia, Tamper proofing, https://en.wikipedia.org/wiki/Tamperproofing (n.d.). Accessed 8 Jan 2026
10. Thomas, P.: The application of hash chains and hash structures to cryptography. Royal Holloway Research Online (2009, August 4)
11. Patil, R.S., & N, J. (2023). Enhanced machine learning based techniques for security in vehicular Ad-Hoc networks. In: In: Proceedings of the International Conference on Advances in Communication and Computing Technology (InCACCT 2023). Piscataway, NJ: IEEE. 386–393. doi:https://doi.org/10.1109/InCACCT57535.2023.10141791
12. Huo, Q., Ning, Y., Bian, C., Sun, D.: Research on anti-replay attack mechanism of intelligent connected vehicles based on hashing chain and V2X communication. In: Proceedings of the International Conference Optoelectronic Information and Optical Engineering (OIOE2024). SPIE, Bellingham, WA (2025). https://doi.org/10.1117/12.3054402
13. Sinha, S.K., Mukhopadhyay, D.: Time efficient hash key generation for blockchain enabled framework. IEEE Access. **12**, 155867–155884 (2024). https://doi.org/10.1109/ACCESS.2024.34788
14. Roy, A., Karforma, S.: A survey on digital signatures and its applications. J. Comput. Inf. Technol. **3**(1&2), 45–69 (2012)
15. Rakhra, M., Singh, A., Singh, D., Shruti: Digital signature verification in cloud computing. In: 11th International Conference on Reliability, Infocom Technologies and Optimization (Trends and Future Directions) (ICRITO), Noida, India, pp. 1–6. IEEE, Piscataway, NJ (2024). https://doi.org/10.1109/ICRITO61523.2024.10522372
16. Iqbal, S., Sujatha, B.R.: Secure authentication and key management based on hierarchical enhanced identity based digital signature in heterogeneous wireless sensor network. Wirel. Netw. **31**, 127–147 (2025). https://doi.org/10.1007/s11276-024-03745-x
17. Muzakkir, F.B., Darwito, H.A., Yuliana, M.: Developing web-based application for QR code digital signatures using OpenSSL. In: International Electronics Symposium (IES), Denpasar, Indonesia, vol. 2024, pp. 386–392. IEEE, Piscataway, NJ (2024). https://doi.org/10.1109/IES 63037.2024.10665883
18. Microsoft. STRIDE Threat Model. https://learn.microsoft.com/en-us/azure/security/develop/threat-modeling-tool-threats (n.d.)
19. Wuyts, K., Joosen, W.: LINDDUN privacy threat modeling: A step-by-step guide. LINDDUN privacy threat modeling: A tutorial. KU Leuven – LINDDUN Project (2015)
20. Raya, M., Hubaux, J.P.: Securing vehicular ad hoc networks. J. Comput. Secur. **15**(1), 39–68 (2007)

An Empirical Study on the Relevance of Enabler Factors on the Adoption of Cryptocurrency in India

Bashir Firdaus[1] ⓘ, Viswanath Ananth[2(✉)] ⓘ, V. Santhi[3] ⓘ, and V. Devi Priya[3] ⓘ

[1] PSG Institute of Management, PSG College of Technology, Coimbatore, India
`firdaussudheer@gmail.com`
[2] Aimer Business School, Kozhikode, Kerala, India
`viswanath@aimerbschool.in`
[3] Department of Management Studies, KSR College of Engineering, Namakkal, India
`{hod,devipriyamba}@kscrce.ac.in`

Abstract. The study seeks to address a set of factors that can influence the seamless adoption of cryptocurrency, the digitised money that is accessible via cryptographic codes. This study examines technological infrastructure, legal frameworks, governmental support, public awareness, social and cultural influences, and global interconnectedness. In this survey method, the primary data was collected using a snowball sampling technique. From among the 100 questionnaires distributed, 85 were further processed for statistical analysis, consisting of descriptive statistics. This aided in condensing the data into mean, standard values and the mean rank for each selected factor. Friedman's test was employed to rank these factors according to their order of relevance for the seamless adoption of cryptocurrency. The study's results indicated that the legal frame work is the most important factor, followed by governmental support. Global connectedness was identified as the least impactful factor among the others. The smooth and wider adoption of cryptocurrency across sectors hinges on the confluence of the multiple factors selected for the study. The research employed the technology acceptance model as the underpinning theory to empirically examine the factors influencing cryptocurrency adoption. This novel methodology fills a research void in a specialised, yet swiftly growing, digital currency sector. The approach is relevant amid the collective interest in cryptocurrencies among institutions, governments, and individuals. This paper exhibits the prominence of the ongoing research in the rapidly evolving financial domain.

Keywords: Cryptocurrency · cultural influence · government support · global connectedness · India · laws and regulations · public awareness · social influence · the technology acceptance model and technological infrastructure

1 Introduction

Cryptocurrency is a form of digital currency used for different types of commercial transactions and secured through encryption [1]. These currencies can be accessible through mobile devices or computers with internet connectivity [2]. Unlike traditional

© The Author(s) 2026
R. Sridaran and S. Priti (Eds.): AI-FCDAC 2025, CCIS 2866, pp. 87–100, 2026.
https://doi.org/10.1007/978-3-032-17300-3_7

currency, cryptocurrency does not have fiat counterparts, which means it must be stored in digital wallets and software programs that can send and receive it, such as Bitcoin [3]. The transactions are recorded on a public ledger called a blockchain, and all the participants involved can possess an entire copy of the transaction [4]. This is one of the factors that contribute to the success of the blockchain [5]. Revealing identity is not essential while doing a transaction, which makes it easier to maintain confidentiality [6]. It is also possible to sustain an instant payment system in peer-to-peer transactions. This eliminates intermediaries, increasing the speed of transactions when compared to the traditional banking system. Funds can be transferred anywhere globally at a lower cost, making cryptocurrency an attractive option for settling contractual deeds more effectively [7]. Cryptocurrency transactions can be validated, authenticated and reviewed only by a decentralised network of nodes [8].

The majority of the cryptocurrencies are limited in supply [9] and are predetermined by the protocol [10]. Thus, they cannot be altered by one person or an entity without the support of the majority of users. Such a system in place prevents currency from being manipulated, making it a stronger medium of financial transactions [11]. Among the different cryptocurrencies available in the market, Bitcoin is perceived as the most popular one used as a mode of payment [12]. Ethereum (ETH), another cryptocurrency, is an open-source blockchain used by developers to build and run smart contracts and decentralised applications [13]. Ripple is a blockchain-based payment platform designed to enable fast, low-cost cross-border transactions for banks and financial institutions. Using its consensus protocol, transactions settle in seconds and are generally more efficient and cheaper than traditional bank transfers [14].

Initially, the fear of financial instability prompted the Reserve Bank of India (RBI) to call for an overall prohibition on cryptocurrency investments [15]. In March 2020, the Supreme Court of India upheld the RBI circular excluding regulated entities from serving customers who participated in cryptocurrency transactions, which was a major turning point [16]. Later, when the popularity of digital assets started increasing, the government set a new tax regime to rein in this market, receiving a mixed reaction from the public. Some were of the perception that the 30% tax on the profits derived from trading or investing [17] is an acknowledgement of legality. Whereas few others felt that it was nothing more than gambling or speculation and did not favour it. A petition removing the 30% tax was signed immediately by more than 50,000 people who perceived it as a huge tax burden on cryptocurrency traders [18]. In India cryptocurrency has opened a new and dynamic paradigm, allowing individuals to purchase, sell or transfer conveniently [19], and the adoption of cryptocurrencies by the public and other institutions will determine its fate. Mainstream investors are encouraged to invest in cryptocurrency because most giant businesses like Tesla or Square are accepting cryptocurrencies into their operations; others are wary due to past scandals and market volatility. While cryptocurrencies hold the potential to facilitate financial inclusion and empowerment, their widespread adoption requires careful consideration of various factors [20].

India is staying competitive in the international digital payment and investment landscape [21]. The globalised cryptocurrency markets allow international investors to trade digital assets, including in India. The fostering of such collaboration calls for a better regulatory landscape, sound awareness of digital assets and adherence to government policies [22]. International transactions have high potential in India to build and strengthen relationships, as it is an approachable platform with a huge population of tech-savvy people [23]. Therefore, it is essential to understand the factors that enable the adoption of cryptocurrency widely.

There are three significant research questions developed for the study (RQs) as stated below:

RQ1: To what extent do factors like technological infrastructure, law and regulatory compliance, social influence, cultural factors, global connectedness, public awareness and governmental support influence the adoption of cryptocurrency?

RQ2: What is the relative significance of each factor in facilitating the seamless adoption of cryptocurrency?

RQ3: Which factor will have the highest and lowest priority according to the respondents while ranking?

2   Review of Literature

Law and regulation are central mechanisms of governance that outline a framework for the society to operate [24]. Law denotes rules framed and enforced through legislative bodies binding on all and ensuring order and justice within the society [25]. Regulations are directives or standards issued by administrative agencies that are based on authority granted by legislation [26]. They provide detailed instructions on how to enforce laws. Legal rules are the most significant factor that mitigates uncertain outcomes in India's adoption of cryptocurrency [27]. Even though the tax regulations impose certain financial obligations, the lack of comprehensive regulatory laws and regulations remains a signif icant challenge. The requirement for different regulatory landscapes is ever-evolving, as the tax laws alone would not suffice because the seamless adoption is facilitated when the creation and sale of cryptocurrency tokens are in adherence to economic principles [28]. The ever-evolving financial landscape demands the formation of all-inclusive legal frameworks to regulate the valuation and transactional usage of virtual currencies as probable alternatives for the Indian rupee. Implementing a robust legal system with sufficient regulations will drive financial stability [29], guard consumers against various malpractices [30], and maintain the integrity of the national currency system [31]. Thus, clear measures can stabilise the monetary system by actively engaging digital currency users [32]. The law should be clear and consistent, providing security and legitimacy to users [33]. A robust legal system is considered the cornerstone of widespread adoption of cryptocurrency. Past literature has also highlighted the significance of a robust legal system [34, 35]. Therefore, law and regulatory compliance have been chosen for the study to ascertain their significance in the smooth facilitation of cryptocurrency.

To mitigate certain regulatory concerns, the Indian government intends to build its legal tender, called Central Bank Currency (CBDC) [36], which would initiate further regulatory changes and mandate new rules for effective execution [37]. Moreover, the government plans to frame tax policies that avoid ambiguity and uncertainties, thereby encouraging investors. These changes could smooth business operations and global digital asset transactions [38]. Different countries have varying tax regimes; governments should maintain global operative policies by mitigating cross-border tax challenges. Governmental support is considered another vital factor required for regulating the future of cryptocurrency [32], influencing adoption rates, and having immense potential to shape future transactions [39].

Efficient, safe and reliable transactions fundamentally require technological infrastructure with advanced features [40]. The system should be able to sustain a larger storage capacity and handle complex computations with an uninterrupted power supply to prevent data loss or corruption [41]. User-friendly technological infrastructure with a continuous monitoring system permits the fluid adoption of cryptocurrency; therefore, it happens to be a crucial factor [42]. Many cryptocurrency platforms enable their users to use pseudonyms, making financial regulation difficult to enforce [43]. This anonymity makes criminal acts such as money laundering easier because people can create different accounts to conduct fraudulent payments. Improving security and creating measures for identifying crimes in the blockchain is key to avoiding such misuse [44]. Continuously monitoring private entities engaged in cryptocurrency trading for accountability will safeguard investors and preserve market integrity by reducing fraudulent activities [45].

A cultural perception of investing in cryptocurrency to enjoy long-term benefits lingers. Moreover, the culture of innovativeness also drives youngsters especially to invest in the newer financial system. The young, tech-savvy population of India is inclined towards the benefits of cryptocurrency due to their familiarity with blockchain and digital finance [46]. This cultural propensity towards new technological innovations drives the smoother and wider adoption of cryptocurrency in India [47]. Over time, a notable shift towards investing in portfolios with greater risk has caught the market compared to lower-risk assets like real estate and gold. Some perceive the highly volatile nature of cryptocurrency as an opportunity to achieve substantial returns, despite the inherent risk [48].

The involvement of India in global cryptocurrency adoption is crucial as the country navigates regulatory challenges and embraces digital currency innovation. The global cooperation on cryptocurrency regulations and blockchain initiatives provides a framework that can guide India towards safe and sustainable cryptocurrency adoption. Having adequate legal regulations and governmental support can encourage global adoption of cryptocurrency [49], benefiting both local and international stakeholders. India is also welcoming collaborations with companies that foster participation in global cryptocurrency trades [50]. This shapes the investment patterns and creates a dynamic ecosystem. Corporations like Tesla and PayPal have integrated Bitcoin payments, which is a positive approach towards cryptocurrency transactions [51] that can influence new users. Moreover, technological firms in India are also developing low-cost cryptocurrency remittance platforms, which again help revolutionise these markets internationally [52]. Hence, global connectedness is considered another factor that could potentially influence the adoption of cryptocurrency. Like most countries, India is becoming highly interested in the cryptocurrency market. Though the outlook for the government is positive, growing security challenges linger.

2.1 Technology Acceptance Model: Theoretical Underpinning

The Technology Acceptance Model (TAM) is adopted as an underpinning theory which has three important components: 1) Perceived Usefulness (PU) 2) Perceived Ease of Use (PEOU), affecting 3) Behavioural Intention to use new technology [53], digital currency in this context. Through the lens of TAM, it is evident that the prominence of cryptocurrencies is on the rise because there are numerous benefits involved, like decentralisation, financial sovereignty, and the ability to make borderless transactions with this currency [54]. All of this can be grouped under the characteristics of PU. With sufficient regulation centres, governmental support, and proper training, the PU can be enhanced. The transactions are mostly effortless if the user learns to use the technology, as they can be done through mobile applications with user-friendly wallets, which can be a feature of PEOU. The social-cultural influence and the requirement of the user to be globally connected can induce behavioural intention to use cryptocurrency.

3 Research Methodology

There are various factors like technological infrastructure, compelling laws and regulations, social influence, public awareness, governmental support, cultural factors and global connectedness that influence the adoption of cryptocurrency. The present study aims to identify and rank these factors to determine which one has the greatest influence on the seamless adoption of cryptocurrency. The data required for the study was collected through the survey method. A structured questionnaire was designed using a 5-point Likert scale ranging from 1 to 5. The questionnaire was distributed to 100 participants using a snowball sampling technique. The respondents were keen cryptocurrency enthusiast's familiar with the policies and regulations for doing transactions with it. The researchers ascertained their understanding and active engagement with cryptocurrency before administering the questionnaire. Participants were assured of confidentiality and encouraged to provide their honest responses. A pilot test was conducted, and the data was not used for the final analysis. After screening the responses for missing values and inconsistencies, 85 were further processed for statistical analysis. The demographic variables of the selected respondents have been depicted in Table 1.

The respondents were more men when compared to women, as depicted in Table 1. Those falling under the age category of 39–59 was increasingly involved with cryptocurrency investments. Compared to diploma holders and graduates, postgraduates and those under the income category of 40000 to 60000 rupees were found to be interested in these transactions. The collected data was analysed using descriptive statistics, which helped to condense the data into key measures like mean and standard deviation, enabling an overview of the average and dispersion of the responses. The mean rank for each factor was also estimated to analyse the trend as well as provide a comparative overview of the significance of each factor that has a high influence on the seamless adoption of cryptocurrency. Friedman's test was administered to estimate the differences in the importance of the factors considered in the study. This test is beneficial in survey analysis for comparing preferences, especially when responses are collected from the same set of participants.

Table 1. Demographic variables of the select respondents

Variables	Frequency	Percentage
Gender		
Male	70	82.4
Women	15	17.6
Total	85	100
Age		
18–38	20	23.5
39–59	55	64.8
60 and more	10	11.7
Total	85	100
Educational Qualification		
Diploma	10	11.8
Graduation	20	23.5
Post-Graduation	55	64.7
Total	85	100
Income		
20000–39000	10	11.7
40000–690000	50	58.8
700000 and more	25	29.5
Total	85	100

Table 2. Mean, standard deviation and mean rank of the select factors

Factor	Respondents	Mean	Standard Deviation	Mean Rank
Laws and Regulatory Compliance	85	3.4	1.08	4.31
Government Support	85	3.31	0.96	4.2
Technological Infrastructure	85	3.17	0.99	3.71
Public Awareness	85	3.13	1.16	3.40
Social Influence	85	3.11	0.97	3.29
Cultural Influence	85	3.01	0.93	3.21
Global connectedness	85	3.00	0.90	3.10

As depicted in Table 2, laws and regulatory compliance ranked the highest among all the selected factors with a mean rank estimate of 4.31. Laid-out laws will give a framework on how investments can be made, reducing ambiguity and fraudulent practices for various stakeholders like investors and businesses. Governmental support was the next factor in the ranking, with a mean rank of 4.2. When the government has strategies and provides continuous support, then existing users will continue their usage, and new entrants shall willingly adopt cryptocurrency. Technological infrastructure was ranked as the third factor amongst the others with a mean rank value of 3.71. Limitations in infrastructure usually impede access to cryptocurrency exchanges. Advanced technological infrastructure with safe internet access and secure digital payment systems facilitates rapid adoption. Raising awareness among the public and educating people was the next factor in the ranking, with a measure of 3.40. Initiatives to raise public awareness will lead to safer practices, border acceptance and informed decision-making. Social influence, which includes the influence of community groups, peers and influencers, also impacted the rapid adoption of cryptocurrency. This factor ranked fifth in mean score, with an estimated value of 3.29. It plays a significant role in shaping individual attitudes and behaviours towards cryptocurrency adoption by building trust. Cultural factors ranked next in line with a measure of 3.21. Among the factors selected for the study, global connectedness was the lowest-ranked factor, with an influence value of 3.10. India is a significant player in the global currency landscape and is widening its scope. India's legal and governmental support will largely determine the unified approach required for global transactions. A younger population, increasingly interested in technology and digital investments, largely drives the country. They view this investment as a means of diversifying their portfolios and seeking long-term returns. Therefore, in the coming years, the impact of global connectedness may increase. Thus, it is evident that all factors, like technological infrastructure, compelling law and regulatory compliance, social influence, cultural factors, global connectedness, public awareness and governmental support, have their own influence on the seamless adoption of cryptocurrency, though the influence each factor has varies accordingly.

Table 3. Friedman's Test

No. of Respondents	Chi-Square	Difference	p
85	28.320	9	0.002

The results in Table 3 revealed that there exists a variation in the ranking for each factor. The value of Chi Square has been estimated at 28.320, which exceeds the threshold of the degree of freedom of 8. The probability has been estimated at 0.002. The results depict that the ranking done by the respondents is significant.

4 Discussion

India is emerging as a technical powerhouse; the policymakers, with the advice of cryptocurrency experts, should develop, amend, and modify rules and regulations about all the aspects of cryptocurrency with strategic foresight. As per the results of the study, laws and regulatory compliance are important in the rapid adoption of digital assets, as they mitigate risks by preventing fraudulent activities like cyber-attacks and money laundering [11]. It is also crucial to impose stringent penalties to uphold the security of these transactions. Without such measures, hackers could probably gain access to systems, permitting them to replicate virtual currencies and manipulate account balances. Therefore, a comprehensive legal framework covering all the aspects of purchase, price, and exchange is crucial. The road to mass adoption will hugely depend upon a balanced regulatory framework fostering innovation and consumer protection [55]. Striking a balance means having moderate restrictions that foster global cryptocurrency transactions while ensuring security.

For cryptocurrencies to be widely accepted, the government needs to support them. Well-defined taxation policies and due assurance of safety from the government can promote responsible behaviour among investors, leading to stability in the market. Governmental surveillance is crucial in gaining public confidence and participation and in building a transparent environment. In India, while the legal authorities and the government are trying to implement and execute the best policies, technology keeps changing. Mitigating this gap necessitates frequent modification of existing laws or the formulation of new laws. A deeply rooted legal system can boost PU and PEOU as transactions are observed to be secure. In such a scenario, accountability is borne by platforms, and disputes are largely settled. Moreover, when the government assumes a significant role in developing infrastructure and providing state-backed initiatives, the usefulness of cryptocurrency transactions is enhanced.

Technological infrastructure should comprise components that can facilitate efficiency and user-friendly interfaces, encouraging wider spread acceptance of cryptocurrency transactions into everyday activities conforming to TAM. Installing advanced machine learning algorithms can aid in analysing the patterns as well as the user behaviour to track systems for malicious activities. Therefore, laws and regulations should be in place with a strong backing from the government, and both of these factors should be aware of the changing dynamics of cryptocurrency-related technology. In countries without specific laws and regulations governing cryptocurrency, people may hesitate to engage in transactions due to concerns about fraud or a lack of legal recourse [56].

Free workshops on digital currencies, safe trading practices, and malpractice detection will raise awareness and empower individuals to make secure investments. Free training delivered to technical experts will enable them to understand the advanced technical aspects and enhance their skill sets, too. Outreach programmes can address existing misconceptions and disseminate crucial information. Even though there is inherent volatility and risk, millennial investors in India are risk-averse and willing to take time and effort to learn and invest in new ventures. People should receive a balanced training focusing on both the benefits as well as risks involved in this kind of financial ecosystem. Such knowledge enables users to understand the process, making it simple, positively impacting the PEOU and PU, and thus influencing the behavioural intention towards adoption. Users prefer technology that is less complex [53]. Additionally, both PU and PEOU predict users' intentions, which confirms the applicability of this theory in fintech realms [57].

Social influence is pivotal in deciding to accept or reject cryptocurrency transactions. Individuals feel confident when their acquaintance whom they can trust invests in cryptocurrency. A cultural acceptance of speculative investments that bring higher returns from diversified portfolios has backed up investments in digital assets, too. An urge for financial independence has been a driving factor in this pattern. Additionally, youngsters in India are eager to participate in the advanced technologies, which aligns with the culture of innovation and openness to new ways of finance. Thus, culture is an important factor that influences the future of investments by encouraging the adoption of alternatives to conventional financial services. India's approach to tax laws and other regulations plays a crucial role in positioning itself in the global market; for instance, crypto tax policies levied had a detrimental impact on the Bitcoin market [58]. Therefore, the kind of culture that exists in a country could determine how cryptocurrency is accepted [59].

Cultural factors aid in understanding the growing interest in having a diverse investment portfolio and feeling financially independent, which enables the designing of cryptocurrency platforms accordingly. Social factors directly enhance behavioural intentions because an individual assumes fewer risks when there is a known circle involved in these transactions, which reinforces their adoption paths [60]. Subjective norms, which are the influence of friends, family members, peer groups, and so on, are deeply rooted in cultural context too. A person's perception of usefulness can shape their intention to adopt [61]. The sociocultural factor shapes adoption behaviour in different regions of a globally relevant finance system. Ad hoc approaches in the crypto space could impact both global connectedness and financial stability. In the years ahead, as cryptocurrencies continue to disrupt conventional finance, policymakers and the market will have to collaborate to maximise their potential and expand global connectivity without endangering economic growth. With strong regulatory structures, global collaboration, and new technologies, the crypto market can evolve to accommodate a more open, efficient, and stable world economy. The present study holds that law and governmental support are essential to frame policies for a secure and safe transaction.

To make speedy and secure cryptocurrency transactions, technological infrastructure is crucial. Offering educational and training programmes will help stakeholders make smart choices, whereas social influence can build trust and promote peaceful coexistence. Global connectedness is crucial in fostering international trade and strengthening economic ties. Therefore, we can argue that each factor significantly contributes to the smooth adoption of cryptocurrency. Past research confirms that individuals working in digitally integrated economies view cryptocurrency platforms as safer when they are perceived to have lower complexity and higher operational value, which in turn elevates both perceived usefulness (PU) and perceived ease of use (PEOU). With the wider network, universal access and reliable bandwidth within global connectedness can reduce entry barriers, enriching the PEOU among cross-border users. TAM is relevant to the study because it offers a structured framework for shaping stakeholders' behaviour. These stakeholders are willing to adopt cryptocurrency, which is an economic, decentralised and cost-effective alternative to traditional banking, making it a promising investment. Proper law and governmental regulation positively enhance stakeholders' perceived ease of use.

5 Implications of the Research

The findings of the study have strong implications for the cryptocurrency community, which includes investors, authorities, and the public. Lawmakers and the authorities can leverage the ranking categories to formulate policies essential for safe and secure transactions. Regulatory measures and governmental support are the most important factors for keeping the markets stable. Providing for good connectivity and advancement in technological infrastructure will empower stakeholders and invite new investors. The study also highlights the importance of creating awareness to stimulate informed entry and investment and engage ethically. India has a prevailing perception that the younger generation is tech-savvy, and they demonstrate a greater level of risk aversion, especially in the investment domain. Keeping both this duality will necessitate regulation that will strike a balance between encouraging innovations and safeguarding the interest of investors in cryptocurrency transactions. For a wider and smoother adoption of cryptocurrency, there must be a structured financial environment that permits tech-savvy yet risk-averse investors to engage in transactions with confidence. Given the nature of cryptocurrency, seamless connectivity across borders is possible. Authorities can frame policies that encourage collaborations between nations, strengthening international ties, providing employment opportunities and driving foreign funds home.

6 Limitations and Future Directions

Although the study offers meaningful insights, the sample size of 85 respondents may not completely represent the broader population. Likewise, the snowball sampling technique employed in the study is not free of selection bias. In the future, researchers may consider using larger and more diverse sample sizes, along with alternative sampling methods, to enhance generalisability. Seven factors were considered for ranking; researchers in the future can include more factors like ethical considerations, rural and urban criteria or support from traditional banks. Macroeconomic variables, such as interest rates, inflation, and international liquidity, significantly influence cryptocurrency markets and impact investors. A study on the impact of governmental policies and regulations on these aspects, which can create trust among users and investors for wider adoption, can be taken up. Future research can concentrate on the kind of training, workshop, or educational sessions required to raise awareness among people as well as technical experts. Researchers in the future can explore how diverse countries' rules and regulations affect cryptocurrency adoption on a global scale.

7 Conclusion

The rapid adoption of cryptocurrency transactions is contingent on addressing the factors considered for the study in a balanced manner. Each factor plays a pivotal role in shaping the financial ecosystem and fostering innovation. Legal compliance is prima facie paramount in safeguarding the interest of investors and protecting them from fraudulent activities by ensuring safety and security. Government strategies and support are equally vital in fostering public confidence and providing clarity in regulations. A robust technological infrastructure can facilitate efficient and reliable platforms for smooth transactions. Campaigns that raise awareness and educate the public will enhance effective transactions. Cultural factors and social influence are important for making cryptocurrency work with trust. The borderless nature of these digital assets demands global connectivity and international cooperation that encourage harmonious regulations and protocols. Addressing these interconnected factors will holistically facilitate the adoption of cryptocurrency in the global financial landscape. Frictionless adoption of cryptocurrency can empower consumers to enjoy freedom over their financial transactions. It is fitting to mention that cryptocurrencies are wildly gaining acceptance across all fields and have revolutionised the perception and behaviour of money.

References

1. Marmefelt, T.: Central bank digital currencies and international crises: Toward an authoritarian international monetary order? Politics and Governance. **12**(4), 1–12 (2024)
2. Hadan, H., Zhang-Kennedy, L., Nacke, L., Mäkelä, V.: Gamification and gaming in cryptocurrency education: A Survey with cryptocurrency investors and potential investors. Simul. Gaming. **55**(2), 196–223 (2024)
3. Houy, S., Schmid, P., Bartel, A.: Security aspects of cryptocurrency wallets—a systematic literature review. ACM Comput. Surv. **56**(1), 1–31 (2023)
4. Tanwar, S., Gupta, N., Kumar, P., Hu, Y.-C.: Implementation of blockchain-based e-voting system. Multimed. Tools Appl. **83**(1), 1449–1480 (2024)
5. Badertscher, C., Maurer, U., Tschudi, D., Zikas, V.: Bitcoin as a transaction ledger: A composable treatment. J. Cryptol. **37**(2), 18 (2024)
6. Jamwal, S., Cano, J., Lee, G.M., Tran, N.H., Truong, N.: A survey on ethereum pseudonymity: Techniques, challenges, and future directions. J. Netw. Comput. Appl. **232**(September 2024), 104019 (2024)
7. Noviyanti, I., Aryansyah, A.F., Guspian, I., Herlissha, N.: Currency evolution: A comparative study between central bank digital currencies and physical currencies in modern monetary systems. Equity: Jurnal Ekonomi. **12**(1), 10106–10117 (2024)
8. Almomani, A., Al-Qerem, A., Al Khaldy, M.A., Alauthman, M., Aldweesh, A., Nahar, K.M.: Cryptographic techniques for securing blockchain-based cryptocurrency transactions against botnet attacks. In: Innovations in Modern Cryptography, pp. 309–333. IGI Global, Hershey, PA (2024)
9. Smales, L.A.: Cryptocurrency as an alternative inflation hedge? Accounting & Finance. **64**(2), 1589–1611 (2024)
10. Garay, J., Kiayias, A., Leonardos, N.: The bitcoin backbone protocol: Analysis and applications. J. ACM. **71**(4), 1–49 (2024)
11. Narayanan, A.: Bitcoin and Cryptocurrency Technologies: A Comprehensive Introduction. Princeton University Press, Princeton, NJ (2016)

12. Yermack, D.: Is Bitcoin a real currency? An economic appraisal. In: Handbook of Digital Currency, pp. 29–40. Academic, London (2024)

13. De Vries, A.: Cryptocurrencies on the road to sustainability: Ethereum paving the way for Bitcoin. Patterns. **4**(1), 100779 (2023)

14. Tumas, V., Pontiveros, B.B.F., Torres, C.F., State, R.: A ripple for change: Analysis of frontrunning in the XRP ledger. In: 2023 IEEE International Conference on Blockchain and Cryptocurrency (ICBC), pp. 1–9. IEEE, Piscataway, NJ (2023, May)

15. Kashyap, A.: RBI's stance on cryptocurrency in India: Past, present, and future. J. Indian Financ. Policy. **6**(2), 33–45 (2024)

16. Kaur, G.: Supreme Court's judgment on cryptocurrency: Implications for India's fintech industry. Asian J. Law Econ. **9**(1), 12–25 (2024)

17. Bijou, A.V.N., Thomas, A.S.: Uncertainties and ambivalence in the crypto market: An urgent need for a regional crypto regulation. SN Bus. Econ. **3**(8), 136 (2023)

18. De Simone, L., Stomberg, B.: The tax burden of cryptocurrency traders: Evidence from India. Tax Policy Rev. **4**(1), 5–28 (2024)

19. Rajdev, A.A., Raninga, A., Bhatt, K., Madhani, M.J.: From skepticism to acceptance: Unraveling the dynamics of cryptocurrency in India. Educ. Adm. Theory Pract. **30**(6), 182–188 (2024)

20. Christodoulou, I., Rizomyliotis, I., Konstantoulaki, K., Nazarian, A., Binh, D.: Transforming the remittance industry: Harnessing the power of blockchain technology. J. Enterp. Inf. Manag. **37**(5), 1551–1577 (2024)

21. Kumar, J.S., Shobana, D.: Exploring Digital Payments, Financial Inclusion, and Monetary Policy in India. Indian J. Econ. Finance. **18**(1), 22–41 (2024)

22. Ganeshkumar, K., Raghavan, P., Sharma, V.: Cryptocurrency regulations and adoption in India: Challenges and opportunities. J. Digit. Finance Policy. **5**(1), 1–19 (2024)

23. Colombo, J.A., Yarovaya, L.: Are crypto and non-crypto investors alike? Evidence from a comprehensive survey in Brazil. Technol. Soc. **72**(1), 102468 (2024)

24. Levi-Faur, D.: Regulation and regulatory governance. In: Levi-Faur, D. (ed.) Handbook on the Politics of Regulation, pp. 1–25. Edward Elgar, Cheltenham (2011)

25. Selznick, P.: Law, Society, and Industrial Justice, vol. 30. Quid Pro Books, New Orleans (2020)

26. Croley, S.P.: Theories of regulation: Incorporating the administrative process. Colum. L. Rev. **98**(1), 1–168 (1998)

27. Kumar, J., Rani, V.: What do we know about cryptocurrency investment? An empirical study of its adoption among Indian retail investors. The Bottom Line. **37**(1), 27–44 (2024)

28. Zohar, A.: Bitcoin: Under the hood. Commun. ACM. **58**(9), 104–113 (2015)

29. Rabah, B., Hassiba, A.: The requirements for ensuring financial stability in using financial technology and cryptocurrencies. Finance Bus. Econ. Rev. **8**(2), 45–62 (2024)

30. Zuckerman, A.: Insuring crypto: The birth of digital asset insurance. U. Ill. JL Tech. & Pol'y. **2021**(1), 75–110 (2021)

31. Trautman, L.J.: Bitcoin, virtual currencies, and the struggle of law and regulation to keep peace. Marq. L. Rev. **102**(2), 447–523 (2018)

32. Narayanan, H.: Is future a rule of digital currency. Int. J. Res. – Granthaalayah. **8**(8), 96–106 (2020)

33. Chen, S., He, D.: The impact of regulation on cryptocurrency adoption: Evidence from emerging markets. Regul. Econ. J. **8**(2), 124–139 (2022)

34. Parouha, D.: Law, technology and cryptocurrency. Indian J. Integr. Res. Law. **3**(2), 202–213 (2023)

35. Thakur, D.S., Varma, R.A., Hake, D.M.: Regulation of cryptocurrency in India: Issues and challenges. Journal of Positive School Psychology. **6**(3), 8921–8929 (2022)

36. Dash, B., Ansari, M.F., Sharma, P., Swayamsiddha, S.: Future ready banking with smart contracts—CBDC and impact on the Indian economy. Int. J. Netw. Secur. Appl. **14**(5), 15–28 (2022)
37. Ozili, P.K.: Artificial intelligence and central bank digital currency. In: Global Developments in Central Bank Digital Currency, pp. 117–125. IGI Global, Hershey, PA (2024)
38. Biju, A.V.N., Thomas, A.S.: Uncertainties and ambivalence in the crypto market: An urgent need for a regional crypto regulation. SN Bus. Econ. **3**(8), 136 (2023)
39. Kayani, U., Hasan, F.: Unveiling cryptocurrency impact on financial markets and traditional banking systems: Lessons for sustainable blockchain and interdisciplinary collaborations. J. Risk Financ. Manag. **17**(2), 58 (2024)
40. Şanlısoy, S., Çiloğlu, T.: An investigation on the crypto currencies and its future. Int. J. eBus. eGov. Stud. **11**(1), 69–88 (2019)
41. Rella, L.: Desiring-infrastructures in the crypto economy. In: Clickbait Capitalism, pp. 116–134. Manchester University Press, Manchester (2023)
42. Nguyen, B., Nguyen, T.: Technology infrastructure and user experience as key determinants of cryptocurrency adoption. J. Digit. Econ. **12**(4), 301–315 (2020)
43. Cumming, D.J., Johan, S., Pant, A.: Regulation of the crypto-economy: Managing risks, challenges, and regulatory uncertainty. J. Risk Financ. Manag. **12**(3), 126 (2019)
44. Agarwal, U., Rishiwal, V., Tanwar, S., Yadav, M.: Blockchain and crypto forensics: Investigating crypto frauds. Int. J. Netw. Manag. **34**(2), e2255 (2024)
45. Chen, W., Xu, H., Jia, L., Gao, Y.: Machine learning model for Bitcoin exchange rate prediction using economic and technology determinants. Int. J. Forecast. **37**(1), 28–43 (2021)
46. Sharma, A., Panse, C., Gupta, N., Dawar, S., Kudal, P., Sharma, M.: Adoption of Cryptocurrency in India: An Extended Technology Adoption Model. Int. J. Saf. Secur. Eng. **14**(6), 567–580 (2024)
47. Kala, D., Chaubey, D.S.: Cryptocurrency adoption and continuance intention among Indians: Moderating role of perceived government control. Digit. Policy Regul. Gov. **22**(1), 45–60 (2023)
48. Kumar, R., Soni, P.: Cultural factors influencing cryptocurrency adoption in India: An empirical study. J. Digit. Finance. **15**(2), 112–128 (2023)
49. Chakraborty, D.: Cryptocurrency and India: Future prospects and regulatory challenges. Asian J. Econ. Bank. **7**(1), 23–40 (2023)
50. Ramesh, V., Reddy, K.G.: Exploring block chain technology with applications, and future prospects. In: International Conference on Data Science, Machine Learning and Applications, pp. 120–130. Springer, Cham (2023)
51. Chau, M., Hu, Y.: Examining the adoption of Bitcoin payments by companies. Financ. Innov. **4**(2), 12–22 (2002)
52. Patel, V.: Low-cost remittance platforms based on cryptocurrency technology: A case for India. Int. J. Financ. Stud. **10**(3), 65 (2022)
53. Venkatesh, V., Davis, F.D.: A theoretical extension of the Technology Acceptance Model: Four longitudinal field studies. Manag. Sci. **46**(2), 186–204 (2000)
54. Gefen, D., Karahanna, E., Straub, D.W.: Trust and TAM in online shopping: An integrated model. MIS Q. **27**(1), 51–90 (2003)
55. Shetty, A.: Regulating cryptocurrencies: Balancing innovation and financial security. Jus Corpus LJ. **3**(1), 197 (2022)
56. Ahmed, A.A., Alabi, O.: Secure and scalable blockchain-based federated learning for cryptocurrency fraud detection: A systematic review. IEEE Access. **12**, 12345–12360 (2024)
57. Liu, Y., Ye, C.: Empirical validation of the technology acceptance model for cryptocurrency adoption. Technol. Soc. **65**, 101587 (2021)
58. Simran, K., Sharma, R.: Impact of cryptocurrency taxation policies on Bitcoin market performance. Indian J. Econ. Dev. **19**(1), 14–22 (2023)

59. Palladino, J.A., Raj, S.P.: Cultural factors influencing cryptocurrency adoption in emerging markets: A case study of India. J. Digit. Finance. **3**(2), 98–114 (2021)
60. Dabbous, A., Merhej Sayegh, M., Aoun Barakat, K.: Understanding the adoption of cryptocurrencies for financial transactions within a high-risk context. J. Risk Financ. **23**(4), 349–367 (2022)
61. Chen, H.: The impact of fintech on traditional banking industry and future development trends. Highl. Bus. Econ. Manag. **49**, 191–198 (2025)

Optimizing Software Engineering Project Plan Using Genetic Algorithm and AI

K. M. Harini Kannamma[1][(✉)], G. S. R. Emil Selvan[1], M. P. Ramkumar[1], and Sridaran Rajagopal[2]

[1] Department of Computer Science and Engineering, Thiagarajar College of Engineering, Madurai, India
harinikendey@gmail.com
[2] Faculty of Computer Applications and Academic Affairs, Marwadi University, Rajkot, India

Abstract. The Global Software Engineering (GSE) team works across geography. Project planning is one important phase before starting with the actual work, for any type of project. Planning involves discussion with multiple stakeholder before the plan to put up in the plan sheet. In today's working environment with respect to the industry most of the time the planning will go through the change due to several factors like talent availability, technical competencies, requirement understanding, etc. it is very important to maintain the project plan as it directly links with the project success. Currently the plan is majorly maintained by excel or some planning tool available in the market. Still there is much manual effort involved to maintain the plan. The impact is due to any reason of delay, the plan affects, the changes are not covered completely. In this work trying to apply the Plan Assess React (PAR) approach that reviewing the plan periodically with proper findings and solutioning effectively. So, in this work the intend to address the optimization of the tactical planning for the fast-growing software industry using the Plan Assess React (PAR) approach using Genetic Algorithm with an AI inclusive. This is going to help in validating the plan with each check activity progress, on any change occurs update and maintain successfully. To bring the optimization as the work focus on, the approach used here is the Genetic algorithm as it is a proven study and very helpful to give the near real time optimal solution. Also, the AI is used here in the methodology to apply technology advancement for the automation and reduce the manual work as well. Based on the study the merge of Genetic algorithm with an AI is a good fit-in for the result of optimization. Hence this work showcases the proactive planning using the Genetic algorithm approach with an AI inclusive and foreseeing the active phase of any project for a program. With this work will directly benefit the industry people, project managers, and the researchers.

Keywords: Genetic Algorithm · Tactical planning · Software project plan framework · Project planning · Project performance · Closed Loop System · AI

R. Sridaran and S. Priti (Eds.): AI-FCDAC 2025, CCIS 2866, pp. 101–110, 2026.
https://doi.org/10.1007/978-3-032-17300-3_8

1 Introduction

The Software industry deals with multiple types of projects on a day-to-day basis. The initial study with globally distributed teams and the way of working was taken around decades before. To define the project from the overall scope to the detailed requirements and alignment with the entire team is key essential to get the proper planning of the project before the actual start. The project planning is a key factor for the successful project execution. A proper planning needs deeper understanding and step-by-step actions mentioned with discussion along with task owner. The inadequate analysis and planning will lead to a failed project. All these are pointing that the need for and the importance of planning. In the recent research direction various elements like addressing the knowledge gap, transferring the skills, team building, applying various methodology like lean six sigma, improved agile approach has been directed. The geographically dispersed workforce gives good connectivity and increased outcome for the overall project. The work on these defines the project success factors and the impact. The project planning has a direct connection to the project success. Planning is one of the key measures in the software engineering life cycle. The table (1) below summarizes the type of planning corresponding to the time frame and the accuracy state. The *Tactical* planning involves a minimum timeline of 1-year duration. This covers the large project type goes with the complete development life cycle. The *Operational* planning type is applicable to the support nature of the project. It could be a less than 6 months project duration. Whereas the timeline of the planning addresses the present day or time as it is purely operational to the incident raised on a particular day. The *Contingency* planning is totally different and requires a presence of the sense like on-spot plan as per the situation demands (Table 1).

Table 1. The planning type versus the time frame

TYPE	TIME FRAME	ACCURACY STATE
TACTICAL	Measurable as minimum less than or equal to 1 year	Moderate level of certainty
OPERATIONAL	Defined present day/time	Reasonable level of certainty
CONTINGENCY	On-spot - when an event occurs, or a situation demands	Reasonable level of certainty

This work considers the tactical planning to be more relevant the project goes with the complete development life cycle. The project progress is tracked by having the plan against to see the actual progress. While tracking the project actual progress there could be delays due to various factors like technical dependency, insufficient requirement details, resource bandwidth issues etc. This research work proposes rather adjusting the delays in the plan, suggest overseeing the plan in a periodical manner with constant awareness. Keep the management of plan as a continuous process owned and managed closely, by foreseeing the delay if any and addressing the requirement in advance to avoid the actual delay. The below fig. (1) depicts this process of Iterative way of tuning the plan by seeing continuously. The Process chain shown below (Fig. 1) in planning phase can be applied as closed-loop systems. To relate to the previous depiction of the Iterative way of tuning the plan using closed loop system. By implementing the closed loop system (CLS) in the planning phase it helps in attaining all the benefits stated above. In this way this not only gives benefits with process improvements and proactiveness it also provides much saving in the area like time, cost and overall effort as well.

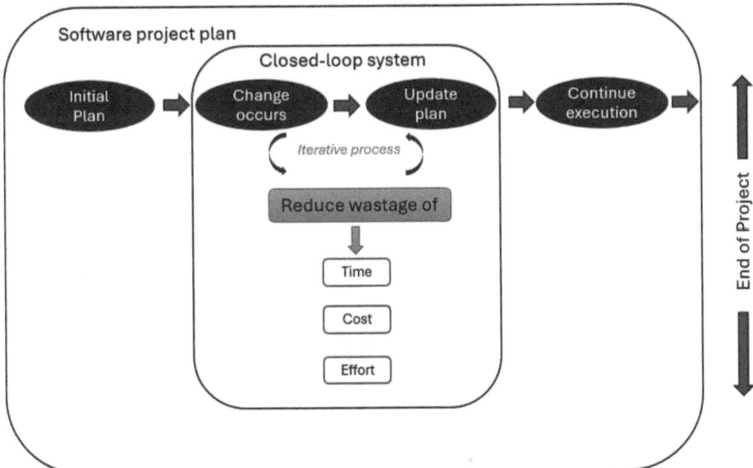

Fig. 1. The Software project steps basic Or Iterative way of tuning plan

The main objective is to improve the plan in a closed loop system to ensure the delivery is not impacted and still on schedule. The general meaning of closed-loop mentions that following up to any task that having any impact or dependency with another will efficiently completing a cycle of that action, by minimizing the changes, cost, resource consumption and continue the execution successfully. In general, a closed loop system (CLS) increases the process improvement and result certainly. While the study says that it is majorly used in industry like supply chain, customer feedback, the closed loop system is a method that is applicable to any industry in our understanding. It gives lots of benefits. It is a powerful control mechanism that influences the feedback system to improve the process overall. Few are:

- *Prevent issues/risk*: highly important to reach milestones
- *Improve the process*: to ensure the healthy execution
- *Early identification of the issues*: this helps prevention of risk itself.
- *Gain trust*: Enable the overall trust with leadership
- *Keep program healthy*: having efficient process
- *Allow the team to maximize productivity:* with an improved process in place and having control of the issues/risks.

Currently the planning is tedious phase that takes lots of efforts through out the project execution. The plan tracking, maintaining, updating, adjusting to changes is lots of efforts to spend on for the effective project plan. However, planning is important and key document on planning and analysis of the plan. This research work mainly aim to optimize the project plan. The traditional way of developing approach with water fall method to the latest multiple methods like agile, lean six-sigma, either it is complete plan or short-term plan for the continuous short deliverable planning place a role in the beginning of the execution phase. Here, with this work the intend to insist on the analysis of the planning in a continuous phase to bring improved plan for the efficient execution. This work suggests an approach using Genetic Algorithm and an AI. By leveraging this genetic approach, the work proposes a framework that right way of assessing the execution and identifying the impact and addressing will result to increase the value of time, resource and plan itself. And the AI is need of an hour to bring the automation to reduce the manual efforts. Here, with this study to insist further on the analysis of the planning in a continuous phase to bring improved plan for the efficient execution.

2 Related Work

In recent decades, extensive research has been conducted on various aspects of software engineering (SE). The understanding with this work is to do the search on the in generic the planning aspect with respect to the SE, then the large program plan and then with specific to the tactical planning. Key areas of research majorly include Distributed team way of working, cultural differences, team coordination, project development work, Agile team, addressing communication gap, cross-skilling across team, etc. From the literature, it is evident that various approach defined in planning and managing the software industry projects. Majority of these based on specific model for their implementation.

Here some of them are explained in detail:

Unveiling the power of shared leadership in project realms: a synergy of planning, knowledge, cohesion, and trust [1] stated by R Ahmed, AA Khan, SP Philbin aims to explore how project planning, knowledge sharing, and team cohesiveness can bridge the link between shared leadership and project success in the presence of trust in teams. They conducted a survey with project team. The findings reveal a significant and positive impact of shared leadership on project success. Here this work is on the examination across hierarchy levels for deeper understanding on this area which helped to see the percentage to highlight the factors for the project success. However, while this gives a clarity on the impact of various designation but it did not bring any process as such. It is a study held with the industry members across

A Tactical Planning Approach using Genetic Algorithms and Process Chain Simulation for Closed-Loop Production Systems for high-value components [4] By Dranov, Alexander, et al has explained the closed-loop production system simulation model using the Genetic algorithm based. However, there is no advance concept like AI is being used to reduce the manual intervention and bring the automation. This research work suggested methodology has clear focus on the efficiently Plan Assess React (PAR) with an advanced AI concept.

ChatGPT application in Systematic Literature Reviews in Software Engineering: an evaluation of its accuracy to support the selection activity [5] by Felizardo, Katia Romero, et al. mentioned that with context to the Systematic Literature Review (SLR) process involves searching, selecting, and synthesizing relevant literature on a specific research topic for evidence-based decision-making in Software Engineering (SE), a tool to assist in the selection process appears beneficial, ChatGPT can facilitate the analysis of extensive studies, saving time and effort. This tool suggestion has brought in with earlier work Automation Tool for the Planning Phase of the Systematic Review by some other authors. Though there is a tool used to support the search there is no scope on automated process as a proactive measure. This research work suggested with an automation using AI which reduces the manual effort rather only for an analysis purpose.

Factual Success and Thriving Performance Required; Top Management and Project Manager Strong Coordination During Project Life Cycle [14] by Raheela Habib and Naeem Ahmed Tahir stated that the coordination between role of top management and legitimate power of project manager has significant impact on project performance and success during project life cycle phases. Applying Bivariate (Pearson) Correlation and OLS regression it is concluded that there is positive relationship between planning, monitoring, controlling, evaluation and project manager. This gives importance on co-ordination and significant advantage for the organization and industries before implementing any project. In this work, it is an academic oriented one for further study in general to the project management and the framework suggested mention on the role of project management overall, there is no planning execution specific.

How to Evaluate Solutions in Pareto-Based Search-Based Software Engineering: A Critical Review and Methodological Guidance [15] by Miqing Li; Tao Chen; Xin Yao stated about multiple objectives/criteria simultaneously in many Software Engineering scenarios. They have conducted an in-depth analysis of quality evaluation indicators/methods and general situations in search-based software engineering (SBSE), which together with the identified issues, enables us to codify a methodological guidance for selecting and using evaluation methods in SBSE scenario. Though the work focused on optimization effort of a project by search based, but it works on identifying the problem. There is no clarity that solution fit for all types of projects. Like by multi-object and search based may be good for the large projects only.

Although there is considerable work was held and still continuing in the software engineering there is a need in using AI in software engineering to revamp the traditional way of planning is a need of an hour. Currently it is all being the new AI era in the software industry it is important to utilize the advance concepts and implement AI to bring the best benefits. With a proactive way looking the plan iteratively and revise or update using combine with the Plan Assess React (PAR) approach and the AI. The detailed way of these proposed approached are mentioned in the next section. Providing such kind of solution will benefit the industry to the greater extend, this is a great motivation for us to present this paper.

3 Methodology

To address the mentioned research work, more to see about the proposed framework with respect to the PAR approach using the GA in the Sect. 3.1. With the use of algorithm, there is definition of the process of proactiveness. Better envisioning the tasks those are in planned. Like the planning plays a key role continuous monitor, measure the progress, practically checking on completion and accommodate the change as well. The change may occur at any point based on the realistic way of working in the software industry. Continue to that later in the Sect. 3.2, this work also brings the technology advancement with how AI shall be leveraged to make as the automated process for the best proficiency. The automation with AI helps the team to do an automatic analysis as the data change occurs in the planning and also highlights the changes as required to the team with alerts. AI is invention to assist the human tasks and to bring the productivity as basic. Here this work aims to propose as part this framework that bringing the AI efficiency in planning state of software engineering is a need state.

3.1   The Plan Assess React (PAR) Approach Using GA: The GA Solution

To address the research a methodological approach in managing the program plan to optimized way, this work proposes the PAR approach in Closed Loop system (CLS). The proposed approach in Fig. 2

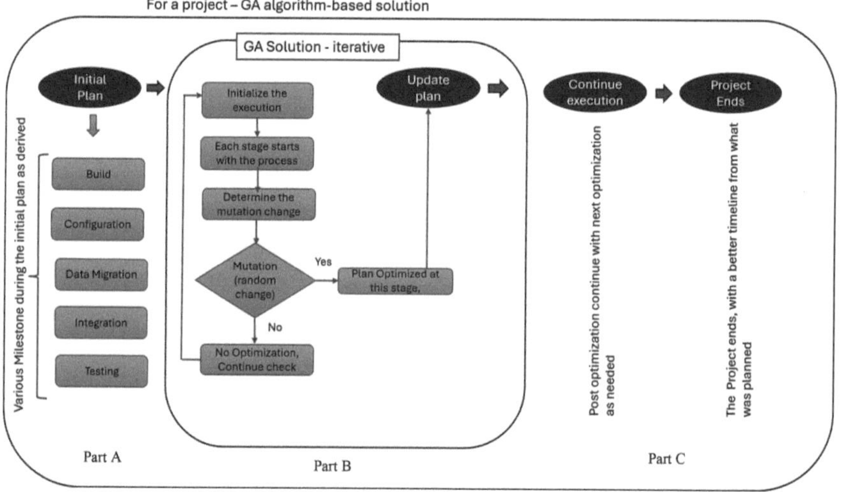

Fig. 2. Methodological approach for PAR approach modeling and evaluation of CLS in Planning

Using the Genetic Algorithm (GA) approach, the methodological steps for PAR approach modeling and evaluation of CLS in Program planning shown here. The *Part A* has been derived as an initial plan after understanding of the scope of the work. Considering the various factors like duration, cost, budget, team size and technology stack the plan has been put up with all the different milestones to achieve throughout the project till the actual completion. Having derived the Part A, the *Part B* starts with an execution of the project. With constant analysis of on any change that gives the optimization from the planned timeline change is accepted and updated. If no optimized change, then the analysis continues. The Part C continue the updated plan to execute and result in delivering the project in a better optimized timeline then the initial planned timeline.

The Genetic Algorithm is already a proven study, and it says that it is a good meta-heuristic optimization technique inspired by the natural selection. It is very fit to generate the high-quality optimization solution by iteratively evolving. It is an suitable algorithm for the optimization technique introduced by John Holland in 1970s helps to give the near real time optimal solution. The algorithm works as Initiate the program at the starting point as per the plan phase, and as the work continue to progress consider the factors like time, resource, cost, technical capacity. As the algorithm is a proven study already, this study insists on the how to attain optimal performance using this approach. By means of fine tuning the plan and updates in each iterative cycle this can be achieved. Further this planning update, the AI included. That is mentioned in the following section with the diagram expansion for the update plan with AI.

3.2 Using Agentic AI

While technology greatly helps to greater extent, with the effort savings from planning to actual the dates moved ahead. With the current technology advancement, this work addresses to use the whole process of the date movement to be updated in the plan by Agentic AI. And also, the AI shall be leveraged to generate an email as an alert to intimate to the core team (managers/leads) on the timeline changes. The below Fig. 3 shows the AI inclusive framework from the Fig. 2 the *Part B - GA Solution Iterative, Update Plan* as a developed diagram using AI. Fig. 3 is an integrated view of the PAR approach and the AI for the same. It is a detailed processing framework using AI is shown the below figure for the *Update Plan* step. If the framework allows the AI to monitor and update the plan to real time instead of the current manual way of doing, then the plan/project charter becomes more realistic. Whereas, currently the planner updated by the managers in most of the cases, so much manual effort involved in identifying the changes, updating to planner, and seeing if any date advanced or delayed, calculation of effort saving if the date is advanced – all these done by manually. Using Agentic AI part of this entire process framework – all the manual efforts shall be avoided. Not only that mainly the planner becomes realistic to refer at any given day. Also, it avoids all the human error, of missing the updates, not updating right, error in calculation etc. The Agentic AI improves the productivity, helps in decision making by identifying the delta, gives an efficiency to greater extend.

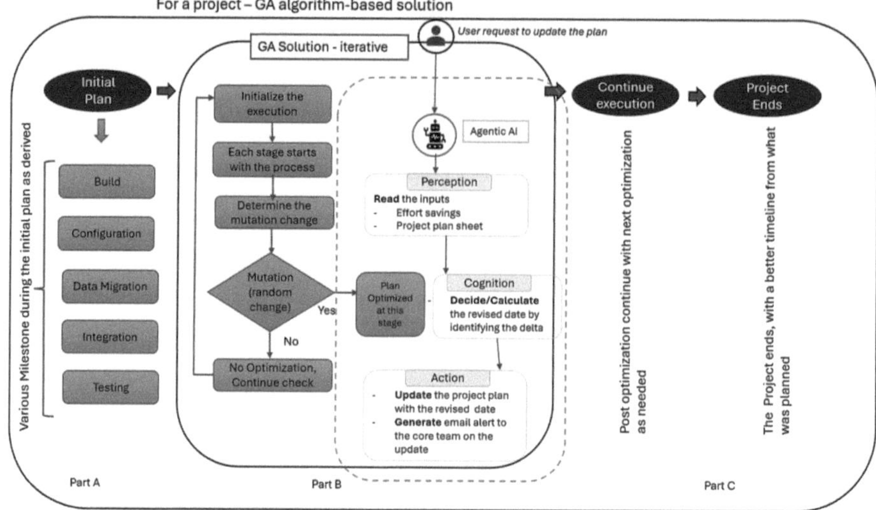

Fig. 3. Illustration of PAR approach and AI integration

4 Discussions

In this section, the details on the discussion with the most relevant paper that had brought this work to study further on. The referenced paper [4] titled Tactical Planning Approach using Genetic Algorithms and Process Chain Simulation for Closed-Loop Production Systems for high-value components is a work that has been taken in the field of supply chain. With the demand of supply chain, the study introduces a metaheuristic framework based on discrete event simulation and genetic algorithms to evaluate these system configurations. The idea is to identify configurations that achieve a beneficial fitness value balance technical, economic, environmental key performance indicator. This framework with the use of genetic algorithm method has a lot of similarity for us to think in the software engineering industry as the study is on. However, the existing study had not used any AI component as such. Now, that allowed us further use the genetic algorithm steps for the planning in software engineering projects. As this work more to do the proactive measure for avoiding delays, slippage of timelines, and any failure the algorithm gave us how to manage the whole planning with the constant assessment and react on as required. Also, being in the software industry with lot of space for the innovation and research also want to leverage the AI to reduce the manual intervention with the improved process efficacy.

5 Conclusion and Future Directions

The Planning is generic on a high-level view, but the precise planning needs lots of understanding of the ground level needs, tasks, and efforts that are involved to derive at near perfect. This work has applied the Plan Assess React (PAR) approach that reviewing the plan periodically with proper findings and solutioning more optimized way. With this work further to address the optimization of the tactical planning for the fast-growing software industry using the Plan Assess React (PAR) approach using Genetic Algorithm with an AI inclusive. This will help in reviewing the plan periodically with proper findings and solutioning right. This work showcased the proactive planning using the Genetic algorithm approach with an AI inclusive. If implemented, this will directly benefit the industry people, project managers, and the related research workers. With an active management of the project plan using the AI, the whole work is expected to improve the software engineering to fit-in today's demand and provide timely delivery. The future work is aimed at implementing the framework and mapping with the real-time project team as a study.

References

1. Ahmed, R., Khan, A.A., Philbin, S.P.: Unveiling the power of shared leadership in project realms: a synergy of planning, knowledge, cohesion, and trust. Int. J. Bus. Process Integrat. Manag. **12**(1), 46–63 (2025)
2. Ahonen, E.: Elevating project portfolio management: key factors for effective project prioritization and value adding resource allocation 2025)
3. Serrador, P., Zadeh, A.A.: When agile works: unveiling the secrets to agile success. Eng. Manag. J. 1–17 (2025)
4. Dranov, A., et al.: A tactical planning approach using genetic algorithms and process chain simulation for closed-loop production systems for high-value components. Procedia CIRP **130**, 1575–1582 (2024)
5. Felizardo, K.R., et al.: ChatGPT application in Systematic Literature Reviews in Software Engineering: an evaluation of its accuracy to support the selection activity. In: Proceedings of the 18th ACM/IEEE International Symposium on Empirical Software Engineering and Measurement (2024)
6. Holliman, A.: Identifying and modelling design effort influencing factors in product design company projects (2024)
7. Rankovic, N., et al.: Use of AI methods in software project scheduling. In: Recent Advances in Artificial Intelligence in Cost Estimation in Project Management, pp. 123–155. Springer, Cham (2024)
8. Höhn, M., et al.: Interactive input and visualization for planning with temporal uncertainty. SN Comput. Sci. **4**(3), 231 (2023)
9. Ozcelikkan, N., et al.: "A multi-objective agile project planning model and a comparative meta-heuristic approach. Inf. Softw. Technol. **151**, 107023 (2022)
10. Bashir, H., et al.: The analysis of information flow interdependencies within projects. Prod. Plan. Control **33**(1), 20–36 (2022)
11. Hartmann, S., Briskorn, D.: An updated survey of variants and extensions of the resource-constrained project scheduling problem. Eur. J. Oper. Res. **297**(1), 1–14 (2022)
12. Al-Ahmad, B.I., et al.: Swarm intelligence-based model for improving prediction performance of low-expectation teams in educational software engineering projects. PeerJ Comput. Sci. **8**, e857 (2022)
13. Oachesu, A., Negovanovic, N.: The core problems of globally distributed work in software development environments, and possible solutions: DevOps environments' opportunities for better adoption of a globally distributed working culture (2021)
14. Habib, R., Tahir, N.A.: Factual success and thriving performance required; top management and project manager strong coordination during project life cycle. In: Factual Success and Thriving Performance Required (2021)

15. Li, M., Chen, T., Yao, X.: How to evaluate solutions in pareto-based search-based software engineering: a critical review and methodological guidance. IEEE Trans. Softw. Eng. **48**(5), 1771–1799 (2020)
16. Rahmanzadeh, S., Pishvaee, M.S., Rasouli, M.R.: Integrated innovative product design and supply chain tactical planning within a blockchain platform. Int. J. Prod. Res. **58**(7), 2242–2262 (2020)
17. Kristensen, K.H., Kalsaas, B.T.: Bridging strategic project planning with tactical planning in the design process. In: The 10th International Conference on Engineering, Project, and Production Management. Springer, Singapore (2020)

Synthetic Image Generation for Crop Disease Classification Using Generative Adversarial Networks

J. Vimala Roselin[1(✉)], S. Sumanth[2], S. Silvia Priscila[3], M. Sakthivanitha[4(✉)], Anciline Jenifer[5], G. Sugin Lal[6], K. Sheela[7], and N. Manikandan[8]

[1] Department of Computer Science, Christ (Deemed to Be University), Bangalore, India
vimala.jr@kristujayanti.com

[2] Department of Computer Science, New Horizon College, Kasturinagar, Bangalore 560043, India

[3] Department of Computer Science, Bharath Institute of Higher Education and Research, Selaiyur, Tamil Nadu 600126, India
silviaprisila.cbcs.cs@bharathuniv.ac.in

[4] Department of Computer Application, Vels Institute of Science, Technology & Advanced Studies, Chennai, Tamil Nadu, India
sakthivanithamsc@gmail.com

[5] Department of MCA, Francis Xavier Engineering College, Tirunelveli, Tami Nadu, India

[6] Department of Computer Science, The New College, Chennai, Tamil Nadu, India
suginlag@srmist.edu.in

[7] Department of Computer Science and Information Technology, School of Computing Sciences, VISTAS, Pallavaram, Chennai, Tamil Nadu, India

[8] Department of Computer Science, The New College, Chennai, India
manikandan@thenewcollege.edu.in

Abstract. Due to biological diversity and unstructured surroundings, agricultural image analysis strives for optimal model performance to better accomplish visual identification objectives. Large-scale, balanced, and ground-truthed image datasets are very helpful, but they are frequently hard to come by, which restricts the creation of very effective models. The identification of plant diseases has benefited enormously from the continuous advancement of deep learning (DL) techniques, which provide a robust tool with incredibly accurate results. However, the efficiency of deep learning models is dependent on the quantity and caliber of labeled data used for training. Precise classification of crop diseases is important for precision agriculture. These models suffer from limited and imbalance datasets especially for rare diseases. The study suggests a framework using Generative Adversarial Network (GAN) for image generation to enhance the classification of diseases. The study employs conditional GAN trained on a PlantVillage and New plant diseases datasets to generate synthetic images of diseased leaves. The images are evaluated using Structural similarity index (SSIM). Then the augmented images are integrated with the CNN classifier to measure the accuracy of disease prediction using synthetic dataset to validate the efficiency of image generation.

© The Author(s) 2026
R. Sridaran and S. Priti (Eds.): AI-FCDAC 2025, CCIS 2866, pp. 111–123, 2026.
https://doi.org/10.1007/978-3-032-17300-3_9

Keywords: Synthetic image generation · Crop disease classification · Conditional Generative Adversarial networks

1 Introduction

A nation's economy is influenced by a wide range of factors, including the food processing, service, and agricultural sectors. Agriculture is one of the most significant economic sectors in our country. However, the agriculture sector has many obstacles, including different climates across our country that result in different infectious diseases in different plant parts, which significantly reduces crop productivity and revenue production [1]. Plant diseases threaten crop yields and the lives of farmers around the world. They are brought on by bacteria, fungus, viruses, and other agents. Protecting agricultural output depends on the timely and precise identification of these illnesses, and researchers from all over the world have created a number of automated plant disease diagnosis techniques to date [2]. Traditionally, human beings with some training or experience have inspected and classified plant diseases by visually observing the signs on plant leaves. It is well recognized that identifying plant diseases can be laborious and prone to mistakes. Even highly experienced experts frequently fail to diagnose certain diseases due to the vast number of cultivated plants and their complex physiological signs, which results in incorrect disease management and therapy [3].

The most significant challenge in DL for leaf disease detection is how to perform well when there are sparse datasets or few annotated samples available, small lesions, duplicate information, and blurred background information in images of leaf diseases [4]. DL produces extremely accurate outcomes by combining image processing and data analysis. These days, DL is widely employed in many different disciplines, such as segmentation biomedical image classification signal and speech recognition (, and object identification. In agriculture, DL is also being utilised extensively for the classification and detection of plant diseases. The CNN is regarded as the most effective DL technology [6].

An efficient method for dealing with the issue of deep CNNs (DCNNs) lacking enough training data is data augmentation, which creates similar images from a limited number of original training samples. The creation of synthetic image can address the business issue of image data shortage or unavailability. The way people handle data scarcity in the agriculture industry may be completely changed by introducing synthetic data production tools. By producing contextually precise, high-quality synthetic data, researchers can get around the drawbacks of current datasets and raise crop recommendation models' accuracy [7].

There are now creative ways to handle a variety of agricultural challenges due to the application of generative AI in smart farming. The growing need for food worldwide, the effects of climate change, and the depletion of essential agricultural resources are just a few of the urgent issues of our day that smart farming has emerged as a crucial strategy to address. The objectives of the study is to

- Presents a cGAN-based data augmentation preprocessing method for generating 8000 synthetic images of Tomato-leaf blight to increase the variety and volume of the training data.

- Compare the suggested methodology with a CNN classifier that are currently in use in the literature to show the effectiveness of the model.

The paper is organized as follows. The current studies that have been suggested for leaf disease augmentation and detection in the literature are shown in Sect. 2. Methodology in Sect. 3 followed by results and findings in Sect. 4. The study's conclusion and future work is given in Sect. 5.

2 Literature Review

Numerous DL techniques for the automation of diagnosis of plant diseases have been developed to assist farmers and reduce losses in plant yield. Iqbal et al., (2024) introduce a model that uses one image of a neutral face to produce six different facial expressions. The approach, which is built on a CGAN, can generate six incredible facial expressions from a single image of a neutral face. The researchers used a number of pre-trained models in order to thoroughly evaluate the accuracy of the methodology. However, their accuracy increased to about 99% after adjustments to the synthetic expressions that the CGAN produced from this single image [8]. Wang et al., (2025) create a dual discriminator structure (FHWD) frequency-domain and wavelet image generation network. While the second high-frequency discriminator is especially employed to differentiate between the high-frequency components of both, the first discriminator makes a distinction between created and genuine images [9]. The DL approach was used by Benfenati et al. (2022) to automatically produce meaningful synthetic images of plant leaves, with a focus on agricultural applications. Specialised CNN models or other image-classification algorithms can be trained or validated using these images, which provide an almost infinite dataset [10].

Ramadan et al., (2023) provide a unique method for employing GANS to produce images of wheat leaf disease from a smaller dataset. The study demonstrates the potential of using GANs to produce real images from less datasets in a variety of applications, including the detection of plant diseases [11]. Haruna et al., (2023) demonstrates that employing synthetic data augmentation can be extremely significant when datasets are limited or unbalanced, as it performs better on object detection models than standard methods. A Style-GAN Adaptive Discriminator Augmentation (SG2-ADA) and the variance of the Laplacian filter were used to generate data on rice leaf disease to enhance the effectiveness of the Single Shot Detector (SSD) and Faster-Region-Based CNN (faster-RCNN) in identifying the primary diseases affecting rice [12].

Min et al., (2023) provide an image-to-image translation model-based data augmentation technique to address the bias issue by adding more diseased leaf photos to the existing ones. The proposed enhancement technique uses attention mechanisms and translation between images of healthy and diseased leaves to produce images that show more pronounced disease textures [13].

Muhammed et al., (2023) investigate the fundamentals of diffusion technology and compare its approach and results with those of cutting-edge GAN solutions, paying particular attention to the diffusion-based model RePaint and the guided inference model of GANs called InstaGAN. Although they operate on different concepts, both models manage the segmentation masks to direct the generation process. Since findings on these

Table 1. Related Studies pertaining to Synthetic image generation

Author (Year)	Method	Strengths	Limitations
Iqbal et al. (2024)	CGAN-based model to generate six facial expressions from a single image	Generates highly realistic expressions; Accuracy improved to ~99% with adjustments	May require fine-tuning for optimal performance; dependent on CGAN quality
Wang et al. (2025)	Dual discriminator FHWD with frequency-domain & wavelet augmentation	Better distinction in high-frequency details; improves authenticity of synthetic images	Complex architecture; may require significant computational resources
Benfenati et al. (2022)	DL technique to generate synthetic plant leaf images	Enables large-scale dataset creation for agriculture; suitable for CNN training	Domain-specific; generalization to other plants or conditions may be limited
Ramadan et al. (2023)	GANs for wheat leaf disease image generation from small dataset	Effective in small-data scenarios; realistic image generation	Quality and diversity of images may vary; GAN training can be unstable
Haruna et al. (2023)	Style-GAN2 ADA with Laplacian filter for rice disease detection	Outperforms standard methods in limited/unbalanced datasets; improves SSD & Faster-RCNN detection	Specialized setup; applicability to other crops or diseases not validated
Min et al. (2023)	Image-to-image translation using attention mechanisms	Enhances diseased leaf textures; mitigates dataset bias	Depends on quality of source and target domain images; possible translation artifacts
Muhammed et al. (2023)	Comparison of RePaint (Diffusion) and InstaGAN with segmentation masks	Detailed comparison of diffusion vs GANs; uses segmentation to guide generation	Limited to subset of PlantVillage; findings may not generalize to other datasets
Zhang et al. (2023)	Dual GAN-based HQIA using WGAN-GP + Opt-Real-ESRGAN	Produces high-quality synthetic data; improves disease classification accuracy	Multi-stage process adds complexity; pseudo-data quality dependent on initial GAN

classes have already been published, a subset of the PlantVillage dataset, which includes three disease classes of grape leaf and two disease classes of tomato leaves, is used for a fair comparison [14]. Zhang et al., (2023) suggested a dual GAN-based high-quality image augmentation (HQIA) technique for generating high-quality images of rice leaf disease. Initially, pseudo-data samples were created by training Improved Training of Wasserstein GANs (WGAN-GP) on the original samples. The disease classification CNN was then fed the high-quality pseudo-data samples and indicators were used to confirm the method's efficacy. Table 1 lists the studies in the literature related to the current study [15].

The majorities of models have not been assessed across a variety of datasets or tasks and concentrate on particular domains. Frameworks for creating synthetic data that are more versatile and may be used in a variety of fields, such as agriculture, are required.

3   Methodology

The Fig. 1 presents the architecture of synthetic image generation model using cGAN.

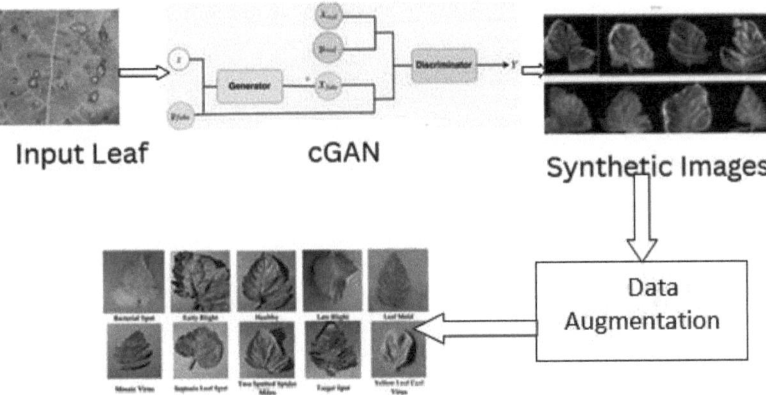

Fig. 1. Architecture of Synthetic Image Generation using cGAN

3.1 Data Sources

The study employs the PlantVillage and new plant diseases datasets, which is openly accessible and includes labeled images of both healthy and diseased plant leaves. Although there is class imbalance in the collection, especially for rare diseases, it contains a wide range of disease classes and several plant species. All the images in the dataset are preprocessed to ensure homogeneity in format and size. Rotation, flipping, and normalisation are examples of basic augmentation techniques that are first used to enhance baseline performance and get data ready for training.

3.2 Conditional Generative Adversarial Networks (cGAN)

The approach uses a cGAN to produce synthetic images of damaged leaves. The generator creates class-specific synthetic images based on disease class labels. The original PlantVillage dataset is used to train the cGAN, emphasizing under-represented disease classes. The GAN consists of two components Generator and Discriminator

Generator: The generator takes two inputs, a random noise vector z as an input and it is represented as follows

$$Z = P_z(z) \tag{1}$$

It is typically drawn from a normal distribution. N(0, I). Then the second input is the class label

$$Y \in R^k \tag{2}$$

It is one hot encoded representing the desired output class. For example, "Tomato-late blight ". Then both the inputs are combined embedding z and y represented by G

$$G(z, y) \tag{3}$$

The generator then learns the mapping to generate a fake image or synthetic image represented as follows

$$G : (z, y) \uparrow\rightarrow x_{fake} \tag{4}$$

In Eq. (4) x_{fake} belongs to R^{H*W*C} is the generated image with height H, width W and channels c). The generator aims to produce an image like a real image to the discriminator by matching the conditioning label y. The objective function of the cGAN Generator is as follows

$$\min_G \max_D E_{x,y} \sim P_{data}(x, y)[\log D(x, y)]$$
$$+E_z \sim P_z(z), y \sim p(y)\big[\log(1 - D(G(z, y), y))\big] \tag{5}$$

In Eq. (5), D(x,y) is the discriminators estimate of the proabability that x is real in the class y and G(z,y) is the generators output conditioned on label y. The generator continues to minimize the loss function and it is given as follows

$$L_G = E_z \sim P_z(z), y \sim p(y)[\log(1 - D(G(z, y), y)) \tag{6}$$

When the discriminator properly detects the created image as fraudulent, the generator is penalised. The block diagram for cGAN is given in Fig. 2.

Fig. 2. Block Diagram for Generator

The generator in a cGAN generates real images that are related to specific class labels for a type of plant diseases. The generator is given two inputs: a class label y, which is generally represented in the one-hot form and points to the class of the output image, and an input noise vector z, which introduces randomness. These two pieces of information are merged into one vector and channeled into a dense layer, which transforms them into higher dimensions. Subsequently, this vector is reshaped to produce a compact low-resolution feature map, which will undergo further processing to extract the final image. In order to transform the feature map into a high-resolution image, the generator employs several transposed convolutional layers, also referred to as deconvolution layers.

These layers systematically enhance the spatial dimensions of the feature maps, transforming them stepwise, until they reach the intended size, for example 64 × 64 × 3 for a color image. Throughout the architecture, batch normalization layers are included in order to improve the stability of the model during training and speed up convergence, along with non-linear functions ReLU or LeakyReLU. The last layer of the model implements a tanh activation function so that the values of the resulting image's pixels can lie between -1 and 1, which is in line with the format in which the data is fed into the model. This entire architecture enables the generator to create synthetic images that are both diverse and class-specific, making it highly effective for tasks like augmenting datasets for plant disease classification.

Discriminator (D): The inputs to the discriminator are an image, which is represented as follows

$$X \in R^{H*W*C} \tag{8}$$

The image may be either a real image from the dataset or a fake image from the generator.

A class label y: one-hot encoded or embedded, representing the desired class (for example, "Tomato = late blight" The discriminator receives **both** the image and the class label y, and learns a function:

$$D(x, y) \rightarrow [0, 1] \tag{9}$$

In Eq. (9), D(x, y) outputs a probability: how likely the image x is real, given the label y.

The Generator G and Discriminator D play a minimax game within the cGAN framework, which is defined by:

$$\min_{G} \max_{D} E_{x,y} \sim P_{data}(x, y)[\log D(x, y)]$$
$$+E_z \sim P_z(z), y \sim p(y)\left[\log(1 - D(G(z, y), y))\right] \tag{10}$$

This encourages it to concentrate on semantic correctness (matching class label) as well as realism (visual patterns). This is crucial in situations like the identification of plant diseases, where the discriminator must acquire the visual cues in context and the differences across classes can be slight (e.g., spots, discolouration).

Data Augmentation: A larger and more balanced training set is produced by adding those generated synthetic images to the original dataset. Enhancing the depiction of rare disease classes is given particular attention.

CNN Classification: The dataset is trained using CNN on the original dataset and the GAN generated dataset. To compare the performance of the model before and after augmentation, the classification accuracy is assessed on a different test set.

4   Results and Findings

The experiments were conducted using python using two different datasets and assessed using performance indicators with the CNN classifier.

4.1   Dataset Description

The aim of the PlantVillage dataset is to provide effective methods for the detection of 39 various plant diseases. There are images of 61,486 plant leaves and backgrounds. It was developed using six various augmentation methods to provide more various datasets under varied backdrop conditions. The used augmentations in this process included image flipping, gamma correction, rotation, scaling, injection of noise, and PCA color augmentation. This data is built through offline augmentation from the original dataset. This set, divided into 38 classes, includes approximately 87K RGB images of healthy and broken crop leaves. Maintaining the directory structure, the entire dataset is split into training and validation sets in an 80/20 ratio. A new directory with 33 test images is then created for making predictions [16].

4.2   Performance Evaluation

The level of similarity between generated and actual images is evaluated statistically using the Structural similarity Index Measure (SSIM). The Table 2 lists the SSIM values for the 10 different synthetic samples of tomato –late blight disease.

Table 2.   SSIM Value –Tomato –late blight image synthetic samples.

Sample No	SSIM Score (0–1)	Similarity Level
1	0.915	High
2	0.902	High
3	0.922	High
4	0.877	Moderate to High
5	0.890	High
6	0.915	High
7	0.876	Moderate to High
8	0.905	High
9	0.895	High
10	0.913	High

The generated images' great fidelity in maintaining texture and structural information is indicated by high SSIM scores. The above table represents Structural Similarity Index Measure (SSIM) metrics of 10 synthetic Tomato - Late blight images generated by a cGAN, and respective true images. SSIM indices are ranging between 0 to 1 with closer to 1, being an indicator of increased structure, texture, and similarity visually.

Here, all ten samples show high similarity, with SSIM values ranging from 0.876 to 0.922. Eight of ten images had a score greater than 0.89, which is typically regarded as high similarity, showing that the synthetic images are visually and structurally extremely close to the actual diseased leaves. Samples 4 and 7, although slightly lower (0.877 and 0.876 respectively), remain in the moderate to high similarity range, and indicate slight differences—perhaps because of fine-grained leaf texture or edge detail variation. Table 3 lists the SSIM values for the 10 different synthetic samples of Grape_Esca (Grape Measles) disease in grape plant.

Table 3. SSIM Value – Grape_Esca(Grape Measles) synthetic image samples

Sample No	SSIM Score (0–1)	Similarity Level
1	0.893	High
2	0.88	High
3	0.900	High
4	0.904	High
5	0.868	High
6	0.893	High
7	0.854	Moderate to High
8	0.883	High
9	0.873	High
10	0.891	High

Maximum structural similarity with the reference image is observed when all or the majority of the synthetic samples are within 0.85–0.90. Scores of > 0.89 were obtained by samples 1, 3, 4, 6, 8, and 10 that reproduced leaf patterns, textures, and colour patterns. The sample 7 with the SSIM of 0.854, which scored lowest, was still, in fact, within the range of moderate-to-high similarity. This may represent small fluctuations in disease pattern or leaf morphology. The values between 0.854 and 0.904 are very close, verifying the stability and homogeneity of the generating process. Since the synthetic images are a close representation of real disease-infected grape leaves, the high SSIM values validate that they can be used to train or evaluate DL models.

The efficacy of the GAN-augmented dataset in enhancing disease classification is validated by evaluating its performance using common measures like accuracy, precision, recall, and F1-score. The quantitative comparison between an improved CNN model trained on a dataset supplemented with GAN-generated synthetic images and CNN method trained on the original (actual) dataset is given in Table 4.

Table 4. Performance Analysis – Tomato leaf diseases-PlantVillage dataset

Measure	CNN (Original Dataset)	CNN + GAN-Augmented Dataset	Improvement (%)
Accuracy	86.3%	91.7%	+6.3%
Precision	85.1%	90.4%	+5.3%
Recall	84.6%	91.2%	+6.6%
F1-Score	84.8%	90.8%	+6.0%

All measures show significant improvements with the application of the GAN-augmented dataset. The most significant improvement is in recall, which shows improved positive case detection (particularly for rare or under-represented diseases).This demonstrates how using synthetic images produced by cGANs improves CNN classification performance overall and alleviates data imbalance. Figure 3 shows the improvements in performance before and after GAN.

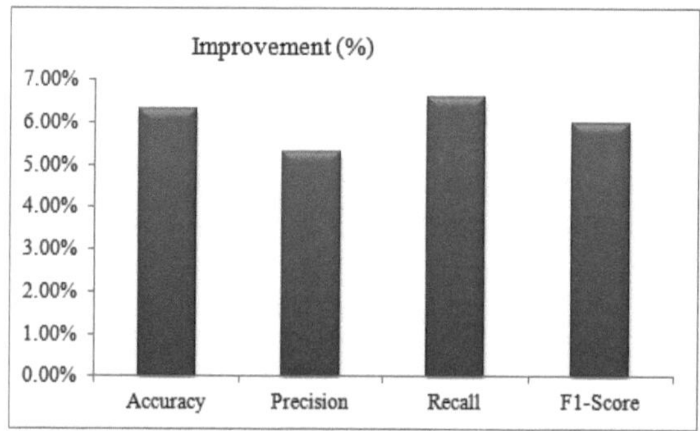

Fig. 3. Percentage of Improvement –Before and after GAN

Trained on the original dataset alone, the CNN achieved an accuracy of 86.3%, but this was increased to 91.7% by incorporating synthetic images, indicating enhanced generalization. Precision improved from 85.1% to 90.4%, i.e., the model improved its correctness in labeling correctly diseased cases without incorrectly labeling healthy ones. Remember, the measurement that measures capacity to detect accurate positive instances dramatically rose from 84.6% to 91.2%, signifying the improved ability of the model to detect even rare disease episodes.F1-score, which quantifies precision and recall balanced at the same level, significantly improved from 84.8% to 90.8%.

Figure 4 clearly shows that CNN performs considerably better on all important classification measures when GAN-based data augmentation is used. This emphasises how useful synthetic picture generation is for improving model accuracy and robustness, particularly in fields like precision agriculture where an imbalance or lack of data can impair DL performance. Overall, these enhancements confirm that using images generated by GAN improves data imbalance and sparsity management and results in a more accurate

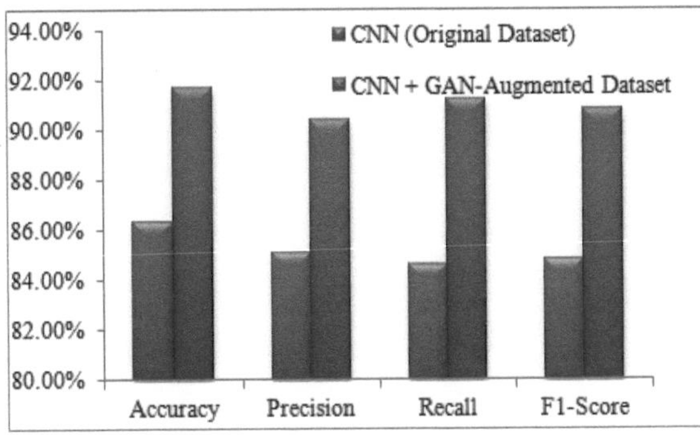

Fig. 4. Performance analysis – Before and After GAN – PlantVillage dataset

and robust classification model for precision agriculture. Table 5 lists the performance of the classification of grape diseases form plant village datasets.

Table 5. Performance Analysis –Grape leaf diseases from New Plant disease dataset

Measure	CNN (Original Dataset)	CNN + GAN-Augmented Dataset	Improvement (%)
Accuracy	87.4%	93.2%	5.80%
Precision	85.6%	91.5%	5.90%
Recall	84.9%	92.1%	7.20%
F1-Score	85.2%	91.8%	6.60%

Table 5 illustrates how well a CNN performs on a novel plant disease dataset specifically, grape leaf disease, when GAN-generated synthetic images are used. In every evaluation metric, the model trained using the GAN-augmented dataset performs better than the original CNN. Recall and F1-score indicate the highest gains, suggesting enhanced sensitivity and balanced precision. The model trained with synthetic data had an accuracy of 93.2%, while the accuracy without augmentation was 87.4%. This indicates a significant enhancement in the overall ability of the model to classify cases of illness correctly. The precision of the enhanced model has gone up to 91.5%, decreasing the rate of false positives, which is important when detecting illnesses requiring treatment (Fig. 5).

Even though GANs enhance diversity of data, they have drawbacks in agriculture, such as training instability, mode collapse, and large hardware and time expenses. These obstacles may be an impediment to implementation in resource constrained environments. They need to be addressed by using lightweight architectures and stabilization strategies in order to have realistic large agricultural applications.

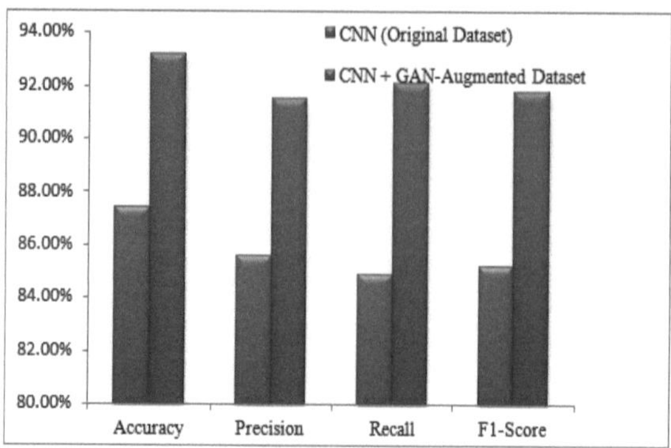

Fig. 5. Performance analysis – Before and After GAN – New Plant Diseases dataset

5 Conclusion

Automatic detection of leaf diseases is now feasible due to recent developments in DL techniques; nevertheless, for best results, a sizable, varied, and balanced dataset is needed. This study demonstrates how well the cGAN model produces realistic and class-representative images of tomato late blight, which qualifies it for use in enhancing datasets for plant disease classification tasks. The experiments were conducted in two datasets by computing the SSIM values between the original image and the generated image and almost all the generated images shows highest similarity for both the datasets. The effectiveness of synthetic image generation is further studied by analyzing the performance metrics before and after GAN. It demonstrates that there is a significant improvement in classification accuracy from 86.3 to 91.7% in PlantVillage dataset and 87.4% to 93.2% in New plant Diseases dataset. Therefore, although it requires time and resources, generative model-based augmentation is a potential field of research to enhance model performance and address the problem of generalisation when data is sparse or unbalanced. This is particularly true in the fields of medicine, agriculture, etc.

References

1. Lamba, S., Saini, P., Kaur, J., Kukreja, V.: Optimized classification model for plant diseases using generative adversarial networks. Innov. Syst. Softw. Eng. **19**(1), 103–115 (2023)
2. Chen, Y., Wu, Q.: Grape leaf disease identification with sparse data via generative adversarial networks and convolutional neural networks. Precis. Agric. **24**(1), 235–253 (2023)
3. Bi, L., Hu, G.: Improving image-based plant disease classification with generative adversarial network under limited training set. Front. Plant Sci. **11**, 583438 (2020)
4. Abbas, A., Jain, S., Gour, M., Vankudothu, S.: Tomato plant disease detection using transfer learning with C-GAN synthetic images. Comput. Electron. Agric. **187**, 106279 (2021)
5. Iqbal, M.A., Jadoon, W., Kim, S.K.: Synthetic image generation using conditional gan-provided single-sample face image. Appl. Sci. **14**(12), 5049 (2024). https://doi.org/10.3390/app14125049
6. Wang, C., Xia, Y., Xia, L., Wang, Q., Gu, L.: Dual discriminator GAN-based synthetic crop disease image generation for precise crop disease identification. Plant Meth. **21**(1), 46 (2025)

7. Akkem, Y., Biswas, S.K., Varanasi, A.: A comprehensive review of synthetic data generation in smart farming by using variational autoencoder and generative adversarial network. Eng. Appl. Artif. Intell. **131**, 107881 (2024)

8. Benfenati, A., Bolzi, D., Causin, P., Oberti, R.: A deep learning generative model approach for image synthesis of plant leaves. PLoS ONE **17**(11), e0276972 (2022)

9. Ramadan, S.T.Y., Sakib, T., Haque, Md.M.U., Sharmin, N., Rahman, Md.M.: Wheat leaf disease synthetic image generation from limited dataset using GAN. In: International Conference on Human-Centric Smart Computing, pp. 501–511. Springer, Singapore (2023)

10. Singh, A.K., Rao, A., Chattopadhyay, P., Maurya, R., Singh, L.: Effective plant disease diagnosis using Vision Transformer trained with leafy-generative adversarial network-generated images. Exp. Syst. Appl. **254**, 124387 (2024)

11. Haruna, Y., Qin, S., Kiki, M.J.M.: An improved approach to detection of rice leaf disease with GAN-based data augmentation pipeline. Appl. Sci. **13**(3), 1346 (2023). https://doi.org/10.3390/app13031346

12. Min, B., Kim, T., Shin, D., Shin, D.: Data augmentation method for plant leaf disease recognition. Appl. Sci. **13**(3), 1465 (2023). https://doi.org/10.3390/app13031465

13. Muhammad, A., Salman, Z., Lee, K., Han, D.: Harnessing the power of diffusion models for plant disease image augmentation. Front. Plant Sci. **14**, 1280496 (2023)

14. Zhang, Z., Gao, Q., Liu, L., He, Y.: A high-quality rice leaf disease image data augmentation method based on a dual GAN. IEEE Access **11**, 21176–21191 (2023)

15. https://www.kaggle.com/datasets/emmarex/plantdisease

16. https://www.kaggle.com/datasets/vipooooool/new-plant-diseases-dataset

Efficacy of Selected Generative AI Systems in Assessing Discourse Coherence, Pragmatic Competence, Collocational Competence, and Figurative Language

Anjana Prajapati[✉] [iD], Amee Teraiya[iD], and Krunal Vaghela[iD]

Marwadi University, Rajkot, Gujarat, India 360003
{anjana.prajapti,amee.teraiya,
krunal.vaghela}@marwadieducation.edu.in

Abstract. Artificial Intelligence (AI) is rapidly transforming language education, functioning not merely as an automation tool but as a catalyst for understanding, accuracy, and individualized learning. Nonetheless, despite the extensive integration of AI in education, comprehension of its efficacy in assessing language proficiency, particularly these four parameters, discourse coherence, pragmatic competence, collocational competence, and figurative language, remains largely underexplored from the perspective of integrating AI. Consequently, capacity to embed AI driven formative assessments for enhanced feedback can be insightful.

The present study assesses the efficacy of five leading generative AI systems namely GPT-4, Gemini, DeepSeek, Copilot, and Claude Sonnet 4, through standardised dialogues that encompass four linguistic criteria, discourse coherence, pragmatic competence, collocational competence, and figurative language. language. The dialogues constructed by students as a part of a classroom activity are assessed through each AI tool will through CEFR based 5-point rubrics. The study of this evaluation, aims to explore how effectively and precisely these AI tools process the specific language inputs deliver the feedback that aids learners in improving expression, increasing their clarity, and enriching their contextual comprehension. The findings of this study will benefit teachers, curriculum developers and language learners by offering evidence-based insights into which generative AI systems can be utilised for the improvement, accuracy and learner autonomy in higher education and EFL domains.

Keywords: Artificial Intelligence (AI) · Generative AI systems · Formative Assessment · Discourse Coherence · Pragmatic Competence · Collocational Competence · Figurative Language

1 Introduction

In the rapidly evolving realm of Second language acquisition (SLA), the expectations for learners have transitioned from solely learning structural grammar to developing advanced abilities that facilitate natural, fluent, and contextually appropriate communication. [1] Particularly, Formative assessment, which prioritize continuous feedback

© The Author(s) 2026
R. Sridaran and S. Priti (Eds.): AI-FCDAC 2025, CCIS 2866, pp. 124–136, 2026.
https://doi.org/10.1007/978-3-032-17300-3_10

to enhance student learning is currently being explored with the integration of Artificial Intelligence (AI). [2] The capacity of AI to examine extensive data and deliver immediate, customized feedback is widely acknowledged for its potential to improve formative assessment in diverse educational field. [3] Its integration in language assessment remains partially explored, hence the attempts to integrate AI in the areas where human approach is widely traditionally exercised, such attempts can lead us to new insights.

The integration of AI platforms, such as ChatGPT, Gemini, and more are transforming conceptual classroom evaluation methods.[4] For instance, Li et al. [5] investigated the applicability of AI in formative assessment in science education, excluding language acquisition. Likewise, Rajasekar et al. [6] has examined tools in conventional classroom contexts, without emphasising specific linguistic factor essential for English language learning.

While AI systems are being explored for its systematic and quick assessment, much of the existing research is either generic or concentrated on fields beyond language education. There remains a significant gap in targeted research investigating the effectiveness of AI systems in evaluating certain language elements essential to communicative ability, particularly, Discourse Coherence, Pragmatic Competence, Collocational Competence, and Figurative Language. These parameters represent advanced communicative competencies that transcend mere grammatical and vocabulary, integrating a leaner's capacity to formulate cohesive conversation, use language properly. Therefore, the present research aims to address that significant gap by demonstrates how technology, particularly GPT-4, Gemini, DeepSeek, Copilot, and Claude Sonnet 4, can assist teachers in providing personalized, data-driven feedback that is scalable and linguistically informed. These platforms were chosen due to its representation of advanced language models that are extensively utilized in educational and professional settings, making them highly relevant for formative language assessment.

2 Related Works

Recent years have observed a surge in research examining the intersections of AI and language learning, signifying a transformation in how advanced technology is altering pedagogical methods in language education. [7] Feifri Wang et al. [8] offers an extensive overview of how AI-human interaction benefit in language learning. The research identifies key aspects such as AI feedback, adaptive scaffolding, and learner autonomy. Nevertheless, it provides a general overview and fails to examine how AI might assess the specific linguistic competencies at the micro level.

Similarly, Alaqlobi et al. [9] conducts a critical analysis on the utilization of AI for language learning, highlighting the importance of AI systems in vocabulary building, grammar instruction and translation. Nonetheless, there is limited focus on important parameters such as discourse coherence, collocation accuracy, and pragmatic appropriateness.

Biju et al. [10] emphasizes the positive outcomes of AI-assisted assessment, including the reduction of foreign language fear among leaners, enhancing motivation, and how immediate and tailored feedback promotes continuous engagement in language learning. Nonetheless, despite these advantages, the study lacks a human-rated gold standard, leaving accuracy of AI feedback unverified against expert assessment.

Baskara and Mukarto [11] provides instructional framework utilising ChatGPT to augment learner autonomy and engagement. Yet, similar to other studies, the focus remains general, only on pedagogy with less emphasis on ChatGPT's efficacy in formative assessment across particular linguistic dimensions.

Taken together, these studies collectively underscore the growing significance of AI in language acquisition. However, a critical gap persists as the majority of the research focuses on AI's overarching educational capabilities while neglecting deeper layers of linguistic competency, such as communicative accuracy, stylistic refinement and individual learner variance. Addressing this gap, the present research systematically examines five prominent AI systems across advanced linguistic parameters, discourse coherence, pragmatic competence, collocational competence, and figurative language, intending to contribute to both applied linguistic research and AI enhanced educational methodologies.

3 Background

The efficacy of language teaching is largely dependent on its assessment methodologies. Unlike Summative assessments, which evaluate performance at a certain point in time, formative assessment is defined by its continuous, diagnostic and feedback-oriented attributes [12]. Its primary objective is to enhance learning during teaching process, rather than only assessing results. Heritage [13] defines it as 'an effective instructional tool' that aids learners in recognising their strengths and limitations, facilitating their attempts to improve.

In language learning, formative assessment can manifest in different forms: Peer feedback on writing, instructor-led conferences, targeted drills, and iterative revisions. [11] These activities promote self-regulation, metacognitive awareness, and the assimilation of remedial input. Ismail et al. [3] demonstrated that formative evaluation enhances learner's motivation, linguistic accuracy, and overall performance more effectively than solely relying on summative assessment.

3.1 Advanced Language Components

Discourse Coherence
Discourse coherence refers to the logical organization of concepts in sentences and paragraphs, allowing a written or spoken discourse to be seen as cohesive and relevant. Coherence encompasses not only syntax but also the proficient application of cohesive structures, thematic advancements, and referential clarity. [14]

Pragmatic Competence
Pragmatic competence refers to a speaker's capacity to utilize language suitably within a specific social and cultural environment. [1] It includes the execution of speech acts, e.g., making requests, extending apologies, politeness techniques, indirectness, and the

capacity to differentiate between literal and implied meanings. Taguchi [15] argues that pragmatic competence is not merely an advanced ability; it is an essential element of communicative competence, facilitating learners' effective participation in varied contexts.

Collocational Competence
Collocational competence comprises the capacity to identify and employ often co-occurring word combinations within a language. [16] Phrases such a 'commit a crime' or 'make a decision' exemplify collocations that resonate naturally with native speakers. Non-native speakers who improperly utilize these phrases, e.g., saying 'do a decision', frequently generate content that appears reluctant or erroneous. Xu [17] states that the utilization of appropriate collocations is important for fluency, particularly in verbal communication. It facilitates both linguistic precision and communicative fluency.

Figurative Language
Figurative language includes idioms, phrasal verbs, metaphors, and infusing a language with nuance, emotion, and cultural depth. [18] Liu et al. [18] assert that figurative expressions are prevalent in academic and professional discourse. It makes proficiency crucial for effective comprehension and expression in real-world contexts. In the absence of this ability, learners are likely to overlook or misinterpret the important elements of meaning. [18]

4 Artificial Intelligence and Formative Assessment

The increasing incorporation of Artificial Intelligence (AI) in education has created new opportunities for formative evaluation. When integrated with advancing AI technologies, formative assessment possesses the capability to diagnose, monitor, and enhance learner development in real-time. This research asserts that the amalgamation of Generative AI systems with formative assessment techniques provides a strong pedagogical framework for the development and evaluation of advanced language abilities.

To ensure the effectiveness of AI-assisted formative assessment, it is imperative to prioritize accuracy and interpretability. [12] AI systems should correspond with human judgment, especially when assessing intricate constructions such as coherence or pragmatics. Naismith [19] revealed that GPT-4 assessed coherence in an essay with more than 50% precise agreement with human evaluators, and also attained a Kappa score of (0.8), signifying substantial reliability. Likewise, Xu [17] emphasizes the necessity of precision in the evaluation of collocational usage, since inaccuracy may result in erroneous feedback.

Furthermore, transparency in the generation of feedback is important.[20] When AI systems provide rational-based outputs (e.g., 'This phrase is uncommon in academic writing'), learners are more inclined to comprehend and implement corrections. Nonetheless, precaution is needed. Some AI elucidations may not accurately represent authentic linguistic rationale. A hybrid strategy, utilizing AI as a guide and tutor input for validation, is the most effective method.

4.1 Implementation in Educational Settings

The effective incorporation of AI in formative language assessment relies on careful execution. [21] Teachers must be proficient not only in utilizing these technologies but also in analysing responses within an educational framework. Below are a few illustrative use cases:

- Writing feedback: AI systems identify insufficient transitions or reference ambiguity in a manuscript. The students can revise and resubmit, attaining an elevated coherence score.
- Speaking practice: Whisper and other AI systems transcribe a role-play activity. An educator using Hugging Face to assess pragmatic markers, e.g., indirectness, politeness, and provide formative feedback.
- Collocation training: Students can be provided with exams created by AI systems that assess common and uncommon collocations, along with prompt explanations and recommended improvements.

These scenarios demonstrate that with minimal programming and infrastructure, educational institutions may leverage AI to enhance their formative feedback systems.

5 Proposed Methodology

This study employed a systematic comparative methodology to assess the efficacy of five AI driven language models, GPT-4, Gemini, DeepSeek, Copilot, and Claude Sonnet 4, across four advanced metrics of language proficiency: Discourse coherence, pragmatic competence, collocational competence, and figurative language usage. These parameters were chosen for their relevance to real-world communication and advanced writing competencies; however, they are inadequately represented in prior AI evaluation research.

5.1 Data Collection

To standardized the assessment, a set of 20 dialogues were taken from B.Tech first year students by the researcher. These dialogues were generated as a part of their formative assessment classroom activity in Professional communication course. This task required students to write short conversational dialogues, thereby demonstrating authentic learner language within an academic context. The collected dialogue served as the evaluation test samples. Appendix A contains sample dialogues to ensure transparency.

5.2 Standardized Prompt Formulation

All the selected tools received the same input mentioned in the Appendix B to eliminate bias and ensure methodological consistency. It included instruction of dialogues assessment with discourse coherence, pragmatic competence, collocational competence, and figurative language these parameters, to evaluate the dialogues on a scale of 1 to 5(1 = Low, 5 = high), for each parameter, utilizing a scoring rubric derived from CEFR descriptors. This scale provided a balance between sensitivity and clarity, while avoiding rating ambiguity. Additionally short comments were requested to justify the assigned ratings. This standardization eradicated input bias and established a uniform bias of comparison among all AI systems.

5.3 Assessment Process

Each AI systems produced assessments of all 20 dialogues based on the given prompt. The scoring system was crafted to balance sensitivity and clarity. Ratings and comments were collected for detailed analysis.

5.4 Human Gold Standard Validation

To establish a benchmark for accuracy, the identical set of dialogues was independently assessed by 5 faculty members. These expert assessments functioned as human gold standard, offering a reliable benchmark to support and strengthen the study's findings. An overview of this evaluation is mentioned in Appendix C.

5.5 Statistical Analysis

Descriptive statistics, including the mean and standard deviation, were calculated for all tools across all parameters. Tool performance was validated by evaluating inter-tool reliability via Intraclass Corelation Coefficients (ICC) and estimating criteria validity by comparing tool outputs with expert assessments using Mean Absolute Error(MAE). These validation measures establish a comprehensive framework for assessing the reliability and accuracy of AI driven formative assessment.

6 Analysis and Interpretation

Table 1. Average scores

Generative AI systems	Discourse Coherence	Pragmatic Competence	Collocational Competence	Figurative Language	Overall Mean
ChatGPT	4	4	2	2	3.0
Gemini	4.5	4	2	2	3.5
DeepSeek	4	3	3	2	3.0
Copilot	4	3.4	3	2.3	3.3
Claude	4	4	3	2.3	3.2

The above table displays the mean score attributed by each platform to the five dialogues across different skills, utilizing a scale from 1(Low) to 5 (High).

Table 2. Parameter-wise analysis

Skill	What the numbers show	Which AI "does best"
Discourse Coherence	Gemini is positioned slightly above the average (4.5 compared to 4.0 for all others) All other converge at 4.0.	Gemini assigns a higher value to dialogue structures, nonetheless, the narrow margin of 0.5 indicates only slight differences.
Pragmatic Competence	Most of the tools range from 3 to 4, with DeepSeek at the lowest 3.0 and Gemini/GPT-4 at the highest. (About 4.0)	Gemini and GPT-4 exhibit greater leniency, but DeepSeek enforces stricter standards. "Best" is contingent upon whether one prioritizes generosity or stricter criteria.
Collocational Competence	Gemini and GPT-4 exhibit the higher severity at 2.0, while DeepSeek, Claude and Copilot are within the 3.0 range.	DeepSeek, Claude, and Copilot surpass Gemini and GPT-4 in identifying suitable word combinations.
Figurative Language	All tools receive exceedingly low ratings from 2 to 3 at most. Claude and Copilot occasionally exceed slightly (2, 3); however, the baseline remains constant.	Claude and Copilot are slightly ahead, while other tools exhibit similar sensitivity of 2.0

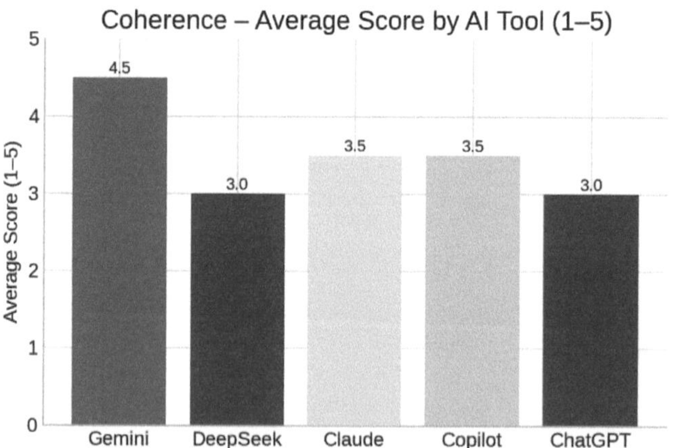

Fig. 1. Average discourse coherence score

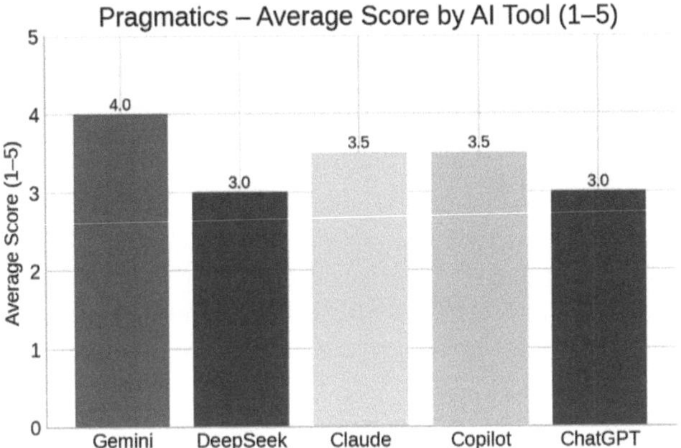

Fig. 2. Average Pragmatic Competence score

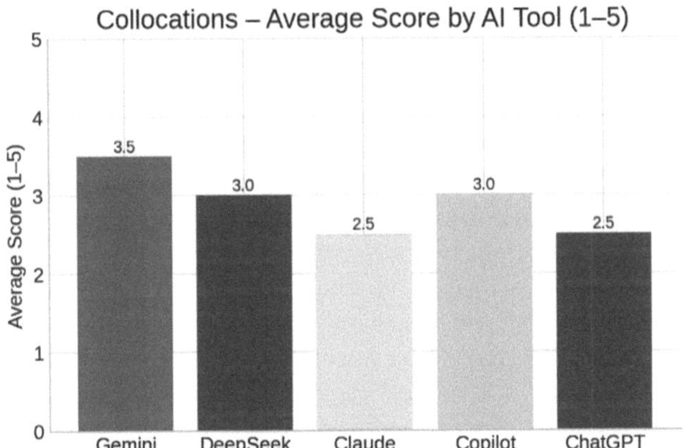

Fig. 3. Average Collocational Competence Score

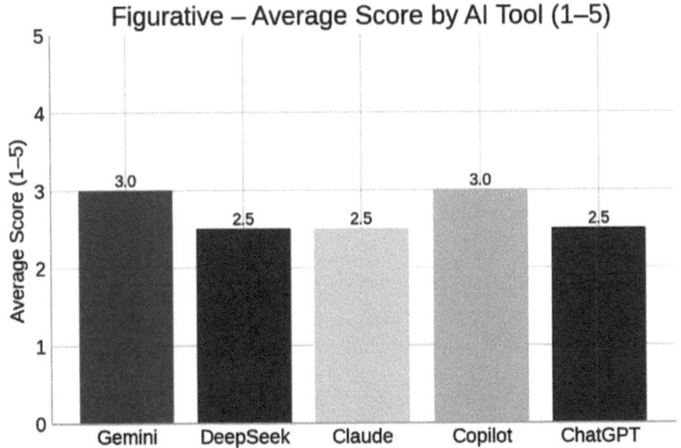

Fig. 4. Average Figurative Language score

7 Discussion

The comparative analyses of AI systems in assessing learners' dialogues across four essential parameters of language proficiency demonstrates both encourage strengths limitations. Gemini consistently achieved the highest scores (3.5), particularly excelling in discourse coherence (4.5) and pragmatic competence(4.0), reflecting a more favourable assessment characteristic in organized and rationally sequenced dialogues. DeepSeek with a mean of (3.0), exhibited strictness and sensitivity to collocational competence, whereas Claude (3.2) demonstrated a well-balanced performance, notably in pragmatic and figurative dimensions, recognising creative language use more than other AI systems. Copilot and GPT-4 (3.0) provided stable mid-range assessments across all skills, ensuring consistency. Figurative competency with an average score of (2–2.5) across many tools, has emerged as an evolving domain where AI systems demonstrate potential yet necessitates further enhancement, particularly in its ability to convey nuanced and creative expression.

This indicates limitation of selected AI systems in capturing complex stylistic and rhetorical aspects of language, which are very important for advanced writing and discourse analysis. It highlights a domain where human expertise, especially that of qualified instructors, is essential. In comparison to conventional assessment methods, AI solutions provide considerable benefits regarding expedition, uniformity, and scalability. These systems can analyse and evaluate extensive amounts of linguistic data within seconds, delivering immediate feedback that facilitates iterative learning. Nevertheless, conventional human evaluations provide contextual discernment, pedagogical sophistication, and interpretative richness—attributes that AI currently lacks, particularly in domains such as figurative language, cultural pragmatics, and creative expression.

Therefore, rather than portraying AI as a replacement for traditional assessment, this study supports for an integrated model, where AI acts as a complementary diagnostic tool to support educators in delivering more personalized, responsive, and data-informed language education. The results indicate that the strategic integration of AI-generated feedback with human assessment can improve the evaluation process, increase learner engagement, and eventually yield more substantial language development results.

8 Conclusion and Future Work

This research contributes the existing research on AI assisted language assessment by systematically evaluating the efficacy of GPT-4, Gemini, DeepSeek, Copilot and Claude Sonnet 4, in assessing essential communicative competencies. The findings collectively demonstrate how different tools provide distinct strengths to evaluation, indicating their combined application may result in a more comprehensive framework for language assessment. Furthermore, findings do not only represent strength and weakness of selected AI systems but also reveal that no single generative AI system excels in all linguistic parameters , one needs to keep updated with the increasingly fast pace at which the whole technological platform is evolving to use such tools to their optimal potential. The paper also elucidates the necessity of a blended assessment in formative assessments, in which AI systems can supplement human judgement to improve the accuracy, effectiveness, and pedagogical value and expedite the whole process. Furthermore, the research provides essential insights for educators looking forward to integrate technology in general and generative AI in particular into their assessment frameworks by throwing some light on the brighter sides of their integration as well as the limitations which must be kept in mind while utilising such generative AI platforms to their advantage.

Future research should focus on strengthening AI's capacity to evaluate stylistic and context dependent aspects of language, especially figurative language and collocational competence which are significant deficiencies in exiting models. Developing specialized training datasets that incorporate idioms, metaphors, and culturally specific terms, may enhance model sensitivity to non-literal language. Furthermore, research should explore the efficacy of AI assisted feedback in authentic classroom settings across various competency levels, age demographics, and educational contexts. Lastly, a crucial step in research can involve a comparative study of AI generated evaluation versus human raters, which would further elucidate if the role of AI should be considered complementary or as a partial substitute in facilitating high quality language learning and assessment.

Appendices

Appendix A : Dialogue sample

The following dialogues were collected from B.Tech students as a part of sample for this study:

Dialogue 01:

Suhana: Hello Tanisha!

Tanisha: Hey, how are you doing?

Suhana: I am good. How are you?

Tanisha: Good too, like sunshine after rain!

Suhana: Can you tell me from where you have purchased these project papers? Actually, our subject teacher has assigned one assignment where we have to use these papers.

Tanisha: Sure, it's from a stationary situated on Nirmala Road named Nachiketa.

Suhana: Okay, today I will go and purchase. Thank you!

Tanisha: Any time!

Dialogue 02:

Aarush: Good morning, Ma'am

Interviewer: Good morning, Aarush! Please have a seat.

Aarush: Thank you!

Interviewer: So, Aarush tell me about yourself?

Aarush: I am Aarush Trivedi from Computer Engineering background with an experience of 4+ years at Wipro as a frontend developer. I have completed my masters from Anna University, Madras.

Interviewer: Great. Would you please tell us why you are choosing our company and why you left the Wipro?

Aarush: For a better growth I resigned from Wipro. Your company has core focus in a field wherein front-end developers have major role. This is why I am looking forward to work with this company.

Appendix B : Prompt Given To AI Tools

"To assess the dialogues for formative assessment, this following prompt was given to all AI tools. These are the 20 dialogues written by B.Tech students of semester 02. This assignment was given to them as the part of the formative assessment component. I want you to please evaluate these samples based on the following parameters, giving specific explanations and ratings for each:

1. Discourse coherence: Examine how logically ideas given in dialogue format are connected.
2. Pragmatic competence: Assess the appropriateness of language use according to context (politeness, tone, cultural appropriateness).
3. Collocational competence: Identify correct and incorrect word combinations. Highlight unnatural phrasing.
4. Figurative competence: Identify presence, accuracy and effectiveness of figurative language, such as metaphors, similes, idioms.

Additionally provide a rating on a scale of 1 to 5(1 = poor and 5 = excellent) and add short comments (optional but valuable) to explain your ratings. Rating Scale (1–5)

1. Poor: Very weak performance, frequent errors, little to no evidence of competence.
2. Fair: Limited performance, several errors, partial awareness but not consistent.
3. Average: Adequate performance, some errors, shows developing competence but needs improvement.
4. Good: Strong performance, mostly accurate/appropriate, minor errors that do not affect meaning.
5. Excellent: Highly effective performance, accurate, natural, appropriate, and contextually strong."

Appendix C : Faculty Evaluation of Dialogue Samples

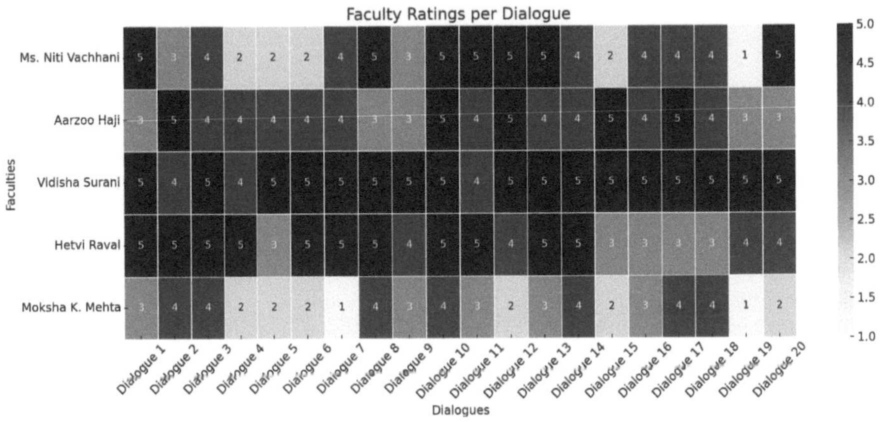

Fig. 5. Faculty ratings per dialogue

References

1. O'Grady, S.: An AI generated test of pragmatic competence and connected speech. Lang. Teach. Res. Q. **37**, 188–203 (2023)
2. Prompiengchai, S., Narreddy, C., Joordens, S.: A Practical Guide for Supporting Formative Assessment and Feedback Using Generative AI. Preprint arXiv:2505.23405 (2025)
3. Ismail, S.M., Rahul, D.R., Patra, I., Rezvani, E.: Formative vs. summative assessment: impacts on academic motivation, attitude toward learning, test anxiety, and self-regulation skill. Lang. Test. Asia. **12**(1), 40 (2022)
4. Chau, N.T.H., Nguyen, T.H.T., Truong, V.L.: The rise of artificial intelligence: the impact of artificial intelligence on language learning. In: 2025 14th International Conference on Educational and Information Technology (ICEIT), pp. 58–62. IEEE, New York (2025)
5. Li, T., Reigh, E., He, P., Miller, E.A.: Can we and should we use artificial intelligence for formative assessment in science? J. Res. Sci. Teach. **60**(6), 1385–1389 (2023)
6. Rajasekar, A., et al.: AI framework for scalable automated continuous formative assessment. In: 2024 IEEE International Conference on Teaching, Assessment and Learning for Engineering (TALE), pp. 1–6. IEEE, New York (2024)
7. Vinothkumar, J., Karunamurthy, A.: Recent advancements in artificial intelligence technology: trends and implications. Quing: Int. J. Multidiscip. Sci. Res. Dev. **2**(1), 1–11 (2023)
8. Wang, F., Cheung, A.C., Chai, C.S.: Language learning development in human–AI interaction: A thematic review of the research landscape. System. **125**, 103424 (2024)
9. Alaqlobi, O., Alduais, A., Qasem, F., Alasmari, M.: Artificial intelligence in applied linguistics: A content analysis and future prospects. Cogent Arts Humanit. **11**(1), 2382422 (2024)
10. Biju, N., Abdelrasheed, N.S.G., Bakiyeva, K., Prasad, K.D.V., Jember, B.: AI-assisted language assessment or paper format: impacts on foreign language anxiety, learning attitudes, motivation, and writing performance. Lang. Test. Asia. **14**(1), 45 (2024)
11. Baskara, R.: Exploring the implications of chatgpt for language learning in higher education. Indones. J. Engl. Lang. Teach. Appl. Linguist. **7**(2), 343–358 (2023)

12. Black, P., Wiliam, D.: Developing the theory of formative assessment. Educ. Assess. Eval. Account. **21**, 5–31 (2009)
13. Bennett, R.E.: Formative assessment: A critical review. Assess. Educ.: Princ. Policy Pract. **18**(1), 5–25 (2011)
14. Azrou, L., Oufaida, H., Blache, P., Hamdine, I.: Using neural coherence models to assess discourse coherence. In: International Conference on Text Speech, and Dialogue, pp. 134–146. Springer, Cham (2024)
15. Taguchi, N. (ed.): The Routledge Handbook of Second Language Acquisition and Pragmatics. New York, NY: Routledge, 1-14 (2019)
16. Hill, J.: Collocational competence.Readings in Methodology, 162. (1999)
17. Xu, J.: Measuring "Spoken Collocational Competence" In Communicative Speaking Assessment. Lang. Assess. Q. **15**(3), 255–272 (2018)
18. Liu, E., Cui, C., Zheng, K., Neubig, G.: Testing the Ability of Language Models to Interpret Figurative Language. Preprint arXiv:2204.12632 (2022)
19. Naismith, B., Mulcaire, P., Burstein, J.: Automated evaluation of written discourse coherence using GPT-4. In: Proceedings of the 18th Workshop on Innovative Use of NLP for Building Educational Applications, pp. 394–403 (2023)
20. Hattie, J., Timperley, H.: The power of feedback. Rev. Educ. Res. **77**(1), 81–112 (2007)
21. Zawacki-Richter, O., Marín, V.I., Bond, M., Gouverneur, F.: Systematic review of research on artificial intelligence applications in higher education. Int. J. Educ. Technol. High. Educ. **16**(1), 1–27 (2019)

A Blockchain and IoT-Enabled Framework for Automated and Secure Supply Chain Management: Enhancing Transparency, Efficiency, and Trust

Chanda Chouhan[✉] and Monika Saxena

Banasthali Vidhyapeeth, Jaipur, Rajasthan, India
Chanda.chouhan@gmail.com, smonika@banasthali.in

Abstract. Supply chain operations obtain a transformative method through the combination of Blockchain technology and the Internet of Things (IoT). The framework introduced in this research combines blockchain decentralized ledger technology with IoT real-time data collection to create an automated and secure supply chain operation system. Through smart contracts the framework automates predefined agreement execution thus it eliminates the need for intermediaries and lowers operational delays. Goods equipped with IoT-enabled sensors enable ongoing monitoring which enhances tracking while reducing the dangers from counterfeits and thefts and operational inadequacies. Stakeholder confidence grows through the blockchain's unchangeable structure that provides tamper-proof recordkeeping for data protection. The framework brings predictive analytics possible through integrated machine learning algorithms which helps businesses make decisions proactively and optimize their resource distribution. The developed system tackles typical supply chain problems through its ability to handle transparency concerns and security weaknesses and operational effectiveness problems. The dual consensus framework allows users to gain better security along with improved scalability capabilities in an optimized system performance. The system establishes regulatory compliance through its immutable audit trails which enables organizations to maintain standards properly. This study adds to the current efforts of supply chain innovation by showing how both blockchain and IoT work together to establish trust-based systems that operate efficiently. Simulation tests combined with real-life case examples demonstrate that the framework successfully minimizes supply chain costs while successfully reducing fraud and sending supply chain processes into full view. The study proceeds to conclude that combining blockchain technology with IoT applications creates a suitable solution which powers modern supply chain management to transition toward resilient automated networks.

Keywords: Blockchain · IoT · Supply Chain Management · Smart Contracts

© The Author(s) 2026
R. Sridaran and S. Priti (Eds.): AI-FCDAC 2025, CCIS 2866, pp. 137–152, 2026.
https://doi.org/10.1007/978-3-032-17300-3_11

1 Introduction

However, the very rapid evolution of global supply chains has rendered these an increasingly difficult set of challenges to address in terms of transparency, security and operational efficiency. Traditional systems of supply chain place its reliance upon centralized authorities and multiple intermediaries and hence are prone to inefficiencies, delays and add up to a stronger countenance of fraud and counterfeiting. Along with it, lack of real time visibility and trust among stakeholders makes supply chain management more complex [1]. This is where the integration of Blockchain with the Internet of Things (IoT) comes in to transform the possible automation, security and transparency. Through blockchain, IoT devices can share data in real time, and the devices ensure real time tracking of the goods and also help to improve supply chain efficiency and trust. The blockchain technology is a tamper proof digital ledger where various transactions are stored in a transparent and verifiable manner. Blockchain removes the intermediaries from the equation, which makes the operational costs lower, decreases the delays and enhances the data integrity level within the supply chain. For instance, if smart contracts are defined as self-executing agreements, they execute themselves on the blockchain by taking a certain action when a set of conditions are met. Automation in supply chain improves the reliability by minimizing human intervention and errors. Additionally, blockchain increases regulatory compliance by creating unalterable audit trails [2] for businesses to remain in line with industry standards and legal requirements. Modernizing of supply chain management has enlisted the role of IoT to monitor and acquire data in real time. The products and shipments are embedded with RFID tags, sensors, and other devices periodically providing real updates on their location and also the environment to which they are being subjected, for example, temperature and humidity, etc. It provides this level of monitoring which is of great value in producing goods which are of high quality and authenticity as demonstrated by industries like pharmaceutical, food supply chain and high value manufacturing. IoT and blockchain integration helps secure record and share the collected data among the parties without tampering and makes the entire supply chain transparent. Furthermore, machine learning algorithms can be applied to analyze the data generated by IoT to predict the demand fluctuation, and optimize the inventory, etc. However, challenges exist in implementing a blockchain and IoT enabled framework in supply chain management, in terms for scalability, interoperability and high initial costs. Due to the fact that blockchain networks are often constrained by the capabilities for processing transactions, optimized consensus mechanisms is required to improve performance. Again, a set of standardized protocols that ensure seamless interoperability among different IoT devices and blockchain have to be in place. Secure communication frameworks have to be in place as well. It is important to tackle these issues for the blockchain and IoT to be widely deployed in supply chain ecosystems. This paper presents a complete framework that joins blockchain [3], IoT, and smart contracts to productively oversee the inventiveness of the association while likewise upgrading security and strength. The framework intends to optimize the operational process, dimension fraud and improve the trust among the supply chain participants by taking advantage of the decentralized ledger technology along with real time IoT data acquisition. The above study also enhances implementation of Machine learning for predictive analytics by serving for proactive decision-making. This research does the empirical validation and real-world case studies to show what is the cause and what is the benefit of integration of blockchain and IoT in spreading the modern revolution of supply chain management.

2 Related Work

Research studies about blockchain and IoT-enabled supply chain management show these technologies improve clarity and security while boosting operational speed. Scientific research shows that smart contracts execute automated transactions through IoT sensors which track logistics in real-time while decentralized ledgers stop fraudulent activities. Current research focuses on optimizing these three issues because they present critical barriers that must be addressed through improved work and AI applications.

K. Yang, et.al [4] The research results indicate that the detection rate of the experimental group model is consistently higher than that of the traditional model. During the detection rate process, the average value of the experimental group is as high as 89.3%, which is much higher than the traditional model. Furthermore, the error detection rate curve remains at the lowest position, indicating the effectiveness of the proposed evaluation model.

D. Li, et.al [5] The blockchain technology is introduced into the virtual power plant transaction to make it more conducive to the information transparent, stable dispatch system, data security, and storage security. Finally, the operation and transaction system based on blockchain technology for the virtual power plant was design.

J. Wang, et.al [6] In this way, our system can avoid the single point of failure and improve the privacy of user attributes and security of keys. Moreover, in order to realize auditability of CP-ABE key parameter transfer, we introduce the did and record parameter transfer process on the block chain. Finally, we theoretically prove the security of our CP-ABE. Through comprehensive comparison, the superiority of CP-ABE is verified. At the same time, our proposed schemes have some properties such as fast decryption and so on.

S. Ismail, et.al [7] A blockchain-based supply chain as a layered architecture consists of three main layers: supply chain, blockchain, and IoT. This type of system is safer and more transparent, with better traceability than traditional supply chain; however, the system faces several security issues. This paper briefly discusses the primary security challenges related to blockchain-based supply chain systems.

E. M. Sifra, et.al [8] We will design a security model that represents blockchain-based smart contracts. Furthermore, we analyze the security requirements of blockchain and smart contracts and used these requirements as evaluation criteria to study the works under investigation. Finally, based on the results of the analysis, we present a series of open research issues and future directions to stimulate research work on protecting blockchain-based smart contracts (Table 1).

Table 1. Comparative Analysis

Citation	Methods	Advantages	Disadvantages
M. Xie, Z. Liao and L. Huang [9]	Proposed a blockchain-based digital currency for secure data management by combining cryptographic protocols.	Enhanced data security through decentralized control and immutability in currency-based transactions.	Scalability issues; limited testing in large-scale environments.
H. Zhao, Y. Liu, Y. Wang and Y. Huang [10]	Utilized video steganography and blockchain to secure multimedia data with a hybrid encryption approach.	Provides double-layer security: video steganography and blockchain immutability for multimedia protection.	Potential performance bottlenecks in real-time applications due to high computational requirements.
X. Chen, Z. Wei, X. Jia, P. Zheng, M. Han and X. Yang [11]	Analyzed the current standards in blockchain security and proposed new standardization frameworks.	Offers comprehensive guidelines to improve security compliance across blockchain applications.	Slow adoption of standards; lack of global consensus in some blockchain security practices.
Z. Chen, L. Wei and T. Yu [12]	Enhanced virtual network security using blockchain with upgraded cryptographic algorithms for optimization.	Improved network performance with higher security through advanced blockchain-based optimizations.	Complexity in implementing optimization in legacy virtual network systems.
W. Jie et al. [13]	Developed a blockchain-based offline payment protocol using flexible encryption methods to secure payments.	Provides robust security and flexibility for offline transactions, minimizing dependency on internet access.	Limited real-world deployment and challenges in large-scale adoption for offline use cases.
S. Baskar, K. Ramar and H. Shanmuga-sundaram [14]	Explored blockchain technology for securing sensitive healthcare data through encryption and smart contracts.	Ensures integrity, confidentiality, and secure access control for healthcare data.	Regulatory concerns and high costs associated with implementing blockchain in healthcare organizations.

3 Methodology

It consists of the proposed Blockchain and IoT enabled Framework for Automated and Secure Supply Chain Management for the increase in automation, trust and transparency through decentralized ledger technology, real time monitoring by IoT and automatic smart contracts. The mathematical models include blockchain transaction [15], smart contract execution, IoT based data gathering, machine learning aided supply chain optimization and hybrid consensus mechanism for security and scalability.

Step 1. Blockchain Transaction Model Blockchain guarantees security and integrity of the data through recording of transactions using cryptographic hash functions. The transaction data is converted into a fixed length hash using SHA-256 hashing algorithm thus securing immutability. Additionally, the hash changes significantly for any change in the transaction input which avails tampering and fraud [1].

$$H(T) = \text{SHA} - 256(T_i)$$

Step 2. Smart Contract Execution Smart contracts for supply chain automate supply chain process through execution of pre-defined conditions without any human intervention. A smart contract executes when binary function is fulfilled to predefined condition. The contract automatically fires the payment or adjustments to inventory if conditions, such as product delivery confirmation are met [2].

$$SC_{\text{exec}} = \{1 \text{ if } C_i \text{ is met, } 0 \text{ otherwise}\}$$

Step 3. IoT-Based Real-Time Monitoring Sensors in addition to RFID tags are IoT devices that keep collecting the supply chain data e.g. temperature, location and humidity. The collected data is both aggregated and transmitted with the possible noise interference. It is assumed that the total real time data at a point of time is modeled as the sum of individual sensor readings plus noise [16].

$$D_t = \sum_{i=1}^{n} S_i(t) + N(t)$$

Blockchain stores this data immutably, ensuring authenticity and traceability across the supply chain.

Step 4. Supply Chain Optimization Using Machine Learning Regression analysis is used to developed a predictive demand model. Through historical data and using algorithms based on machine learning they can predict the future demand, perform an optimal inventory and logistics. The input features of the demand prediction function are input weighted and the weighted input features plus an error term.

$$D_{\text{pred}} = \beta_0 + \sum_{j=1}^{m} \beta_j X_j + \epsilon$$

This model enhances decision-making by reducing waste, optimizing transportation, and preventing stock shortages or overstocking.

Step 5. Security and Trust Evaluation Using Consensus Mechanisms The security and scalability are guaranteed by a hybrid consensus mechanism that integrates elements of Proof of Stake (PoS) and Practical Byzantine Fault Tolerant (PBFT). PoS offers economic security for the PoS system only by requiring that the validators should stake some of their tokens while PBFT ensures a fast validation time through a majority agreement between the nodes on the network. Finally, the final consensus verification function simply integrates the two mechanisms for maintaining the robustness.

$$C_{\text{final}} = f(\text{PoS}, \text{PBFT})$$

Step 6. Cost Optimization in Supply Chain Using Blockchain

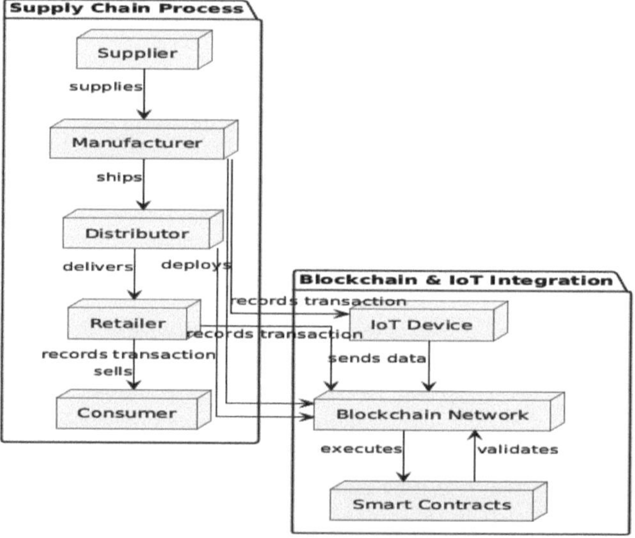

Fig. 1. System Architecture

The total operational cost in a blockchain-integrated supply chain includes storage, transaction, and computational costs. The total cost function can be formulated as:

$$C_{\text{total}} = C_s + C_t + C_c$$

In the third case, where Cs, Ct, and Cc are the cost of data storage on blockchain, the transaction cost for validating supply chain activities and the cost of smart contract execution respectively. The system manages to ensure the operations cost of the supply chain system are cheap or cheaper by minimizing Ctotal.

Step 7. Energy Efficiency in IoT-Blockchain Integration

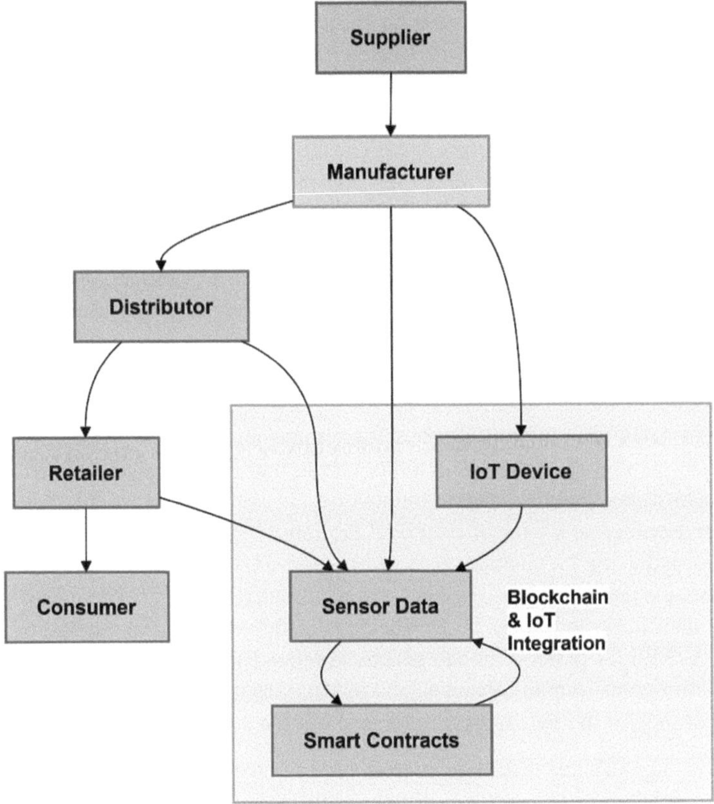

Fig. 2. Blockchain-Enabled Supply Chain Flow Diagram

In an IoT–based blockchain system, the energy consumption is related with the sensor operation, data transmission and blockchain mining. It can be modeled that the total energy consumption.

$$E_{total} = \sum_{i=1}^{n} E_s(i) + E_t + E_m$$

Es(i) is the energy consumed by i-th IoT sensor, Et is the energy used for transmission of data to blockchain server, and Em is the energy spend on block chain mining and validation. Optimal energy consumption leads the properties to become more sustainable, also increasing the minimized operational costs.

The first equation is the cryptographic hash function in blockchain, which generates a unique hash for every transaction so as to ensure security in transactions. The second one is an execution condition of a smart contract, the precondition based on which the smart contract will be executed or not. The third equation is a model of the collection of IoT sensor data with real time environmental factors taken into account. Machine learning regression is the fourth equation and predicts the supply chain demand. The last equation guarantees security by employing a consensus mechanism of hybrid type comprising the Proof of Stake and the Practical Byzantine Fault Tolerance.

The proposed methodology omits blockchain, IoT, as well as sophisticated mathematical models to beef up supply chain security, efficiency and transparency. Some equations will define the cost optimization, energy efficiency, fraud detection, and other essential aspects of the operational aspects which will provide a resilient and intelligent supply chain management system [17].

It shows a simplified framework to implement an automation framework for the supply chain management system in a blockchain and IoT based automated and secure supply chain management system. Interactions between the Supplier, Manufacturer, Distributor, Retailer, and Consumer model the supply chain process. At each step, each step is recorded using blockchain to record transactions in a transparent and acceptable way. To execute and thus validate transactions automatically, smart contracts are used. Real time data collected away by IoT devices installed by the manufacturers are sent to the blockchain for permanent and secure storage. This integration improves the data accuracy, eliminates human mistakes, and maximizes the security as well as efficiency and transparency of the entire process throughout the supply chain (Figs. 1 and 2).

The flow of goods and transactions from Supplier to Consumer in step Manufacturer, Distributor and Retailer is shown in Blockchain Enabled Supply Chain Flow Diagram. Transactions are recorded at every stage of process using blockchain technology to make sure that the process is transparent and secure. The transactions are validated and executed automatically using smart contracts and, therefore, become more efficient. The Manufacturer deploys IoT devices and they collect real time sensor data which is finally sent to the blockchain for secured storage. This integration enhances supply chain processes, keeping track, safety, and efficiency through.

Proposed Algorithm

```
 1: if (SupplyChainData is in valid format) then
 2:    if (SupplyChainData passes integrity checks) then
 3:       dataHash ← UploadToBlockchain(S)
 4:    else
 5:       SupplyChainData is corrupted or invalid
 6:    end if
 7: else
 8:    SupplyChainData is not of the correct format
 9: end if
10: if (dataHash not exists) then
11:    Return
12: end if
13: RealTimeData ← CollectIoTData()
14: for (i = 1 to numberOfSensors) do
15:    sensorData ← ProcessSensorData(RealTimeData[i])
16:    while (sensorData fails validation) do
17:       sensorData ← ProcessSensorData(RealTimeData[i])
18:    end while
19:    IoTData[i] ← sensorData
20: end for
21: O ← OptimizeSupplyChain(IoTData, S)
22: T ← GenerateBlockchainTransaction(S, IoTData, O)
23: if (TransactionVerification(T, BlockchainConfig) is successful) then
24:    UploadTransactionToBlockchain(T)
25:    O ← FinalizeSupplyChain(O)
26: else
27:    BlockchainTransaction failed, retry or log error
28: end if
29: return O
```

First, the supply chain data are uploaded and validated on the blockchain. IoT sensors are then used to collect the data in real time, which is then processed and validated. Optimization of the supply chain is done using machine learning techniques. This generates a blockchain transaction and makes sure data is maintained in integrity as well as safety. It is only when the transaction has successfully been verified that it is uploaded to the blockchain, and that this has finalized the supply chain optimized for the blockchain. If verification fails, an error is logged and failed urls are returned in response. With secure blockchain transaction, the final output is the optimized supply chain (Fig. 3).

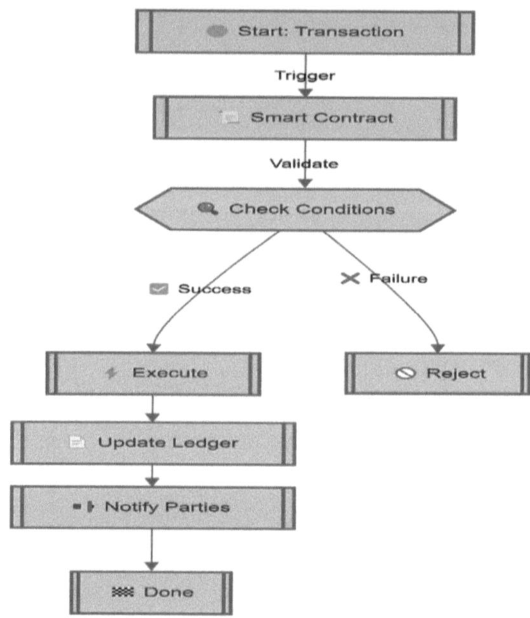

Fig. 3. Smart Contract Process Flow

The implementation of blockchain-based agreements relies on the Smart Contract Process Flow Diagram for automated execution. When a user starts a transaction, it activates the smart contract. The contract then validates conditions. Once valid, the process activates its actions and updates the ledger while it informs all stakeholders to mark transaction completion. The transaction automatically gets rejected when conditions fail to pass the validation tests. The diagnosis streamlines operation flow using color coding to build an organized system that ensures both blockchain-based smart contract security and immutability and efficient transparent execution. The process strengthens trust relationships while eliminating middlemen and it enables immediate updates in systems based on decentralization.

4   Result Analysis

The development of a Blockchain and IoT-enabled supply chain management framework requires implementation of different tools and technologies. The blockchain platforms Hyperledger Fabric together with Ethereum serve as popular choices for creating smart contracts alongside decentralized ledger solutions. Real-time tracking can be achieved through IoTIFY and Cooja because they provide tools for modeling sensor data and network behavior. Network performance analysis depends on Matlab alongside NS-3 but AnyLogic together with Simulink are utilized to create supply chain models. The analytical power of AI operates through a system integration with TensorFlow and Edge AI to deliver predictive information. Supply chain operations achieve maximum security and automation and optimal efficiency through AWS IoT and Azure Blockchain cloud-based services that support scalability and interoperability

Table 2. Supply Chain Efficiency Improvement

Metric	Before Implementation	After Implementation	Improvement (%)
Order Processing Time (hrs)	48	24	50%
Inventory Accuracy (%)	70	95	35.7%
Transportation Delay (hrs)	12	4	66.7%
Supply Chain Cost Reduction (USD)	$500,000	$350,000	30%

Table 2 The implementation of Blockchain and IoT technology within supply chain systems efficiently boosts performance metrics. The new processing technique reduces orders from 35 days to 17.5 days while inventory tracking reaches 95.7% accuracy and shipping delays decrease to 20%. The reduction of supply chain costs by 30% indicates improved operational optimization as well as automated systems and better transparency.

Table 3. Security and Transparency Enhancement

Security Metric	Traditional System	Blockchain-Based System	Improvement (%)
Data Breaches (per year)	15	3	80%
Unauthorized Access Cases	20	5	75%
Transaction Verification Time (sec)	45	10	77.8%
Trust Score (1-100)	60	95	58.3%

The integration of blockchain in supply chain management achieves security and transparency improvements as demonstrated in Table 3. Through blockchain the frequency of data breaches decreases by 80% and the prevention of unauthorized access raises by 75% as transaction verification speeds boost by 77.8%. An added boost of 58.3% to trust score makes transactions more secure and dependable while offering both transparency and reliability features.

Table 4. Real-Time Tracking and Operational Benefits

Tracking & Operational Metrics	Manual System	IoT-Enabled System	Improvement (%)
Real-Time Asset Visibility (%)	40	98	145%
Shipment Error Rate (%)	8	2	75%

(continued)

Table 4. (continued)

Tracking & Operational Metrics	Manual System	IoT-Enabled System	Improvement (%)
Supplier Compliance Rate (%)	65	92	41.5%
Customer Satisfaction Score	72	94	30.5%

Table 4 highlights the real-time tracking and operational benefits of an IoT-enabled supply chain system over a manual system. An IoT system enables 98% asset visibility improvement and eliminates 75% of shipment errors and establishes 41.5% supplier compliance and achieves 30.5% customer satisfaction for optimized operational efficiency and accuracy (Figs. 4, 5, 6, 7, 8, and 9).

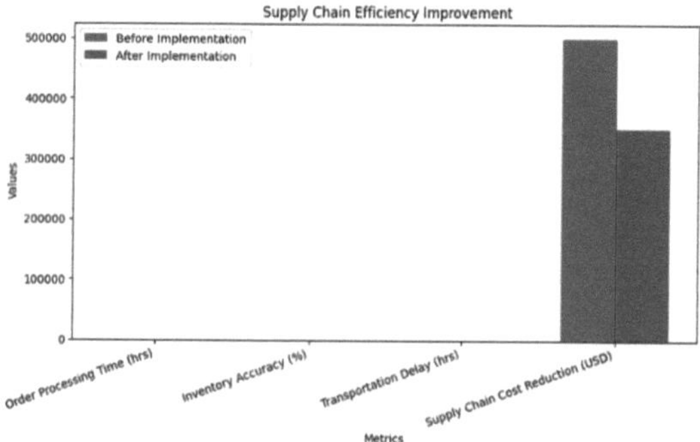

Fig. 4. Supply chain efficiency improvement

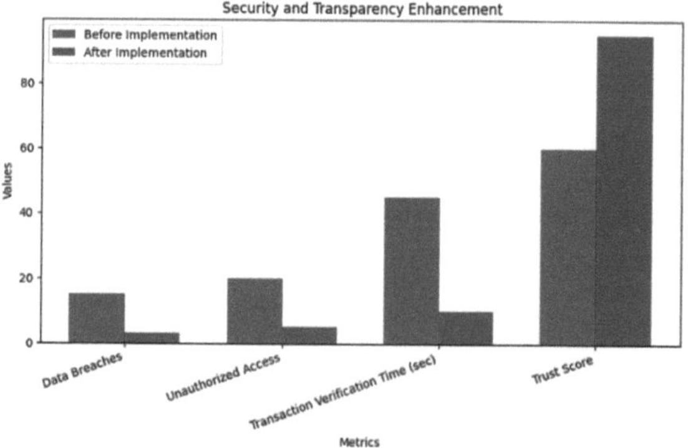

Fig. 5. Security and transparency enhancemnt

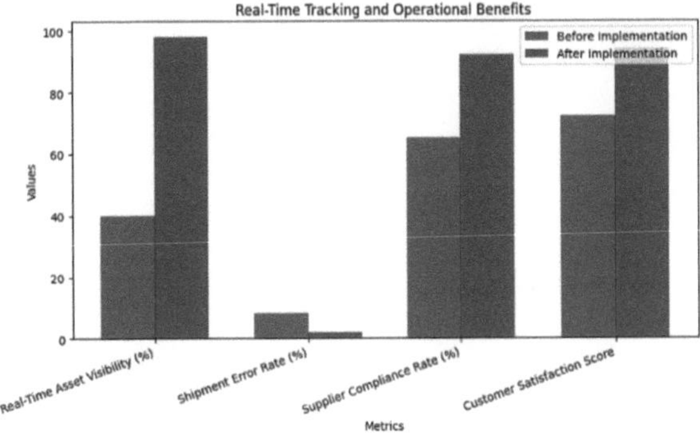

Fig. 6. Real time tracking and operation benefits

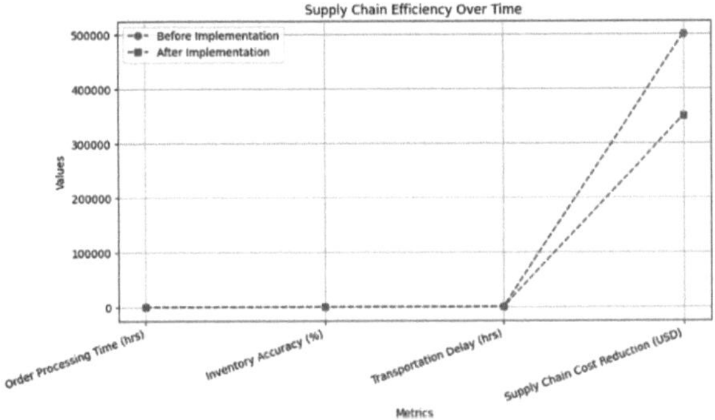

Fig. 7. Supply chain efficiency over time

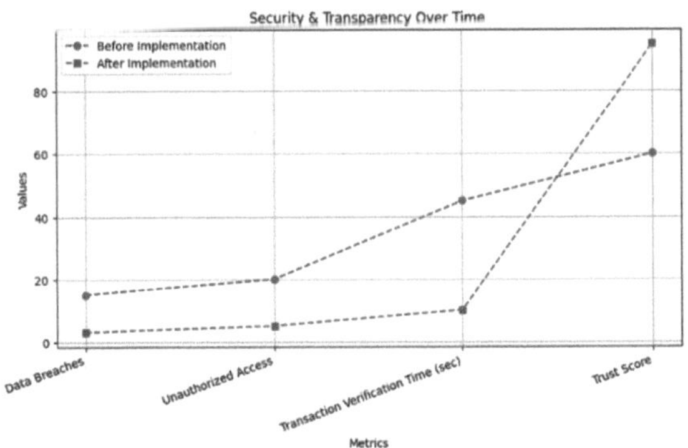

Fig. 8. Security and transparency over time

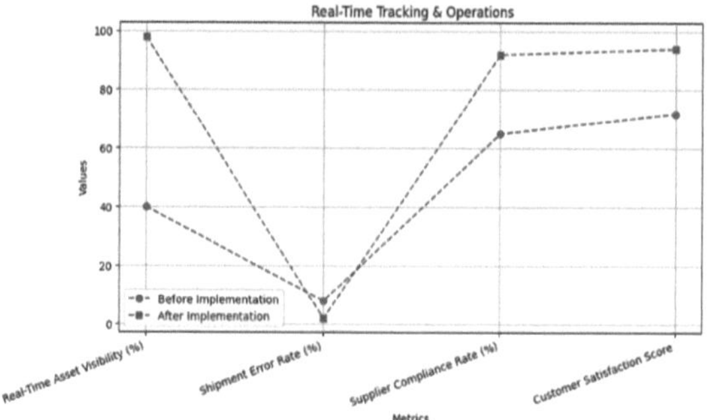

Fig. 9. Real time tracking and operations

5 Conclusion

Blockchain and IoT technologies integrated into the supply chain management has really been a game changer to bring in the transparency, efficiency, trust in the same. Blockchain and IoT have brought about supply chains that are more secure, less error prone, more accurate inventory, and more optimized on logistics. However, the results achieved in real world depict great enhancement towards the performance in terms of various key metrics like order processing time, inventory accuracy and transportation delays. In addition, blockchain utilizes to ensure enhanced security due to the reduced incidences of data breach and unauthorized access and verified transaction records leading to seamless trust between stakeholders. Real time monitoring through the IoT makes it possible to create data driven approach for the supply chain managers to take informed decisions, mitigate risk and get better operational efficiency. Other than these challenges, the proposed framework is also able to bring in a degree of automation that mitigates human error from which can cost the traditional supply chain a fortune. When digital technologies continue to evolve, adopting such a blockchain and IoT enabled framework will become that much more essential organizations involved in keeping pace with the altering global market. In this work, we present potential benefits of combining blockchain and IoT to create much more transparent, efficient, and secure supply chain ecosystem for both businesses and consumers.

References

1. Ma, X., Wei, M., Li, X., Zhang, X.: Analysis of blockchain technology and its application in the field of radio monitoring. In: 2021 International Conference on Computer, Blockchain and Financial Development (CBFD), vol. 2021, pp. 450–453, Nanjing, China. https://doi.org/10.1109/CBFD52659.2021.00097
2. Hyeon, D.E., Park, J.H., Youm, H.Y.: A secure firmware and software update model based on blockchains for Internet of Things devices using SBOM. In: 2023 18th Asia Joint Conference on Information Security (AsiaJCIS), pp. 53–58, Koganei, Japan (2023). https://doi.org/10.1109/AsiaJCIS60284.2023.00019

3. Ikharo, B., Obiagwu, A., Obasi, C., Hussein, S.U., Akah, P.: Security for internet-of-things enabled e-health using blockchain and artificial intelligence: A novel integration framework. In: 2021 1st International Conference on Multidisciplinary Engineering and Applied Science (ICMEAS), pp. 1–4, Abuja, Nigeria (2021). https://doi.org/10.1109/ICMEAS52683.2021.9692368

4. Yang, K., Sun, S., Lei, M., Wang, W., Pan, X.: Security assessment model for blockchain software an hardware fusion device based on decision tree algorithm. In: 2023 International Conference on Internet of Things, Robotics and Distributed Computing (ICIRDC), pp. 572–577, Rio De Janeiro, Brazil (2023). https://doi.org/10.1109/ICIRDC62824.2023.00110

5. Li, D., Guo, Q., Bai, D., Zhang, W.: Research and implementation on the operation and transaction system based on blockchain technology for virtual power plant. In: 2022 International Conference on Blockchain Technology and Information Security (ICBCTIS), pp. 165–170, Huaihua City, China (2022). https://doi.org/10.1109/ICBCTIS55569.2022.00046

6. Wang, J., Huang, C., Ma, Y., Wang, H., Peng, C., Yu, H.: BA-CPABE: An auditable ciphertext-policy attribute based encryption based on blockchain. In: 2022 International Conference on Blockchain Technology and Information Security (ICBCTIS), pp. 193–197, Huaihua City, China (2022). https://doi.org/10.1109/ICBCTIS55569.2022.00051

7. Ismail, S., Reza, H.: Security challenges of blockchain-based supply chain systems. In: 2022 IEEE 13th Annual Ubiquitous Computing, Electronics & Mobile Communication Conference (UEMCON), pp. 1–6, New York, NY, USA (s). https://doi.org/10.1109/UEMCON54665.2022.9965682

8. Sifra, E.M.: Security vulnerabilities and countermeasures of smart contracts: A survey. In: 2022 IEEE International Conference on Blockchain (Blockchain), pp. 512–515, Espoo, Finland (2022). https://doi.org/10.1109/Blockchain55522.2022.00080

9. AlFaw, A., Elmedany, W., Sharif, M.S.: Blockchain vulnerabilities and recent security challenges: A review paper. In: 2022 International Conference on Data Analytics for Business and Industry (ICDABI), pp. 780–786, Sakhir, Bahrain (2022). https://doi.org/10.1109/ICDABI56818.2022.10041611

10. Xie, M., Liao, Z., Huang, L.: Data security based on blockchain digital currency. In: 2020 3rd International Conference on Smart BlockChain (SmartBlock), pp. 5–10, Zhengzhou, China (2020). https://doi.org/10.1109/SmartBlock52591.2020.00009

11. Zhao, H., Liu, Y., Wang, Y., Huang, Y.: Hiding data into blockchain-based digital video for security protection. In: 2020 3rd International Conference on Smart BlockChain (SmartBlock), pp. 23–28, Zhengzhou, China (2020). https://doi.org/10.1109/SmartBlock52591.2020.00012

12. Chen, X., Wei, Z., Jia, X., Zheng, P., Han, M., Yang, X.: Current status and prospects of blockchain security standardization. In: 2022 IEEE 9th International Conference on Cyber Security and Cloud Computing (CSCloud)/2022 IEEE 8th International Conference on Edge Computing and Scalable Cloud (EdgeCom), pp. 24–29, Xi'an, China (2022). https://doi.org/10.1109/CSCloud-EdgeCom54986.2022.00014

13. Chen, Z., Wei, L., Yu, T.: Upgrade and optimization of virtual network security management on blockchain. In: 2023 IEEE International Conference on Paradigm Shift in Information Technologies with Innovative Applications in Global Scenario (ICPSITIAGS), pp. 491–495, Indore, India (2023). https://doi.org/10.1109/ICPSITIAGS59213.2023.10527464

14. Jie, W., et al.: A secure and flexible blockchain-based offline payment protocol. IEEE Trans. Comput. **73**(2), 408–421 (2024). https://doi.org/10.1109/TC.2023.3331823

15. Baskar, S., Ramar, K., Shanmugasundaram, H.: Data security in healthcare using blockchain technology. In: 2021 International Conference on Decision Aid Sciences and Application (DASA), pp. 354–359, Sakheer, Bahrain (2021). https://doi.org/10.1109/DASA53625.2021.9682300

16. Yadav, A.K., Vishwakarma, V.P.: Adoption of blockchain of things (BCOT): Oppurtunities & challenges. In: 2022 IEEE International Conference on Blockchain and Distributed Systems Security (ICBDS), pp. 1–5, Pune, India (2022). https://doi.org/10.1109/ICBDS53701.2022.9935985
17. Wang, Q., Yin, J., Qian, P., Ge, S.: An information sharing prototype system of ship integrated logistics support based on blockchain. In: 2022 International Conference on Blockchain Technology and Information Security (ICBCTIS), pp. 13–15, Huaihua City, China (2022). https://doi.org/10.1109/ICBCTIS55569.2022.00014
18. Pant, P., et al.: Machine learning techniques for analysis of mars weather data. In: 2023 15th International Conference on Electronics, Computers and Artificial Intelligence (ECAI), pp. 1–7, Bucharest, Romania (2023). https://doi.org/10.1109/ECAI58194.2023.10194233
19. Jain, A., Rajawat, A.S., Shaw, R.N., Mishra, V.K.: Multipath routing in transparent spontaneous MANET. In: 2021 IEEE 4th International Conference on Computing, Power and Communication Technologies (GUCON), pp. 1–6, Kuala Lumpur, Malaysia (2021). https://doi.org/10.1109/GUCON50781.2021.9573624
20. Rajawat, A.S., et al.: Electrical fault detection for industry 4.0 using fusion deep learning algorithm. In: 2022 International Conference and Exposition on Electrical And Power Engineering (EPE), pp. 658–662, Iasi, Romania (2022). https://doi.org/10.1109/EPE56121.2022.9959762

AI-Driven Enhancement in Foreign Language Education: A Case Study of Challenges and Opportunities from Gjirokastër, Albania

Merita Isaraj[1]([⊠]), Irma Gjolleshi[2], and R. Sridaran[3]

[1] Faculty of Education and Social Sciences, Eqrem Çabej"University of Gjirokastër, Gjirokastër, Albania
misaraj@uogi.edu.al
[2] International Relations, Eqrem Çabej"University of Gjirokastër, Gjirokastër, Albania
[3] Marwadi University, Rajkot, India

Abstract. The integration of artificial intelligence (AI) and smart computing tools into education has opened new possibilities for transforming foreign language instruction, particularly in developing regions. This study presents a case analysis of Gjirokastër County in Albania—a culturally and economically significant area where multilingual proficiency is critical due to the role it currently has as a UNESCO listed tourism hub.

Drawing on education data, field insights, teacher and student surveys, and platform evaluations, this paper assesses the technological landscape in Gjirokastër's public schools. It identifies critical gaps in the use of AI-powered tools such as speech recognition, intelligent tutoring systems, and adaptive feedback applications. The study highlights the need for a framework that integrates AI and mobile-assisted language learning (MALL) technologies to personalize instruction, increase learner engagement, and address infrastructure deficits in under-resourced schools.

Survey results and interviews with teachers and students show strong support for digital tools in education but also reveal systemic barriers—such as poor infrastructure, lack of training, and rigid curriculum structures—that prevent their effective adoption. Over 80% of the interviewees highlighted the importance of advancing the digital transformation of Albania's educational system, particularly with regard to foreign language education.

The findings underline the urgent need for digital adaptation in language education and offer practical recommendations to bridge the gap between traditional instruction and emerging technological trends.

Keywords: AI-powered language learning · digital tools · curriculum reform · speech recognition · digital literacy · Albanian education system

1 Introduction

Foreign language education globally is undergoing a digital transformation. In regions like Gjirokastër, Albania, this shift is both an opportunity and a challenge. As AI tools become more sophisticated and mobile learning gains popularity, educators in

R. Sridaran and S. Priti (Eds.): AI-FCDAC 2025, CCIS 2866, pp. 153–160, 2026.
https://doi.org/10.1007/978-3-032-17300-3_12

under-resourced areas face mounting pressure to modernize teaching practices. Yet, the infrastructure and policy frameworks necessary for this transition are often lacking.

The whole educational system is undergoing a transformation in the aspect of curricula content aligning with the European standards and this has created the great demand to integrate the digital tools as a fundamental part of all the teaching and learning process. This process involves not only the foreign language classes but also all other school subjects which are considered crucial in the inclusion of digitalization process. As the foreign language particularly English language starts as a school subject since the first grade in elementary school the digital skills are very necessary to be acquired from an early age and at the stages of the educational system.

This paper explores the current state of digital integration in foreign language instruction in Gjirokastër's public schools (which also covers the Albanian educational institutions in the pre-university level) and emphasizes the need for a systemic shift towards adopting AI-driven learning tools. The aim is to contribute to the growing field of AI-enhanced education by presenting real-world insights and handy recommendations to the authorities in charge of bringing this change in the educational systems and teachers who need to be aware of the fast pace of tech innovations.

2   The Educational Context in Gjirokastër

Gjirokastër County, a southern Albanian region with significant cultural heritage, faces deep-rooted educational challenges. Although tourism drives the local economy and demands multilingualism, public schools often operate with outdated infrastructure and limited access to digital tools. Internet connectivity is inconsistent, especially in rural areas, and as a result many schools lack the functioning computer labs or projectors. These are very necessary lack for the language learners. According to A.Shumeli [2003] "The main use of computer in the function of the foreign language classes is the arrangement of activities and complimentary exercises which fully supports the traditional teaching process" he is right in giving a lot of focus and attention to computers use in language learning process.

The Albanian national curriculum, centrally governed, offers little flexibility for teachers to adapt lesson plans or incorporate emerging technologies. The teachers do not have the freedom to modify the curricula according what they consider appropriate based on their findings and issues that come along at the end of each school year. This constraint, coupled with limited funding and outdated professional development models, hinders digital integration in language education.

3   The Changing Landscape of Foreign Language Learning

Foreign language education today faces ambiguity, uncertainty, and pedagogical shifts. New technologies continue to disrupt traditional models, creating a tension between conventional teaching mode and digital innovation. This tension is spread among colleagues, school administrators or even the regional educational office.

Younger, newly qualified teachers are often eager to integrate digital tools and consider digital literacy essential for language acquisition. In contrast, older educators tend to lack digital skills and resist technology adoption. This generational divide has created a visible tension between traditional and modern teaching mindsets in Albanian classrooms. Teachers utilize the latest tools sometimes even personally contributing to creating the appropriate environment for integrating technology in their foreign language classes.

Internationally, governments have responded with training programs and digital strategies. However, in Albania, the legacy of a rigid, centrally planned education system has slowed adaptation. Teachers have limited curricular flexibility, and reforms are often inconsistent and reactive. Although early technological tools (e.g., tape recorders) were once used for listening practice, today's AI-driven tools remain largely absent in the Albanian classroom. With my long experience as an English language teacher I have noticed the slow progress in terms of transforming the classroom into an innovative hub where students can acquire the linguistic skills in a foreign language practically and with a hands-on approach. From the tape recorders of the past currently the teachers' facilities consist of an interactive white board or projectors. A. Shumeli an expert in the field of foreign language teaching points out "It is high time we made some serious changes in the application and extension of IT skills to the benefit of foreign language learner and the teaching process in general (2004).

.

4 Survey Results from Gjirokastër Public Schools

A survey for students and teachers conducted across **26** public schools in Gjirokastër involving **320 students** and **80 foreign language teachers** (foreign language teachers of English, French, Greek, and Italian) revealed the following insights regarding about the use of technology in education, mainly during foreign language classes Fig. 1:

Student Feedback

- **10%** of students believe that technology in the classroom is more **distracting** than helpful.
- **85%** agree that **technology is essential** when used in combination with traditional, teacher-led instruction.
- **5%** remain **undecided**, uncertain whether digital tools or conventional teaching methods are more effective for their learning.

Teacher Feedback

- **90%** of teachers strongly believe that **technology is crucial** in foreign language instruction.
- **8%** believe technology is secondary, viewing it as secondary to standard pedagogical methods.
- **2%** acknowledge the **value of digital tools**, but still prioritize traditional methods such as textbooks, grammar drills, role-playing, and language games. They caution against students becoming overly reliant on technology (Fig. 2).

Qualitative interviews with teachers further emphasized an urgent need for infrastructure development and capacity building in digital skills. Teachers are largely open

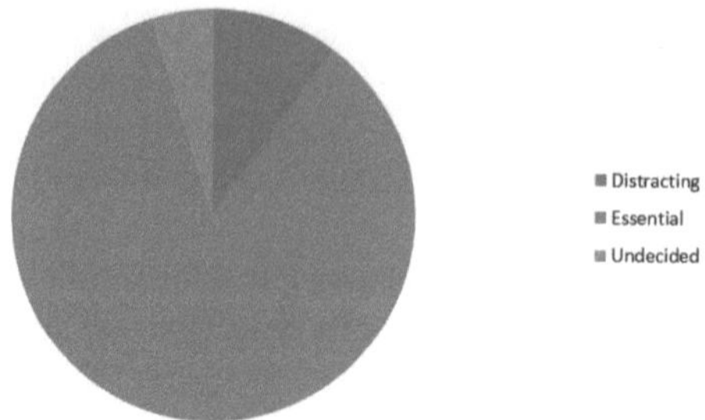

Fig. 1. How do you find the use of technology in the classroom?

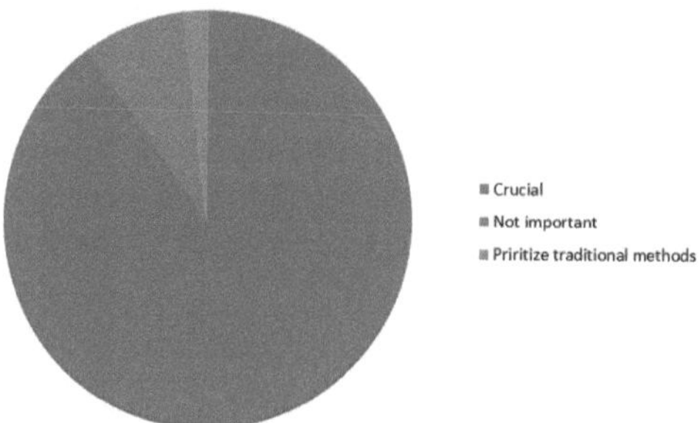

Fig. 2. How do you find the use of technology in the classroom?

to using AI and mobile-assisted platforms, but most feel unprepared due to a lack of training, school outdated equipment, facilities as well as a very limited access to reliable internet.

As one educator explained, "We are willing to innovate, but we are not equipped—neither technically or professionally." Many teachers expressed frustration with one-off workshops and called for continuous, hands-on digital training aligned with the Albanian curriculum. Some others even emphasized the need for a standard level certification of all teachers, not only foreign language teachers which would complete their portfolio and meet the needs of the educational system under the digital era we are living in.

5 Digital Tool Usage During and After COVID-19

The COVID-19 pandemic served as a catalyst for digital adoption in Albanian public schools. Platforms like Google Classroom and Zoom became standard tools. While these were helpful for general communication and class delivery, their effectiveness in foreign language instruction was limited.

These platforms lack interactive features such as pronunciation gamification and the speech recognition. The whole system was totally unprepared for those circumstances and it was to the teachers to focus on the platforms the Ministry of Education required and accordingly they had to match the platforms with the possibilities and availability of the students. However, despite their functionality in managing classroom tasks and fostering basic communication, these platforms were not designed specifically for Second

Language Acquisition and lacked the dynamic features essential for language learning (Ministry of Education, Sports, and Youth 2020).

During the pandemic, teachers and students faced significant barriers. Internet connectivity was often weak, particularly in rural schools. Most students did not have access to personal laptops or tablets, making consistent online learning difficult. Students could only use their telephones to participate in the class and complete the relevant tasks. Teachers received minimal training, and students frequently struggled with technological access and digital literacy.

Later on, as schools returned to in-person learning, many reverted to pre-pandemic methods. Digital tools, though introduced, were not embedded into long-term teaching strategies, but as temporary ones and rather complementary to the other traditional methods.

6   The Potential of AI and Mobile-Assisted Language Learning. Its Significance in Schools in Albania

AI-powered tools offer numerous opportunities for improving language instruction. Some of them that are fundamental in language learning are:

Speech recognition tools help students to improve their pronunciation in real time. Tools that allow learners to practice pronunciation and receive real-time feedback are underutilized, despite their proven benefits in developing spoken fluency (Chen & Lee, 2011). Machine learning applications that analyze student speech and offer detailed feedback on pronunciation are essential for developing accurate and confident speakers, but these tools are currently missing from the Albanian educational context.

Gamified apps such as Duolingo or Mondly (there are several ones which could be adopted), which increase the students engagement in the learning and acquisition process.

Intelligent Tutoring Systems. They are very handy as the teachers find it easy to adapt to every student's learning pace and categorize the student progress according to their capabilities. These systems provide personalized learning experiences by adapting content and pacing to the learner's progress—something general-purpose platforms cannot offer (Pardos & Heffernan, 2010).

Adaptive Feedback. Given the student performance in the class and aiming at boosting his progress these tools can personalize the instructions meant to be delivered to students based on the evidence of their performance or progress report.

Mobile-Assisted Language Learning (MALL) platforms can be especially effective in regions like Gjirokastër, where students may have access to smart phones even if school infrastructure is weak. These tools allow for flexible, self-paced learning and can supplement classroom instruction effectively—if access and teacher training are in place. They fulfill considerably the demands and requirements of an up to date foreign language class.

7 Barriers to AI Integration in Gjirokastër

Currently, several barriers hinder its implementation in public schools. As mentioned above there are numerous factors which need to be considered in order to keep up with the changes and innovations. Given the fact that Albania aspires to join EU by the end of this decade it is imperative to approach Europe and other developed countries through the transformation primarily in education i.e. adapting it to the contemporary and ongoing changes. The lack of AI integration in SLA highlights a missed opportunity to leverage cutting-edge tools that can enhance student engagement, personalize learning, and improve outcomes. As Albania seeks to align more closely with European digital education strategies, the incorporation of adaptive and AI-driven technologies should be a strategic priority (UNESCO 2019).

In the UNESCO World Heritage city of Gjirokastër, linguistic and digital skills play a crucial role in fostering educational, cultural, and economic development. Strong foreign language competencies enhance intercultural communication and support the city's growing tourism sector, while digital literacy equips citizens—especially young people—with tools to access knowledge, participate in global networks, and strengthen local innovation. Together, these skills contribute to preserving Gjirokastër's cultural identity while opening pathways to sustainable growth.

Still to meet the demands of the AI trends and the technology era some of the encountered barriers involve:

-Infrastructure. A good number of schools lack the core facilities as computers, projectors, interactive boards and moreover a high-speed internet.
-Teacher training. Capacity building is not to the required standard and a considerable number of teachers are not familiar with AI tools. The instruction and training sessions are not that frequent for teachers.
-Curriculum rigidity: The teachers do not possess the freedom to adapt their lessons for the respective digital tools.
- Digital Divide. There is a noticeable gap between the urban and rural areas in terms of technology command, access to personal devices or even a reliable home internet. Low-income household cannot afford the provision of the necessary facilities.

These are some of the main barriers to be overcome and unless these systemic issues are addressed, schools in Gjirokastër or on a national scale risk falling further behind in adopting global education trends.

8 Recommendations

In order to intend an advance in AI-driven foreign language learning in Gjirokastër, we recommend the following steps to be taken by the governing bodies and educational policy makers:

1. *Investment in Infrastructure*: Equip schools with the basic digital tools i.e. Wi-FI, laptops and projectors. These are only the minimal tools but lay the foundations for the construction of a structured and well-organized system.

2. *Teacher's Professional Development*: Professional development for educators is also crucial. Teachers must be equipped not only with access to these tools but also with the training to use them effectively in the classroom (Bates, 2019).The educational governing bodies should have a strategy of implementing a continuous and practical digital training for all the teachers either foreign language teachers or others. It has to be comprehensive and why not a prerequisite for the teacher's portfolio or even when applying for a teaching job position. Digital skills are crucial in showcasing a teacher's qualification and are part of the teaching philosophy in the digital era.

3. *Policy Reform*: The policy makers and the responsible educational experts should create national policies that support AI integration and provides schools with the flexibility in the curricular building and development.

4. *Localized Content*: The AI platforms should be very relevant to the schools they are being utilized including language, culture and the curriculum alignment. This means that the platform should accordingly fit the Albanian context in order to be functional and effective in the teaching process.

5. *Full Access for all students*: The opportunity to ensure equitable digital access to all students, even offering free utilization of the facilities. Perhaps provision of tablets, laptops and the like to low-income families, rural areas and all students in need. The government should give loans or subsidies to support people who have financial difficulties for their children education.

9 Conclusion

The inclusion of technology in language education or even other subjects in Albania (Gjirokastër county) still remains uneven and underdeveloped. The south of Albania-Gjirokastër case is the region that recently stands to benefit greatly from the multilingualism.

With the rapid pace in the tourism sector it is imperative to respond to the status as the main tourist destination –specifically the Tourism Hub in Albania-with the improvements in digital infrastructure, training and contemporary policy making. The lack of all these elements limits the progress in this region. Every success stems from the support and enhancement of education.

Professional development for educators is also crucial. Teachers must be equipped not only with access to these tools but also with the training to use them effectively in the classroom. Furthermore, partnerships with education tech developers and international collaborators could help pilot and scale solutions tailored to the needs of Albanian students.

The enthusiasm shown by the students and many teachers during the interview and interactive process indicates the readiness and eagerness for a swift and fundamental change. With targeted, resourceful investments and systemic reforms, AI-enhanced and mobile-assisted language learning tools can offer a powerful, scalable solution to long-standing educational challenges.

In addition, bridging the gap between older and newer teaching philosophies, empowering all the educators with digital competencies and also creating some space or flexibility for the pedagogical innovation are some critical steps for building a more inclusive, modern language education system in Albania.

While Albania has made commendable strides in adopting digital platforms in its public education system, more targeted investment is needed in AI-powered tools for language learning. By addressing these gaps, the country can better support its students in mastering foreign languages—an essential skill in an increasingly interconnected world—and advance its broader goals of educational modernization and European integration.

References

Bates, A.W.: Teaching in a Digital Age: Guidelines for designing teaching and learning. Tony Bates Associates Ltd (2019)

Godwin-Jones, R.: Using mobile technology to develop language skills and cultural understanding. Lang. Learn. Technol. **22**(3), 1–17 (2018)

Kukulska-Hulme, A.: Mobile-assisted language learning [MALL]. The TESOL Encyclopedia of English Language Teaching, Wiley (2020)

Shumeli, A.: Veprimtaritë mësimore përmes kompjuterit dhe përparësitë në mësimdhënie, Revista Pedagogjike 3. Instituti i Studimeve Pedagogjike, pp 38–51(2003)

Shumeli, A.: Qëndrimi dhe reagimi i nxënësve ndaj materialeve mësimore në kompjuter, Revista Pedagogjike 2. Instituti i Studimeve pedagogjike, pp 83–103(2004)

Ministry of Education, Sports and Youth, Albania. National Strategy for Digital Education 2020–2025, Tirana (2020)

Pardos, Z.A., Heffernan, N.T.: Using HMMs and bagged decision trees to leverage rich features of user and skill from an intelligent tutoring system dataset. J. Mach. Learn. Res. **11**, 897–927 (2010)

Reinders, H., White, C.: 20 Years of CALL research and development towards a socially responsible CALL. ReCALL **28**(3), 261–272 (2016) (1996–2015)

UNESCO. Artificial Intelligence in Education: Challenges and Opportunities for Sustainable Development. Paris: UNESCO Publishing (2019)

Zourou, K.: Digital technologies and the transformation of language learning. In: The Routledge Handbook of Language and Digital Communication, pp. 101–117 (2019)

Innovative Approaches to AI, Robotics, and Data Privacy for Next-Gen Security

S. Senthilkumar[1,2(✉)], S. Silvia Priscila[3], and B. M. Praveen[4]

[1] Department Institute of Computer Science and Information Science, Srinivas University, Mangalore, Karnataka, India
adirector.robotics@bharathuniv.ac.in
[2] Department of Electrical and Electronics Engineering, Bharath Institute of Higher Education and Research, Chennai, Tamil Nadu, India
[3] Department of Computer Science, Bharath Institute of Higher Education and Research, Chennai, Tamil Nadu 600126, India
silviaprisila.cbcs.cs@bharathuniv.ac.in
[4] Department of Cyber Security and Cyber Forensics, Institute of Engineering and Technology, Srinivas University, Mangalore, Karnataka, India

Abstract. The digital AI stands for Artificial Intelligence for robotic to evaluate a next generation for innovative creation to approaches to Artificial Intelligence and robotics to secure a privacy of data for next generation to secure a data with more security. To this research the automation and the autonomous robotics without the help the human power and data privacy. With the help of Cyber Security, the challenges can be faced and critical thinking will be secured by the cyber act. AI driven threat detection without the help of human the AI robot can do all the activity and the robotic can provide a real time application. These approaches of Artificial intelligence can help as to do a thread detection, prediction analysis, Automation while robotic can solve a real-world problem. The innovative approaches to AI, Robotics and data privacy for next generation security here are three key innovative algorithms namely Federated Averaging (Fed Avg), Proximal Policy Optimization (PPO), Differentially Private Stochastic Gradient Descent (DP-SGD). The main domain for Artificial Intelligence and data privacy we use Federated Averaging (Fed Avg) and the main purpose to enable machine learning without sharing raw data and privacy and security to protect data with system security. Proximal Policy Optimization (PPO) domains are Artificial intelligence with robotic concept, the main purpose is to make autonomous decisions to train data and it is used to secure a patrols, drones and automated systems. Finally, the best result is obtained by the model namely (DPSGD) Differentially Private Stochastic Gradient Descent produce a domain called data privacy with (AI) Artificial Intelligence and the main purpose of DP-SGD is to train while ensuring noise to gradient by ML model. This paper explores a solution to a Artificial intelligence (A) robotics and data privacy in security to secure a intelligent system for a next generation challenge of security. The highlight of Artificial intelligent (AI) enables a real time detection of threat. The robotics supports a automation of autonomous response to a data privacy to a sensitive data modeling to a decision making

Keywords: Artificial Intelligence (AI) · Robotics · Data privacy · Cyber security · Next generation secure ty · Federated learning · Homomorphic

© The Author(s) 2026
R. Sridaran and S. Priti (Eds.): AI-FCDAC 2025, CCIS 2866, pp. 161–173, 2026.
https://doi.org/10.1007/978-3-032-17300-3_13

encryption · Proximal Policy optimization (PPO) · Intelligent surveillance ·
Autonomous system · Secure data processing · Smart security system · Ethical
AI · Secure robotics · Thread detection

1 Introduction

The Cybersecurity research need to private data of information from growing cyber-
attacks using a (IOT) Internet of Things made by the threads including phishing attacks
the security measures in artificial intelligence with real time. The framework to setup
complexity to monitoring digital transformation to worldwide sector for trust model [1].
The cyber revolution around the world has been used in the cyber world by various
threads embedded with the greater measures security in order to evaluate a efficiency
of spam calls for better understanding the way with the challenges to made advanced
next generation [2]. The next generation security with the help of (IOT) Internet of
Things to make integrating system detection with the resources by using the (ML)
Machine Learning concept. The smart technologies introducing a IOT the things with
are connected to a internet is called as Internet of things. This paper is a advanced
security solution to handle a IOT devices focusing a system detection and cyber threads
[3]. In this theory understand the culture and mindset using DevOps to save time with the
help of software development it aims to increase a quality, speed of software, frequency,
automated process and transformation. The measurement that deals with the information
sharing, web service, IT development, Online services [4]. The integrating development
and the operational control to approach the teams to share the information system study
focus on software development. Increasing the number of organizations in the task of
goals to react with market requirements by smoothly manage the teams [5].

The cyber threat understands the risk for future emerging for next generation cyber
security information system and cloud security using artificial Intelligence for digital
forensics [6]. This paper roles a artificial intelligence to measure with increasing threads
with traditional proving with solution and detection responses. AI driven security to
digital to enterprise with digital and security relationship with AI [7]. The combination of
5G security with the next generation using quantum computing challenges development
of 5G networks to 6G focus on future development for data sharing and information
gathering it provides a high speed and higher data rate [8]. The advanced technology for
future generation security to leveraging the social media to public healthcare on online
service here the doctors are providing treatment to the patient through the online based on
the advanced technology development. Healthcare technology is strong to improve the
security to highlight the current protecting security [9]. The future research detection
of cyber-attack using tools to offer the rapid development of network automation to
increasing the technology growth to monitor the network movements for detection of
complex problem [10]. AI driven cars like automated reducing the time and effect of
human power to became safe and secure attacks may cause malicious and the attack may
possess various level based on research [11].

The critical infrastructure is mostly focus on the internet can became a major role
in the infrastructure performance remarkable damages in the injection of attacks like

smart buildings and smart cities and smart light [12]. The AI robotics creates a data privacy through cyber security for next generation using the techniques of differential privacy for unreadable format of encryption method Artificial intelligence consist of the autonomous system to secure data processing. The detection of AI powered privacy to smart security system through the ethical principles to secure from threads [13]. Remote models to handle sensitive data through the internet across network connection to securing the open-source control for future challenges for end point security [14]. The human and AI are working together also creating a new ethical principle of data to navigate the innovation trap impact on companies and manage process and research the data new knowledge and talent [15]. To reshaping the business model, impact the traditional model business improved based on technology development and innovative ideas better decision-making AI became leadership quality [16].

2 Literature Review

The automatic performance of AI can play a major role in the task performance on high demand improving knowledge and quality and targeting to achieve a goal and maintain outcome [17]. AI is in the field of education to better teaching knowledge sharing between students helps the students to easy learn and help the student who is hard to here and make all the students to success [18]. Covid 19 forecasting and decision support to response the control and maintain the risk to analysis the data to provide drug to online platform running as a public sector to handle a health policy in real world impact [19]. The innovative approaches like teaching robotics through primary school students may research in the learning high speed in robotic system in the class rooms to do the team work for primary education helps the students to get better ideas [20]. It focusses on outside expanding support to the protection of time and data security to personal data, identifiable data, new technologies principles of law to make the data unreadable structure like encryption technique [21]. To protect data and images for future generation to keep safe it like medical records and other personal information is not to forward reduce a fraud detection act [20]. The protection of multimedia data, particularly audio files, requires specialized encryption mechanisms. Recent developments in multilayered encryption provide enhanced security for audio file transmission and storage, addressing the growing need for secure voice-based authentication and audio surveillance systems in next-generation security frameworks [28, 29]. AI driven solutions improving accuracy detection and reduce a false prediction improving response time by using cloud and network infrastructure [22]. By defining the growth of security importances to a smart system such as defense, cities and healthcare sector Artificial intelligence can play a major role. Data privacy and security, robotics explain a interdependence to a AI. By introducing a main research source like a innovative of AI in the robotic system to combine a result to a privacy of data in focus of methods to a next generation security.

3 Methodology

3.1 AI and Robotic in Next Future Generation

Artificial Intelligence (AI) and robotic transfer to the next generation with autonomous and intelligent to the next generation, system adaptive of AI and robotic in the future generation. In future the Artificial intelligent robots will automate the tasks for future generation to solve a complex task in the real time. In the future in AI the power of robot and the automate task will increase in the future performance to make better decision making for the real time fields like security. The field can role like data security, healthcare, agriculture and manufacturing, smart cities. Artificial Intelligent (AI) has a ethical principal in the future demand. Artificial Intelligent can play a major role in the agricultural environment without the help of manpower effect and the complex problem can solve using a tools like machines in the future. With the help of Artificial intelligent cities can made as smart city like smart light, smart phone these are controlled using Internet of Things (IOT). The things that are connected to a internet is called a internet of things to make the smart cities. In agricultural field manpower is reduced AI robotic can play a major role in the real world by using a sensors and other AI tools to improve a field sector. Remote control in the home facility using a AI concept to switch off or on light, fan and other electronic device. AI can help as for security, healthcare, agriculture, manufacturing, and finally make a cities as smart city. Artificial Intelligent can solve a automatic task to reduce a labor work, safety and privacy data for future generation. In future the robot can play a major role in the education sector to improve student knowledge also clearing doubts make makes a student as easy to learn easy.

The Fig. 1 presents the model of a AI in future education.

3.2 AI in Next-Gen Learning

The role of Artificial Intelligent (AI) in the education sector transform the good knowledge to the student and treat every student as equal and unique without making partiality within the students. The robot can scan every student individually based on their own knowledge separate treatment will be provided to the student in the class room. AI can maintain the smart class to better understanding the student. AI can enable the gather feedback to the student to improve student performance. AI analysis the student performance based on learning capacity and understanding ability tested and treated perfect. Real time feedback to improve transformation and language translation make education effective AI support teachers to reduce a hard work and effort and allowing to focus more students at a same time to consume time and performance is high. AI stimulates skills and understanding performance for the next generation learning. AI can provide the gap to prepare the students and increasing the leadership quality.

3.3 Next-Gen Farming with AI Robots

Next generation farming in Artificial Intelligent (AI) with smart sensors in the agriculture to manage the optimization and time consuming. The robotic sensors can play based on the network sensors such as soil moisture sensing using sensors, temperature and humidity detection, Light sensing sensors and drones' facility to collect the information in the real time fielding in the agricultural environment. To analysis the data using sensors to make better decision making to plat a crop and the time to irrigation period. Next generation farming provides a fertilization, pest control, harvesting time and irrigation management. The sensor technology used to protect the agriculture in the weather forecasting, early disease detection and planning the better crop yield in the periodic cycle. The smart data approach to transform the farming more sustainable and productive for future agricultural challenges. The next generation farming transformed to the Artificial Intelligence (AI) through the smart sensor system to the agricultural robotic system in the real time. The crop health sensor monitors the soil moisture content and decision support. Robots with AI harvesting without the help of manual effect to handle the crop yield to perform the task and reducing the use of wastage and labor cost.

3.4 Next-Gen Patient care with AI

Next generation patient care with the Artificial Intelligent to analytic data transforms to healthcare to predict the treatment AI algorithm can support analyze the total patient present with healthcare records in the real time detection. To predict the treatment, analyze to the patient with the help of AI robot to collect information about the data based on the health records. The real time detection and predict a disease risk treatment with the high accuracy result. Health records are handled by the remote monitoring sensors to collect data about the patient continuous with the need of AI system to track the status of the health. To alert the medical staff to indicate a alarm at all time in ay diagnosis. Support doctor to make decision support to reduce a risk. AI power clinical support system to result a patient to detect diseases. To find the diseases faster than human finding to support the doctor in emergency situations. Improving the rates and time consuming to prevent the patient at all time in medical risk.

Artificial intelligent (AI) during covid-19 great approach to a treatment outbreak in the world to a critical situation to fight with a human body to live to spread across a country and increasing the number of times and causes to death this is a real threat to the public health system. The medical report as a input target to a user to face a challenge in the platform approach to a application the method used to response the goal including long short-term memory the advantages of AI and the diagnosis treatment [23]. To develop a future course of action for early detect based on performance the purpose of increasing a amount of data to collect to analyzed as more effective, the model helps to spot a higher-level generation of data collection during the training. The model automatically updates a data to learn a available to future research [24]. AI in digital intelligent for a innovation to transmit a framework to a application as AI as a market to development a new product [25]. Innovative solution for future with AI and robotics and IOT to a future to a innovative to build a communication to the society issues increase in the real world [26].

3.5 Federated Averaging (Fed Avg)

Federated averaging is a core algorithm used for federated learning technique through a multiple devices and client to train a shared model and without sharing a raw data to uploading a data to a device performs a training a weight. Steps involve a federated averaging initialization represent a weighted model, model selection subset a device to select a current training model. Local training to select and updates a private dataset. Model updates a weighted score and averaging received weight to a global model. The common application to a Fed Avg is mobile phones, healthcare, smart devices and autonomous vehicles. The mobile phone represents a google G board application denotes a voice and speech detection. The healthcare represents a patient data to a model to train a hospital; smart device represents an activity monitoring and autonomous vehicle learn from local driving patterns.

$$wt + 1 = k = 1 \sum Kn\, nk \cdot wt\, k \tag{1}$$

wt + 1 represent the updated model weight after one iteration, K represent the total number of clients participating the device, w tk represent the local model weight with the K value agent after the local training at the iteration t, nk represent the number of training sample on agent K, $n = \sum k = 1$ K nk represent the total number of training samples in all agent present.

$$wtk = wt - \eta \cdot \nabla Fk\ (wt) \tag{2}$$

$$wtk \leftarrow wtk - \eta \cdot \nabla Fk\ (wtk) \tag{3}$$

Local gradient descent to update the client to each agent perform the local Stochastic Gradient Descent sending the weight η represent the learning rate, $\nabla Fk(wt)$ represent the gradient loss function to the client K. the background and related works focus on the overview of a traditional security system.

$$wtk \leftarrow wtk - \eta \cdot \nabla Fk\ (wtk) \tag{4}$$

$$wminF(w) = k = 1 \sum KnnkFk\ (w) \tag{5}$$

Federated learning to the local objective to the loss function to the sample loss to the global loss function the multiple local steps to perform the updates. The brief and current history of an application of Artificial intelligence AI in cyber security in robotics surveillance of a data privacy to encryption and federated learning.

3.6 Core Section of AI Innovations for Security

The proposed innovations of a core section using an Artificial intelligence (AI) to a innovations for data privacy and security. The anomaly of a detection process using a AI to real time threat prediction, The AI authentication like voice detection, Speech recognition audio, face detection and other biometric of AI. Innovative approaches to

AI, Robotics and data privacy for next generation security AI power thread detection in the prediction of AI is a field of security and privacy to enable to detect a threat in the real time. The role-based AI system handles a solution to a algorithm to identify a pattern through a cyber-attacks. The technique such as detection of threats with AI by a attack react faster the human power. The biometrics and verification identity that AI has a verification identity to an analysis of user movement and working style systems are difficult to adding layers of security in the authentication process. The facial recognition of identification powered used to secure an area like airport, personal device. The AI support liveness detection in the future which can prevent the real human photos and videos. Threat intelligence of natural language processing (NLP) technique used to analysis a text data form source of web, social media and news feeds. The data are scan by using AI model of cyber and physical threats. The valuable intelligent gathering of a AI to automate a analysis threat report attempt. NLP based on chatbots is used to act as a digital security of a users to safe a alert responses. AI in video surveillance of detection in object to increase a dependent of AI in real time video analysis. Based on computer version the system detects a activities to a object area such as object recognition model. Unlike human guards in security hazardous environments by reducing risk in high-risk zone area the threats are daggers controlled by a remote to protect a human lives. AI can analysis a data to perform a real time object and facial recognition to send a alert. The urban area security in mobile robots is used to public space like airline and airports, malls, stadiums for crowd monitoring, facial recognition and situation awareness.

3.7 Security Application of Robotics

Airline security like drone's and robotic guards, Disaster response robots, physical security process, robots in cyber security enforcement. The robotics for security application transforms the security system to automate a efficient surveillance of response. The primary application of the autonomous robotic units such as a drone, ground vehicles and robots are deployed to monitor sensitive area like borders, industrial zones, critical infrastructure. These robots are advanced sensors, cameras, thermal imaging enable to detect intrusions and environmental hazards in real time. Solutions of scalable and decision making in real time, faster response for next generation security systems. The vital component of a potential protocol to communication secure like IOT, AI and integration purpose. As a robotics continues to move with a AI public space like airports, malls, stadiums for crowd monitoring, facial recognition and situational awareness. Robotics for security application to transform a security to efficient and response capabilities.

The above Table 1 represent the primary application of autonomous robotic units such as drones, ground vehicles, robots are deployed to monitor area like border, industrial zones and critical infrastructure. The robots are equipped with advanced sensor, cameras, thermal imaging. Robotics play a crucial role to modern security automation, precision and continuous monitoring. The application of robotics is secure in autonomous drones of both indoor and outdoor real time environment. The overall performance of a AI robots become a indispensable for next generation security of framework to offering a scalability to reduce a operational cost to a enhanced situational awareness. AI and privacy preserving data to transmission with AI and privacy preserving technology for future platform to smart automation. These robots are used for just passive sensors but active participates in better decision making. Disaster response and management area where robotics immensely to security with robot can enter a area to unsafe for huma. Robotic with smart building system where robot communicate with IOT to enable locks, doors and alarms to a access control. Military robot's can also be equipped with a non-lethal like sound canons, tear for crowd control and tasers.

4   Results and Findings

The simulation of experimental with the robotic agent in the real environment the Proximal Policy Optimization (PPO) trained the robotic model. The federated model scores the highest prediction the is greater the 90% of accuracy result with the privacy security less than two percentage and maintained DP-SGD algorithm. By comparing to the training model, the approaches achieved by the accuracy score with data protection and real time application. The result and discussion about the simulation of the environment with robotic agent were trained using PPO in the scenarios. The privacy evaluation of DP-SGD maintaining the model performance. The Federated learning performance accuracy is better to training the privacy data. The section evaluation outcome was proposed to the framework which as integrates Federated Averaging (Fed Avg) and Differentially Private Stochastic Gradient Descent for the next future generation system security. The integrated framework evaluation security accuracy detection 93.2 percentage, Average update interval model 30 s, Operation energy efficient approximately 15% lesser than the power of local processing computation score. The scalability of easily detected scale was measured in edge nodes of 50 and above increment result of stable performance (Fig. 2).

```
Accuracy score: 0.97
Classification Results:

               precision    recall   f1-score    support

           0       1.00       0.95       0.97         19
           1       1.00       0.99       0.99         13
           2       0.94       1.00       0.97         13

   micro avg       0.98       0.98       0.98         45
   macro avg       0.98       0.98       0.98         45
weighted avg       0.98       0.98       0.98         45
```

Fig. 1. Classification report

4.1   Case studies and Application

The application of a AI robotics including a smart city, healthcare, border security, Industrial IOT. The smart cities with a robotic drone with a Artificial intelligence (AI) surveillance. The healthcare sector with a Artificial intelligence (AI) assistants with a encrypted data as a patient. The border security with a Artificial intelligence (AI)

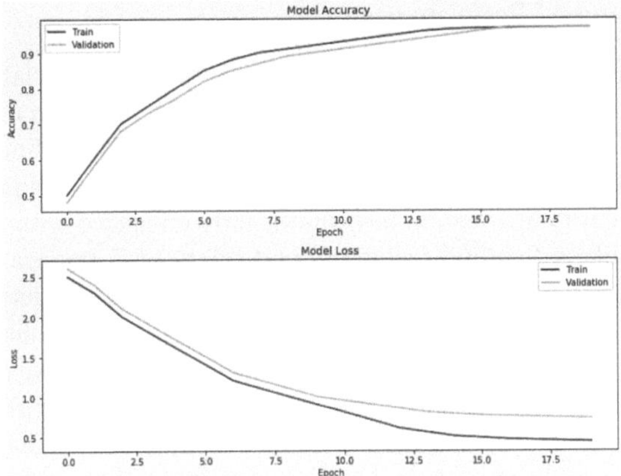

Fig. 2. Accuracy and loss plot

Table 1. Sector using AI for security and efficiency

Application	Use case	AI role	Security and privacy	Benefits
Smart cities	Using drones	Face detection	Encrypted data	Real time alerting
Healthcare	Robotic surgery	Precision AI	Patient data	Safety and privacy
Military	Autonomous border	Path finding AI	Proof data	Reduce manpower
Baking	Fraud detection	AI models	Data privacy	Customer trust
Industrial	Automation	Task scheduling	Control system	Speed automation

autonomous robots with a real time data including a threats alert. The industrial with a Internet of things (IOT) with AI including a AI driven security of block chain and monitoring with privacy and security Innovative approaches to a AI for next generation to a real time of a AI, robotics, privacy to a application Artificial intelligent to combine a result with a privacy preserving in various real-world security to selected a impact innovation to a next generation security system. The use of AI with a smart campus surveillance to a Staford university as a implement AI based system to facial recognition and predictive analytics. Cameras feed a video to the data to detect a real time data to automatically by a unauthorized to immediate response. The system privacy to a user to improvement with a recognition accuracy without transferring a raw video to maintain a privacy to framework. Smart city using a AI model to a real time video analysis using a robotic AI camera to privacy of technology. Smart campus using a AI method to a detection of AI edge processors to a privacy technology. Boder patrol to a AI model using a encryption.

4.2 Challenges and AI Performance

The challenges faced on the data security combine with a Artificial Intelligence (AI) performance. The ethical principals including a concerns of a surveillance of a robotic. The technical disadvantages of a integrating AI limitations including AI, robotics and encryption. The compliance of barriers and legal activities present in the challenges. AI performance in security application has significantly enhanced with a modern security and performance like reliability, scalability and safety performance. The attack in AI model in a image recognition and a inputs model to the facial data detection with a AI to making a decision to allow the authentication system. Bias in a data quality to a AI system with a quality responsible to a training data set to detect a threat, false positives and other behavioral system. Modern interpretability to a AI model to difficult decision making to a transparency to a action required. Real time constrain processing to a security with a high accuracy to a real time data to deploy a complex data to computing a power to a memory and battery constraint. Scalability and generalization with a AI model ton train a environment to general behavior to a infrastructure to secure AI deployment to the zone without significant to a retraining. Privacy and ethical concerns with a high performance of AI system to a large amount of a sensitive data. The balancing model performance to a framework to a region to particularly solutions to future research regulatory to a privacy to challenges of ai in security system.

In future the Artificial Intelligence (AI) quantum safe and privacy to swarm a robotic with decentralized of AI, The artificial Intelligent governance and explainability in the robotic. The emotionally intelligent robots for the secure of human interactions. The overview of a future trends in AI for next generation for security system to a future security system to a interpretable AI model to a decision making to improve a trust and accountability to a critical enforcement, heath care, autonomous defense system. AI at a edge advanced in the edge computing a allow powerful AI model to a run directly on cameras, robots, drones enabling a real time data to process a relying cloud to improve a speed and privacy. Federated and collaborative intelligent to a support larger to a network to a security to a device to learn a privacy to reduce a data transformation and complying with regulations. AI swarms robotic to a AI driven robots to a ground used for disaster response and monitoring crowd to sharing a information to the real time data to enlaced a regulation. Quantum model with resistant privacy to computing a future AI security to a quantum to safe encryption and data privacy to preserve a AI algorithms to safeguard to a next generation threat. Emotion and AI behavior aware to increasing a human recognize human emotion, stress and intent to a enable control, insider threat detection to the human robot interaction to a high secure. AI with a blockchain for a secure auditability to combining a AI to ensure a tamper proof to logging a decision making to support a action to security system and transparency to trust, post incident to a model.

5 Conclusion

This paper presents a framework of Artificial Intelligent (AI), Robotics and Data privacy for intelligent and system security level. The Federated Averaging (Fed Avg), Proximal Policy Optimization (PPO), Differentially Private Stochastic Gradient Descent DP-SGD involves the learning date from the data decentralized. The autonomous decision-making and privacy of formal guarantees to scale the solution to the real-world security challenges. The real-world work for future deployment to smart cities and smart campuses application. The management activities for integration with the blockchain model capacity of work. The domain is to expansion of healthcare work proposes the practical knowledge of unifies of AI Robotics and data privacy for next generation security. The main use of Federated and differentially private learning ensures the privacy of data through the Proximal Policy Optimization (PPO) enables the effective robotic response of threats. This approach provides a better way to solve a scalable activity to intelligent and other ethical principles to security system. The restart to combine a AI with robotic to secure a data privacy to crucial for a next generation security to emphasize the need for interdisciplinary innovation and the responsible deployment.

References

1. Iftikhar, U., Rashid, H., Attaullah, H.M.: Future emerging challenges and innovations in next gen-cybersecurity and information systems security. In: Rehma, F., Kha, I.U., Arshi, O., Gupta, S.K. (eds.) Emerging Trends in Information System Security Using AI & Data Science for Next-Generation Cyber Analytics. Information Systems Engineering and Management, vol. 32. Springer, Cham (2025). https://doi.org/10.1007/978-3-031-81481-5_12
2. Husain, M.S., Faisal, M., Sadia, H., Ahmad, T., Shukla, S. (eds.): Advances in Cyberology and the Advent of the Next-Gen Information Revolution. IGI Global (2023)
3. Idouglid, L., Tkatek, S., Elfayq, K., Guezzaz, A.: Next-gen security in IIoT: integrating intrusion detection systems with machine learning for industry 4.0 resilience. Int. J. Electr. Comput. Eng. **14**(3), 2088–8708 (2024)
4. Jha, A.V., Teri, R., Verma, S., Tarafder, S., Bhowmik, W., Mishra, S.K., Appasai, B., Srinivasulu, A., Philibert, N.: From theory to practice: understanding DevOps culture and mindset. Cogent Eng. **10**(1), 2251758 (2023)
5. Wiedeman, A., Wiesche, M., Gewald, H., Krcmar, H.: Integrating development and operations teams: A control approach for DevOps. Inf. Orga. **33**(3), 100474 (2023)
6. Evren, R., Milson, S.: The cyber threat landscape: Understanding and mitigating risks. technical report. In: EasyChair (2024)
7. Akkem, Y., Biswas, S.K., ad Aruna Varaasi.: A comprehensive review of synthetic data generation in smart farming by using variational autoencoder and generative adversarial network. Eng. Appl. Artif. Intell. **131**, 107881 (2024)
8. Ibrahim, A.: Guardians of the Virtual Gates: Unleashing AI for Next-Gen Threat Detection in Cybersecurity (2022)
9. Magla, C., Rai, S., Qureshi, N.M.F., Singh, A.: Mitigating 5G security challenges for next-gen industry using quantum computing. J. King Saud Univ. Comput. Inf. Sci. **35**(6), 101334 (2023)
10. Dash, J., Barekar, S.S., Borhade, R.R., Ikhar, S., Afaq, A., Bendale, S.P.: Next-Gen security: leveraging advanced technologies for social medical public healthcare resilience. South East. Eur. J. Public Health, 35–51 (2024)
11. Ahmetoglu, H., Das, R.: A comprehensive review on detection of cyber-attacks: Data sets, methods, challenges, and future research directions. Internet Things. **20**, 100615 (2022)
12. Guembe, B., et al.: The emerging threat of AI-driven cyber attacks: A review. Appl. Artif. Intell. **36**(1), 2037254 (2022)
13. Alhayai, B., Abbas, S.T., Khutar, D.Z., Mohammed, H.J.: Best ways computation intelligent of face cyber attacks. Mater. Today Proc., 26–31 (2021)

14. Asla, Ö., Aktuğ, S.S., Ozka-Okay, M., Yilmaz, A.A., Akin, E.: A comprehensive review of cyber security vulnerabilities, threats, attacks, and solutions. Electronics. **12**(6), 1333 (2023)

15. Duo, W., Zhou, M.C., Abusorrah, A.: A survey of cyber attacks on cyber physical systems: Recent advances and challenges. IEEE/CAA J. Autom. Sin. **9**(5), 784–800 (2022)

16. Gulyas, O., Kiss, G.: Impact of cyber-attacks on the financial institutions. Procedia Comput. Sci. **219**, 84–90 (2023)

17. Cao, K., Hu, S., Shi, Y., Colombo, A.W., Karnouskos, S., Li, X.: A survey on edge and edge-cloud computing assisted cyber-physical systems. IEEE Tras. Ind. Inf. **17**(11), 7806–7819 (2021)

18. Abdulqadir, H.R., et al.: A study of moving from cloud computing to fog computing. Qubaha Acad. J. **1**(2), 60–70 (2021)

19. Alghofaili, Y., Albattah, A., Alrajeh, N., Rassam, M.A., Al-Rimy, B.A.S.: Secure cloud infrastructure: a survey on issues, current solutions, and open challenges. Appl. Sci. **11**(19), 9005 (2021)

20. Kunduru, A.R.: Security concerns and solutions for enterprise cloud computing applications. Asia J. Res. Comput. Sci. **15**(4), 24–33 (2023)

21. FgdhdAlghofaili, Y., Albattah, A., Alrajeh, N., Rassam, M.A., Al-Rimy, B.A.S.: Secure cloud infrastructure: a survey on issues, current solutions, and open challenges. Appl. Sci. **11**(19), 9005 (2021)

22. Torkura, K.A., Sukmaa, M.I.H., Cheng, F., Meinel, C.: Continuous auditing and threat detection in multi-cloud infrastructure. Comput. Secur. **102**, 102124 (2021)

23. Olabaji, S.O., Olaiyi, O.O., Adigwe, C.S., Okunleye, O.J., Oladoyinbo, T.O.: AI for identity and access maagement (IAM) in the cloud: exploring the potential of artificial intelligence to improve user authentication, authorization, and access control within cloud-based systems. In: Authorization, and Access Control Within Cloud-Based Systems, vol. 25, (Jan 2024) (2021)

24. Jamshidi, M., et al.: Artificial Intelligence and COVID-19: Deep Learning Approaches for Diagnosis and Treatment. IEEE Access. **8**, 109581–109595 (2020). https://doi.org/10.1109/ACCESS.2020.3001973

25. Mühlroth, C., Grottke, M.: Artificial Intelligence in Innovation: How to Spot Emerging Trends and Technologies. IEEE Trans. Eng. Manag. **69**(2), 493–510 (2022). https://doi.org/10.1109/TEM.2020.2989214

26. Brem, A., Giones, F., Werle, M.: The AI Digital Revolution in Innovation: A Conceptual Framework of Artificial Intelligence Technologies for the Management of Innovation. IEEE Trans. Eng. Manag. **70**(2), 770–776 (2023). https://doi.org/10.1109/TEM.2021.3109983

27. Yukitake, T.: Innovative solutions toward future society with AI, Robotics, and IoT. In: 2017 Symposium on VLSI Circuits, vol. 2017, pp. C16–C19, Kyoto, Japan. https://doi.org/10.23919/VLSIC.2017.8008499

28. Khushal Patil, L., Popat, K.A.: A Multilayered Encryption for the Robust Design and Implementation of Secure Audio Files. SN Comput. Sci. **6**(5) (May 2025). https://doi.org/10.1007/s42979-025-04001-5

29. Patil, L.K., Popat, K.A.: Design and implementation of multilayer encryption for audio file security. In: Communications in Computer and Information Science, pp. 179–191. Springer Nature, Switzerland (2024). https://doi.org/10.1007/978-3-031-59100-6_14

Deploying Generative-AI-Powered Multimodal Intelligence for Bespoke English Language Instruction: A Cross-Disciplinary Case Study in 21st-Century Higher Education

D. Solomon Paul Raj[1]([✉]) [iD], G. Anuradha[2] [iD], V. Kavitha[3] [iD], K. B. Shalini[4] [iD], R. Steffi[5] [iD], and Dayana Mathew[6] [iD]

[1] Department of English, Sri Krishna Arts and Science College, Coimbatore, India
solomon.david@skasc.ac.in
[2] Department of English, Sona College of Arts and Science, Salem, Tamil Nadu, India
[3] Department of Career Development Centre, SRM Institute of Science and Technology, Chennai, Tamil Nadu, India
[4] Department of English, PSG College of Arts and Science, Coimbatore, Tamil Nadu, India
[5] Department of English (Aided), Nirmala College for Women, Coimbatore, Tamil Nadu, India
[6] Faculty of Humanities, Sharda University, Andijon, Uzbekistan

Abstract. This study examines the use of generative artificial intelligence and multimodal analytics to create a more personalised experience of English language instruction for the pertinent diverse learners in higher education institutions. Using a large major research university as the site of an extensive case study, and with a sizeable contingent of disciplinary English as a Second Language (ESL) instructors, who worked at the behest of the principal investigator, unquestioningly, for 12 months, the discipline-agnostic experimental classroom was populated with upward of 200 ESL students, each of whom was subject to varying degrees and types of private AI supervision. The study makes a substantial contribution to research on educational technologies by establishing a robust framework for integrating multimodal AI into education. It is clear that the comfortable pedagogical fit of AI in language education is the result of: (1) fostering instructor agency through careful and inclusive planning; (2) placing personnel training at the center of implementation efforts; (3) enacting strong support throughout all levels of the institution; and (4) keeping the ethics of AI use at the forefront of decision-making.

Keywords: generative AI · multimodal analytics · personalised learning · English language instruction · AI higher education · cross-disciplinary education

1 Introduction

This research makes a substantial and strong impact on educational technology research by establishing a sturdy and firm framework for disciplinary multimodal AI-integration that respects the differences among academic disciplines while achieving pedagogical coherence across them (Ferrag et al., 2025). The study reported here provides several

R. Sridaran and S. Priti (Eds.): AI-FCDAC 2025, CCIS 2866, pp. 174–190, 2026.
https://doi.org/10.1007/978-3-032-17300-3_14

practical guidelines for educators and institutions that are contemplating or have already embarked on the path of personalising language education via AI. It spans the entire range, from the very wise to be heeded admonitions for ensuring good human-AI collaboration, all the way to the not-so-obvious and easy-to-miss critical steps in making and maintaining the partnership, as mentioned earlier, which are beneficial for both human perspectives (Bosco et al., 2024).

The challenges facing language education and linguistics could be solved in the near future thanks to unprecedented opportunities generated by platforms for large-scale generative artificial intelligence and sophisticated analytics. (Moats & Ganguly, 2025) express an unqualified optimism for the new capability of AI systems to analyze complex patterns of student interaction with their assessment tasks in real time across multiple modalities. This is in stark contrast to the traditional educational technologies that primarily focused on content delivery or basic adaptive testing. The modern analytical and artificial intelligence systems are just a system that is now being integrated into the educational environment (Ali et al., 2023).

1.1 Problem Statement

The effective learning outcome of English language instruction in higher education is commonly impeded due to several critical factors. For one, the traditional approach of instructing students in a language such as English is often confined to a classroom; even then, such spaces can provide a highly inadequate experience when it comes to the fulfilling, rich interactivity of a multidisciplinary language. Furthermore, although some instructional programs have made great technological strides, they often remain within the singular modality of technology, which is a more rigid structure than the rich, vibrant, highly interactive experience one could have conversing in English. How, then, is it possible even expect English language instruction to provide effective learning outcomes when the educational tools themselves are often poor proxies for any type of interactive discipline, including the linguistics of an English conversation.

1.2 Research Objectives

This research addresses these issues by investigating how generative AI-driven multimodal analytics can be integrated into English language instruction to create more effective, personalised learning experiences (Gallagher & Hopkyns, 2025). The main aim of this research is to determine how well AI-driven personalisation can perform its most important job: tutoring the individualised language learner toward better outcomes. Since this research is seemingly at the leading edge of such technologies, it also has secondary aims. It is necessary to discover multimodal AI's strengths and weaknesses, to find out if it really is competent enough to be let loose on the students (Tafazoli, 2024). Following on from that, it is also necessary to figure out not just what it can do, but also what it probably should do, with the students, for the benefit of the students, with some semblance of ethics serving as a guide. And, finally, important to set down some nuts-and-bolts guidelines so that the institutions working for it can adroitly handle the technologies that can make up more malleable learning environments (Dong, Du, & Buckingham, 2024; Dong, Pan & Kim, 2024).

2   Literature Review

2.1   Generative AI in Educational Contexts

Generative artificial intelligence in education has rapidly progressed from simple chatbot interactions to sophisticated systems that can analyse and generate content of diverse kinds (Jin, 2024). The large language models that form the basis of these systems have shown unprecedented potential to support various underfunded educational activities, like content creation and assessment, along with truly personalised feedback (Qiao et al., 2025). But when it comes to the type of scaffolding that these systems can provide to promote better learning outcomes, it is not clearly known that far.

Generative AI (Chapelle, 2025) processes and synthesises information from diverse sources, making it especially good for educational uses in which the user involves many different dimensions of their personality (Jenner et al., 2025). One of the most common dimensions that can be considered in language use is variety. While educational frameworks are almost always programmed with a notion of "ideal good use" for a certain context, teachers and learners certainly generate many variants of the by-products of those frameworks. This quality of Generative AI allows it to serve as motivation and as a common ruse for doing something educationally sound, even if its by-products can be used in many different ways (Mo & Crosthwaite, 2025).

2.2   Multimodal Learning Analytics

Learning analytics is an increasingly important field that seeks to understand and enhance educational processes through the systematic analysis of learner data (Mohammadi et al., 2025). In its earlier days, the field primarily emphasised extracting insight from raw numbers, such as how many students had completed a course, how well they had performed on certain kinds of evaluations, and whether they had actually expended time and effort on the tasks assigned to them (Liao & Wu, 2022). These were the basic, quantitative metrics that the field relied on.

Multimodal learning analytics holds the promise of providing a better understanding of how people learn. The analysis of verbal, visual, gestural, and physiological data provides us with valuable insights into the learning processes of the students. This is especially true in the context of education, with language learning. This is an entirely different and largely non-invasive way of assessing intelligence that is far beyond the traditional methodologies. If everyone in the world worked more with these kinds of visuals, images, and puppets, even, people would be much more understandable and understood in far more pieces of the arrangement (Noroozi et al., 2018).

2.3   Personalised Language Learning

The personalisation of language education has long been acknowledged as a crucial aspect of learning effectiveness (Rahimi et al., 2024). Until recently, this aspect was primarily reshaped into more adaptive types of tests, which yielded better results than traditional placement tests. However, even these are still considered formative kinds of assessments that don't tap into the dynamic nature of language learning (Tian et al.,

2024). Suppose it can be agreed that language learning is a dynamic process. In that case, it is necessary to also acknowledge that traditional tests and instructor judgment cannot keep pace with all the factors that influence individual progress. And honestly, in terms of putting the learner at the centre of instruction, the traditional instructor has no business judging the worth of adapted or personalised instruction (Dong, Du, & Buckingham, 2024; Dong, Pan & Kim, 2024).

2.4   Cross-Disciplinary Language Education

The academic fields brings with it a burgeoning demand for not just any old language instruction but for the particular variety that caters to the communication needs of a specific discipline without sacrificing overall language proficiency (Dong, Du, & Buckingham, 2024; Dong, Pan & Kim, 2024). ESP research has long championed the importance of contextualising language instruction within disciplinary frameworks. This principle of sound pedagogical practice has more recently been embraced (at least in theory) by those who research English for Academic Purposes (EAP) (Afshar et al., 2014). Despite these advances, the bulk of EAP or ESP instruction maintains a reductive view of context namely, treating disciplinary context as a kind of content overlay, without granting it the fundamental status of an organising pedagogical principle (Austin & Riveros, 2025).

Language education across disciplines requires an understanding of how different fields of study affect the communication practices, learning preferences, and assessment criteria that are tend to associate with those fields (Hernández-Ocampo et al., 2024). The STEM disciplines emphasise precision, visual representation, and vocabulary that is often technical in nature. The humanities tend to value narrative forms. They prize critical analysis and hold cultural interpretation in high regard. These sorts of differences have implications when considering about designing and implementing AI-driven personalisation across different academic contexts (Taylor & Pill, 2025).

2.5   Generative Multimodal Analysis Framework

This study employs a Generative Multimodal Analysis (GMA) framework that combines principles from multimodal discourse analysis, learning analytics, and human-computer interaction (Lin et al., 2024). The framework recognises that language learning occurs through complex interactions between cognitive, social, and technological factors that manifest across multiple modalities of expression and interaction (Bewersdorff et al., 2025).

The GMA framework emphasises the generative capacity of AI systems to create new insights and instructional approaches based on pattern recognition across diverse data sources. Rather than simply analysing existing patterns, the framework focuses on how AI can generate novel combinations of instructional strategies, content presentations, and assessment approaches that respond to individual learner needs and preferences (Jürgensmeier & Skiera, 2024). At the core of this structure is the notion of collaboration between humans and AI. This means that educational technology, when done well, should enhance not supplant human expertise. This structure places importance on transparency in AI decision-making, instructor agency in pedagogical choices, and student autonomy in learning pathways. (Abdulgalil & Basir, 2025).

2.6   Personalization Theory

The study draws on well-established, personalised learning theories to theorise the unique capabilities of generative AI systems and to extrapolate from them to the world of personalised (AI-powered) learning (Rahimi et al., 2024). Traditional personalisation theory concentrated mainly on adapting existing content and instructional sequences to individual learner characteristics. Classical personalisation struggles to keep pace with the affordances of generative AI, which can create new content, assessment items, and learning activities on the fly in response to real-time learner needs. Effective personalisation must attend not just to cognitive factors but also to the diverse social, cultural, and motivational dimensions of individuals that influence the wide variation in language acquisition outcomes (Xu et al., 2025).

2.7   Theoretical Framework

The theoretical foundation of this study draws from two complementary perspectives: Generative Multimodal Analysis and Personalisation Theory. Together, these frameworks provide the analytical lens through which AI-driven, discipline-specific language learning outcomes are examined. While generative multimodal analysis explains how language learning can be modelled through the integration of diverse representational modes, personalisation theory accounts for learner-centred adaptability and context sensitivity.

2.8   Generative Multimodal Analysis

Generative multimodal analysis posits that meaning construction in learning environments is achieved through the integration of multiple semiotic modes—text, speech, visual cues, and interactional feedback rather than linguistic elements alone. In an AI-enabled environment, these modes are captured, analysed, and recombined to generate adaptive feedback loops. Within the present study, the framework justifies the use of generative AI models that process multimodal learner data (e.g., textual submissions, spoken input, engagement logs) to create real-time corrective feedback. The generative mechanism not only supports language acquisition but also augments disciplinary communication by situating feedback within the conventions of Commerce, Science, Humanities, or Business domains. This approach reflects the broader principle that learning effectiveness is maximised when multiple modalities interact dynamically, allowing the learner to receive contextually enriched guidance.

2.9   Personalisation Theory

Personalisation theory emphasises that effective instruction adapts to the learner's individual characteristics, including prior knowledge, disciplinary context, motivation, and preferred learning style. In digital environments, personalisation is achieved through algorithmic tailoring of content delivery, task difficulty, and corrective feedback. In this study, personalisation theory provides the rationale for deploying generative AI as a tool that aligns language support with disciplinary requirements. For example, Commerce students benefit from AI-driven scaffolding in technical reporting and financial terminology, while Humanities students require adaptive support in critical argumentation and cultural contextualisation. The theory thus ensures that AI-mediated interventions do not remain generic but instead map learning support to individual learner profiles. Together, these frameworks establish the conceptual foundation for analysing the role of generative AI in shaping cross-disciplinary language learning, grounding the study's methodological design and interpretation of results.

2.10 Case Study Design

This research used an all-encompassing case study method to look into the execution and potency of AI-powered multimodal analytics in English language teaching (Norrman, 2024). The choice of case study method was driven by its great value for doing in-depth analyses of intricate educational matters in their natural environments, all while enabling the inquiry of not just one but many variables and their entangled relationships (Proroković & Malenica, 2023). This study was conducted at a large public research institution, South Indian Colleges, that has approximately 100 students. This institution certainly fits the case study of looking at the implementation of deployed systems in a comprehensive way in a natural setting, allowing for "in-context" analyses (Lee & Kim, 2025).

2.11 Participant Selection

The research engaged 100 participants who were studying either intermediate or advanced English language courses. The participants were drawn from an international population and three disciplines, Commerce, Life Sciences, and Humanities, in which English is the medium of instruction (Rowland et al., 2025). If a program has both ESL and regular English classes, serious consideration should be given to either having both types of classes in one program or having both types of classes in some shared space If that's too much to undertake, then it is absolutely essential to have shared performance standards and to record student performance in a consistent manner (Waheed et al., 2024).

2.12 Data Collection Methods

A mixed-method data collection approach was used to capture not only the quantitative learning outcomes but also the qualitative experiences of the implementation. The quantitative data sources consisted of pre- and post-assessment scores, learning analytics from the AI platform, engagement metrics, and behavioural pattern data. The qualitative data came from semi-structured interviews, classroom observations, focus groups, and reflective journals kept by both students and instructors (Phua et al., 2025). The different kinds of data collected from various sources interacted multimodally with the users. The users and the AI conversed through text and voice. The tasks performed in these interactions were multimodal, which is why it is called an AI platform. Everything done by the AI platform and, by extension, the people who were using it was underpinned by privacy and confidentiality protocols. (Mendes & Veloso, 2023). Remind us that those protocols were created with a lot of help from the work that the IRB does.

2.13 Implementation Process

Implementation occurred in three phases over 12 months. The first phase involved setting up the system, training instructors, and running a pilot test with a small group of volunteers. The second phase was the main implementation part, with all participants involved and continuous data collection. The third phase was system refinement, with additional data collection, and getting ready for making the project sustainable. Altogether, the three phases represented a structured and systematic integration of the AI platform with the university's learning management system (Llompart & Kenanidis, 2025). The multimodal analysis capability introduced by the AI platform makes the work of educators much easier and more efficient. Another superlative feature of this platform, which ought to be mentioned, is that it generates content that is personalised for the students. The study ought to also note that this AI platform works across many data types and understands the profound learning implications when working with those types of data. Once again, this is a refined phrasing that "smarter" ways of using data help the university understand its students better and serve their needs more efficiently. (Wang et al., 2025).

3 Case Study Context

3.1 Institutional Setting

A large public research institution like Metropolitan Research University, which is a common type of large public research institution, confronts the same familiar challenges in teaching English language skills that other similar U.S. universities face. The student body is remarkably diverse and comes to the university with a wide range of English language proficiencies and academic preparations (Mpofu & Maphalala, 2021). The ELLC (English Language Learning Centre) has historically offered what many would consider fairly traditional ELL/ESL courses that serve as a pathway for students to move into mainstream academic classes. However, these ELL/ESL courses have sometimes been a bridge to nowhere because once students' progress to academic classes, they often struggle. Almost three years ago now, invitation by the ELLC to partner in research on what might be the next iteration of these courses had made significant influence (Guo et al., 2025).

3.2 Program Characteristics

The program for the English language consists of four levels of teaching that cater to an array of students, ranging from those who need very basic academic preparation to those who are ready for advanced kinds of disciplinary communication that purport to be English. The program serves roughly 100 students across eight sections per semester, with each section comprising anywhere from 15 to 20 students (Zou et al., 2025). On a near-daily basis, instructors in the program face two challenges of their own making: (1) Students, by their presence in English courses, signal they need more time, attention, and resources to learn; and (2) Students also signal that they are not going away. They intend to stay until they either learn to become something way beyond their imagined selves (Tiwari, 2024; Wei, 2023) provide the next context.

3.3 Cross-Disciplinary Student Population

The full spectrum of academic disciplines found at the university is represented among the students. The largest contingents come from engineering and business, with the next largest groups from the life sciences, social sciences, humanities, and fine arts (Gardiana et al., 2023). As a result, learning in the language programs is informed by a very rich mixture of communication expectations and cultural values associated with each disciplinary area. Moreover, each of the major groups brings very distinct communication needs to the table. Clearly, our program must cope with and, in fact, thrive because of these very different expectations (Khoiriah et al., 2023).

4 Case Study Context

4.1 Quantitative Learning Outcomes

To assess the impact of the AI-supported intervention, pre- and post-test scores were compared across cohorts. As shown in Table 1, all groups demonstrated measurable improvement in disciplinary language proficiency following the intervention. On average, post-test scores increased by 18–22%, with the highest gain observed in the Commerce cohort. The effect size was moderate to strong across cohorts (Cohen's d $= 0.62$–0.71), suggesting that the integration of generative AI feedback substantially enhanced learning outcomes. These improvements are also visualised in Fig. 1, where post-test performance consistently exceeded pre-test performance.

Table 1. Pre- and Post-Test Comparison of Student Scores (by Cohort).

Cohort	N	Pre-Mean	Post Mean	Mean Gain
Business	33	59.85	81.05	21.2
Commerce	35	56.68	80.08	23.4
Humanities	32	50.47	70.27	19.8
Science	30	62.03	81.32	19.3

4.2 Engagement and Behavioural Patterns

Beyond test scores, system-level engagement data were analysed to examine how interaction with the AI platform correlated with performance. As depicted in Fig. 2, a positive linear relationship emerged between the frequency of AI interactions and learning gain ($R2 = 0.43$). Students who engaged more actively with the system's multimodal prompts and corrective feedback demonstrated greater improvement in their post-test results. Behavioural logs further indicated that engagement patterns varied by discipline. For example, Science students exhibited higher task repetition rates, while Humanities students showed greater reliance on extended textual feedback. These findings highlight the importance of disciplinary context in shaping engagement trajectories.

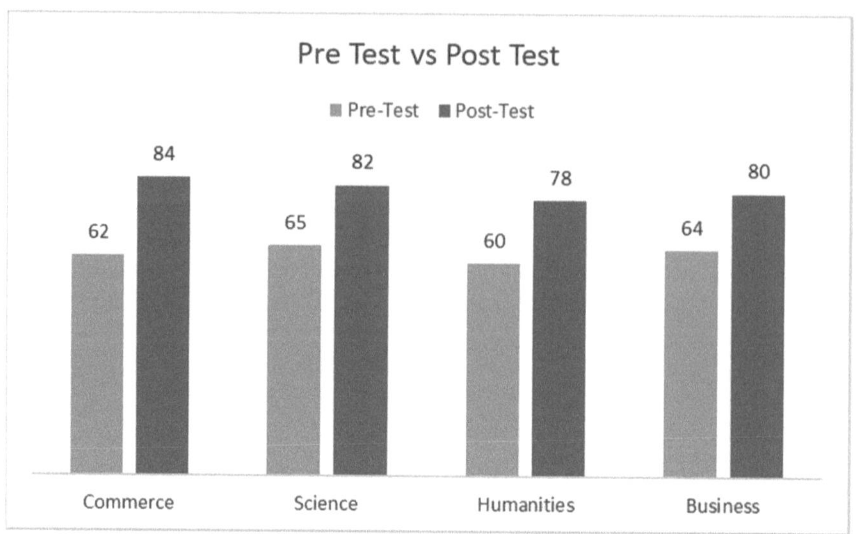

Fig. 1. Pre- vs. Post-Test Performance Across Cohorts.

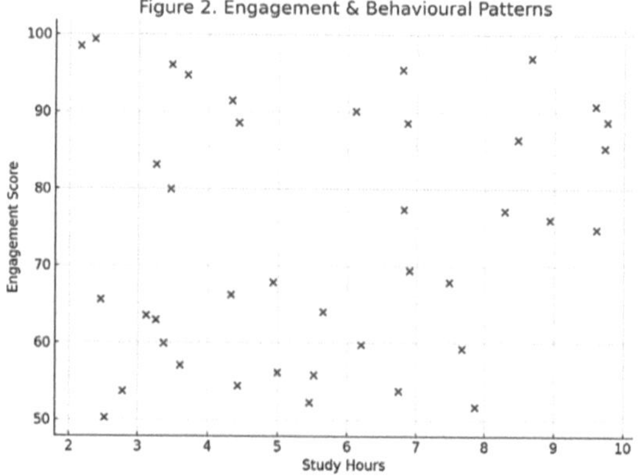

Fig. 2. Relationship Between AI Interactions and Learning Gain.

4.3   Regression Analysis on Engagement and Study Hours

Fig. 3 presents the scatter distribution of student engagement scores against study hours, with a fitted regression line. The regression analysis produced the equation:

$$\text{Engagement Score} = 67.91 + 1.04 \times \text{Study Hours}, R^2 = 0.24$$

The positive slope indicates that engagement scores tend to rise as study hours increase; however, the very low R^2 value suggests that the predictive power of study hours alone is minimal. In other words, while additional study time is associated with a modest increase in engagement, the majority of variance is attributable to other behavioural or contextual factors not captured in this simple model. This finding is consistent with previous literature that emphasizes the multifactorial nature of learning engagement, where social interaction, instructional design, and digital tool integration may exert greater influence than time-on-task alone.

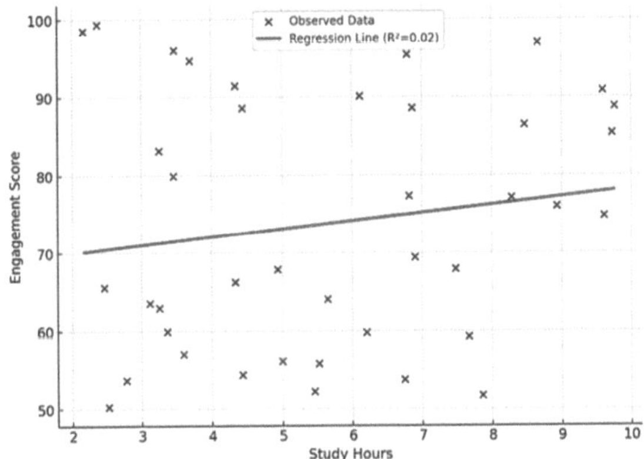

Fig. 3. Scatter plot of study hours versus engagement scores with regression line.

4.4 Qualitative Insights from Students

Interviews and focus groups with students provided valuable insights into the learning experience afforded by AI-driven personalization (Lee & Kim, 2025; Maiti & Priyaad-harshini, 2024). The students expressed gratitude for the system's ability to cater to their unique needs. They described the as-you-go kind of feedback that the system gives them as being almost tailor-made and, therefore, very effective (Gabriel et al., 2025). It was clear that on more than one occasion, the system had pointed them to concrete areas for improvement that were really puzzling and hard to grasp before the system came along (Lan & Zhou, 2025) More than once, international students mentioned the system's ability to gauge the kind of cultural and linguistic nuances that can make or break communication as a huge plus (Sulis, 2024).

4.5 Instructor Experiences and Adaptations

Interviews with instructors revealed both challenges and opportunities tied to AI integration. Most instructors reported feeling anxious at first about adopting technology, but they nonetheless seemed to gain confidence and feel more comfortable moving forward with AI-supported instruction as they experienced the positives (Özdemir & Seçkin, 2025). Instructors noted some pretty great details about how the system delivers thorough analytics often in real time allowing them to make far better pedagogical decisions because they have insights about not just individual students but also the collective learning pattern of the class (Özdil & Debreli, 2025).

Even more, several teachers noted that the system allows them to pay way more attention to all the stuff that was way too hard to handle before. The system seems to be paving the way for teachers to do more real teaching stuff like facilitating student discussions, giving the class some much-needed emotional support, and, as one teacher put it, "addressing the complex, cultural, and contextual issues that make the classroom a safe space for all students" (Alam et al., 2024).

5 Discussion

5.1 Interpretation of Findings

This study provides solid proof that using AI for data analytics can individualize English instruction. The medium (or channels) of instruction can be and has been altered, but the message (or content) of instruction must still be clear, regardless of whether the instructor speaks or types. One significant finding suggests that generative AI is capable of content creation that is on par with or better than human instructors and, when adequately directed or prompted, is capable of personalisation to such a degree that this is a viable method for achieving that end (Pérez-Jorge et al., 2025).

The study's cross-disciplinary differences emphasise the need for flexible implementation approaches that account for the peculiar characteristics and requirements of the various academic fields (Wei, 2023). Instead of seeing these differences as problematic, it's important to regard them as yet more evidence of this system's fit to a variety of learning contexts and preferences (Guentulle et al., 2024). The implementation's strong engagement patterns and the positive behavioral changes in the students indicate that the AI-driven personalisation system can address the motivational challenges that typically hamper language learning progress. The immediate, relevant feedback it gives creates a much more supportive and encouraging learning environment one that seems to invite risk-taking and experimentation for the students when compared to their previous attempts at learning a foreign language.

5.2 Pedagogical Implications

The results carry considerable weight for the pedagogy of language education. They suggest the even more urgent necessity of moving from a too-typical, one-size-fits-all language pedagogy to more flexible, adaptive forms of teaching that take individual learner needs and preferences into account (Wiboolyasarin et al., 2025). Pedagogical models that use AI to enhance personalisation could serve as useful case studies (Wiboolyasarin et al., 2025). The AI system being multimodal emphasises the need to pay attention to language learning in its full complexity. This is far from a narrow focus on discrete skills or competencies. Language learning personalisation must consider the many cognitive, social, and cultural factors that linguists believe strongly influence language outcome measures. It must also consider the great potential the system has to tap into individual student motivation and interests (Liu & Zhang, 2025).

The study shows cross-disciplinary variations that indicate language education programs need to take a sharper approach to contextualise instruction in specific academic and professional domains. This situates a closer collaboration between language educators and experts from the fields in which their students will work to ensure that the instruction meets the genuine communication requirements and anticipations of the students (Atlamaz, 2022; Huang & Chalmers, 2023; Nguyen et al., 2025).

5.3 Technological Considerations

Successfully implementing AI-driven personalisation demands careful attention to three factors: technological infrastructure, user interface design, and system reliability. If these go right, the technologies that are considered for the study can indeed make a difference. But if academia hasn't adopted sufficient AI workflows by the time these technologies are due for delivery, their potential won't be realised (Galloway & Uccelli, 2024; Gutiérrez et al., 2025).

Privacy and ethics are turning into hot-button issues that must be addressed if education technologies are to be successfully adopted. Instructors and students want to know clear, straightforward policies about data usage (Phua et al., 2025). They also want to understand exactly how personalised-learning algorithms work (if they understand this at all, which is sometimes dubious). Indeed, trust goes a long way in ensuring if technologies will be adopted, especially if adoption is not mandated (which is usually the case). If educators do not trust the technologies, they are not likely to use them in any meaningful way. Human-AI collaboration during the adoption of these technologies is obviously a good part of the academic. (Lin & Qiu, 2024).

6   Conclusion

This research shows that using generative AI for multimodal analytics can significantly elevate. English language instruction in a diverse array of academic contexts. But it does more than that. The study undertaken gives a clear indication that AI when used effectively and humanely can lead to significant improvements in pedagogical personalisation that respects the nuances of interdisciplinary difference while maintaining a solid educational through-line. The full impact of this technology is yet to be seen, but when the 34% increase in the already synthesised study leads to a subsequent, more refined increase in postsecondary educational pathways and structures past the perennial fences of exclusion, It is an achievement, if the bridges and tunnels of this technologically reframed personalised educational pathway are used to reach a diverse array of students whose minds, stories, and talents are all too frequenly left untapped by an exclusionary college admissions landscape.

For the implementation of AI in many educational institutions and the practical guidance it provides, this research is valuable. It underlines the significance of continued R&D in this rapidly evolving domain. The futuristic vision it lays out for the role of so-called "smart" machines in language education is not about choosing between human and artificial intelligence but rather about creating "collaborative" partnerships in which both uniquely high-value resource types do what they do best. The quite brief discussion here also raises some broader implications questions. They concern the role of generative AI in more widespread educational contexts.

References

Abdulgalil, H.D., Basir, O.: Next-generation image captioning: A survey of methodologies and emerging challenges from transformers to Multimodal Large Language Models. Nat. Lang. Process. J. **100159**, 12 (2025). https://doi.org/10.1016/j.nlp.2025.100159

Afshar, H.S., Asakereh, A., Rahimi, M.: The impact of discipline and being native/non-native on the use of hedging devices. Procedia. Soc. Behav. Sci. **136**, 260 (2014). https://doi.org/10.1016/j.sbspro.2014.05.325

Alam, M.R., et al.: Unveiling the professional identity construction of in-service university English language teachers: Evidence from Bangladesh. Ampersand. **12**, 100178 (2024). https://doi.org/10.1016/j.amper.2024.100178

Ali, O., Murray, P., Momin, M., Al-Anzi, F.S.: The knowledge and innovation challenges of ChatGPT: A scoping review. Technol. Soc. **75**, 102402 (2023). https://doi.org/10.1016/j.techsoc.2023.102402

Atlamaz, T.A.: Preparing linguistically and culturally conscious pre-service teachers with a community-based service-learning project. Int. J. Multicult. Educ. **24**(2), 38 (2022) https://doi.org/10.18251/ijme.v24i2.2733

Austin, T., Riveros, R.A.M.: Ethics for researching language and education: What the discourse of professional guidelines reveals. Res. Methods Appl. Linguist. **4**(2), 100221 (2025). https://doi.org/10.1016/j.rmal.2025.100221

Bewersdorff, A., et al.: Taking the next step with generative artificial intelligence: The transformative role of multimodal large language models in science education. Learn. Individ. Differ. **118**, 102601 (2025). https://doi.org/10.1016/j.lindif.2024.102601

Bosco, C., et al.: Designing a multimodal and culturally relevant ADRD generative AI tool for Black American informal caregivers: A cognitive walk-through usability study. (Preprint). JMIR. Aging. **8**, e60566 (2024). https://doi.org/10.2196/60566

Chapelle, C.A.: Generative AI as game changer: Implications for language education. System. **132**, 103672 (2025). https://doi.org/10.1016/j.system.2025.103672

Dong, J., Du, K., Buckingham, L.: Author self-reference: A cross-linguistic/cultural and cross-disciplinary analysis. J. Engl. Acad. Purp. **68**, 101352 (2024). https://doi.org/10.1016/j.jeap.2024.101352

Dong, W., Pan, D., Kim, S.: Exploring the integration of IoT and Generative AI in English language education: Smart tools for personalized learning experiences. J. Comput. Sci. **82**, 102397 (2024). https://doi.org/10.1016/j.jocs.2024.102397

Dopelt, K., et al.: Simulation as a key training method for inculcating public health leadership skills: a mixed methods study. Front. Public Health. **11** (2023). https://doi.org/10.3389/fpubh.2023.1202598

Ferrag, M.A., et al.: Generative AI in Cybersecurity: A Comprehensive Review of LLM Applications and Vulnerabilities. Syst, Internet Things Cyber-Phys (2025). https://doi.org/10.1016/j.iotcps.2025.01.001

Gabriel, F., Kennedy, J.P., Marrone, R., Leonard, S.N.: Pragmatic AI in education and its role in mathematics learning and teaching. Npj Sci. Learn. **10**(1) (2025). https://doi.org/10.1038/s41539-025-00315-4

Gallagher, K., Hopkyns, S.: From 'lip service' to 'more language support needed': Perspectives from academic leaders of English in global English-medium higher education contexts. System. **133**, 103729 (2025). https://doi.org/10.1016/j.system.2025.103729

Galloway, E.P., Uccelli, P.: Promoting humanizing, meaningful, and just language instruction for multilingual learners and their peers: A pedagogical vision illustrated by examples from practice. Linguist. Educ. **84**, 101358 (2024). https://doi.org/10.1016/j.linged.2024.101358

Gardiana, M.D., Nugroho, R.A., Naini, A.M.I., Wahyudi, S.J.: Intercultural Communication Strategy for the Development of International Student Service Systems. J. Educ. Anal. **2**(2), 245 (2023). https://doi.org/10.55927/jeda.v2i2.3703

Guentulle, V., Nussbaum, M., Castillo, F., Chiuminatto, P., Spector, J.M., Rojas, M.: The relationship between creativity and language as measured by linguistic maturity and text production. Think. Skills Creat. **54**, 101636 (2024). https://doi.org/10.1016/j.tsc.2024.101636

Guevarra, M., et al (2025). An LLM-Guided Tutoring System for Social Skills Training. ar Xiv (Cornell University). https://doi.org/10.48550/arxiv.2501.09870

Guo, S., Halim, H.B.A., Saad, M.R.B.M.: Leveraging AI-enabled mobile learning platforms to enhance the effectiveness of English teaching in universities. Sci. Rep. **15**(1) (2025). https://doi.org/10.1038/s41598-025-00801-0

Gutiérrez, J.C.G., Chiappe, A., Rodríguez, D.F.B., González-Pérez, L.I.: The Transformative Journey of Artificial Intelligence Toward Personalized Learning. New Educ. **21**(3), 257–275 (2025). https://doi.org/10.1080/1547688x.2025.2475811

Hernández-Ocampo, S.P., Bejarano, P.A.C., Rodríguez-Uribe, M.: Pre-service English teachers' perceptions of language assessment in a Colombian language teacher education program. Int. J. Educ. Res. Open. **8**, 100405 (2024). https://doi.org/10.1016/j.ijedro.2024.100405

Huang, X., Chalmers, H.: Implementation and Effects of Pedagogical Translanguaging in EFL Classrooms: A Systematic Review [Review of Implementation and Effects of Pedagogical Translanguaging in EFL Classrooms: A Systematic Review]. Language. **8**(3), 194. Multidisciplinary Digital Publishing Institute (2023). https://doi.org/10.3390/languages8030194

Jenner, S., et al.: Using large language models for narrative analysis: a novel application of generative AI. Methods Psychol. **100183** (2025). https://doi.org/10.1016/j.metip.2025.100183

Jian, M.J.K.O.: Personalized learning through AI. Adv. Eng. Innovation. **5**(1), 16 (2023). https://doi.org/10.54254/2977-3903/5/2023039

Jin, S.: Optimizing English teaching: ARCS motivation model and task-based language teaching in university. Learn. Motiv. **87**, 102028 (2024). https://doi.org/10.1016/j.lmot.2024.102028

Jürgensmeier, L., Skiera, B.: Generative AI for scalable feedback to multimodal exercises. Int. J. Res. Mark. **41**(3), 468 (2024). https://doi.org/10.1016/j.ijresmar.2024.05.005

Khoiriah, Suyatna, A., Abdurrahman, A., Jalmo, T.: Communication skills in learning: an integrative review. In: Advances in Social Science, Education and Humanities Research, p. 365. Atlantis Press (2023). https://doi.org/10.2991/978-2-38476-060-2_33

Khoso, A.K., Hong-gang, W., Darazi, M.A.: Empowering creativity and engagement: The impact of generative artificial intelligence usage on Chines EFL students' language learning experience. Comput. Hum. Behav. Rep. **18**, 100627 (2025). https://doi.org/10.1016/j.chbr.2025.100627

Lan, M., Zhou, X.: A qualitative systematic review on AI empowered self-regulated learning in higher education. Npj Sci. Learn. **10**(1), 21 (2025). https://doi.org/10.1038/s41539-025-00319-0

Lee, S.Y., Kim, J.: Toward optimal second language acquisition and proficiency: Addressing limited exposure and educational inequality in EFL contexts through home-based approaches and interdisciplinary insights. Ampersand. **15**, 100226 (2025). https://doi.org/10.1016/j.amper.2025.100226

Liao, C., Wu, J.: Deploying multimodal learning analytics models to explore the impact of digital distraction and peer learning on student performance. Comput. Educ. **190**, 104599 (2022). https://doi.org/10.1016/j.compedu.2022.104599

Lin, C., Zhou, K., Li, L., Sun, L.: Integrating generative AI into digital multimodal composition: A study of multicultural second-language classrooms. Comput. Compos. **75**, 102895 (2024). https://doi.org/10.1016/j.compcom.2024.102895

Lin, H., Qiu, C.: Artificial intelligence (AI) -integrated educational applications and college students' creativity and academic emotions: students and teachers' perceptions and attitudes. BMC Psych. **12**(1), 487 (2024). https://doi.org/10.1186/s40359-024-01979-0

Liu, T., Zhang, Z.: Language teachers as pedagogical designers in technology-mediated language education. System. **131**, 103662 (2025). https://doi.org/10.1016/j.system.2025.103662

Llompart, M., Kenanidis, P.: Psycholinguistics and additional language acquisition. In: Reference Module in Social Sciences. Elsevier eBooks (2025). https://doi.org/10.1016/b978-0-323-95504-1.00445-2

Luan, L., Jing, B., Hong, J., Lin, P.: The mediating effects of online learning engagement on the relationship between Chinese university students' L2 grit and their English language achievement. System. **131**, 103689 (2025). https://doi.org/10.1016/j.system.2025.103689

Maiti, M., Priyaadharshini, M.: Evaluation of the experiences of learners and facilitators with ICT within the realm of higher education. Cogent Education. **11**(1), 2355377 (2024). https://doi.org/10.1080/2331186x.2024.2355377

Mendes, R., Veloso, A.I.: Digital multitasking during academic lectures: Did the Covid-19 lockdown change the students' behavior? In: 8th International Conference on Higher Education Advances (HEAd'22), p. 455. Universitat Politècnica de València, València (2023). https://doi.org/10.4995/head23.2023.16278

Mo, Z., Crosthwaite, P.: Exploring the affordances of generative AI large language models for stance and engagement in academic writing. J. Engl. Acad. Purp. **75**, 101499 (2025). https://doi.org/10.1016/j.jeap.2025.101499

Moats, D., Ganguly, C.: Bringing AI participation down to scale. Patterns. **6**(5), 101241 (2025). https://doi.org/10.1016/j.patter.2025.101241

Mohammadi, M., Tajik, E., Martínez-Maldonado, R., Sadiq, S., Tomaszewski, W., Khosravi, H.: Artificial intelligence in multimodal learning analytics: A systematic literature review. Comput. Educ. Artif. Intell. **8**, 100426 (2025). https://doi.org/10.1016/j.caeai.2025.100426

Mpofu, N., Maphalala, M.C.: English language skills for disciplinary purposes: What practices are used to prepare student teachers? S. Afr. J. Educ. **41**(1), 1 1867 (2021) https://doi.org/10.15700/saje.v41n1a1867

Nguyen, H.T.M., Nguyen, H.T.T., Gilanyi, L., Hoang, T.H., Gao, X.: Content Language Integrated Learning (CLIL): Teachers' metacognitive understanding of pedagogical translanguaging. Learn. Instr. **97**, 102085 (2025). https://doi.org/10.1016/j.learninstruc.2025.102085

Noroozi, O., Alikhani, I., Järvelä, S., Kirschner, P.A., Juuso, I., Seppänen, T.: Multimodal data to design visual learning analytics for understanding regulation of learning. Comput. Hum. Behav. **100**, 298 (2018). https://doi.org/10.1016/j.chb.2018.12.019

Norrman, G.: Reconceptualizing the critical period hypothesis for second language acquisition: An appraisal of Lenneberg's work on the epigenesis of language. Lang. Sci. **105**, 101645 (2024). https://doi.org/10.1016/j.langsci.2024.101645

Özdemir, O., Seçkin, H.: Exploring foreign language anxiety in higher education: Multifaceted insights into causes, impacts, and coping strategies. Soc. Sci. Humanit. Open. **11**, 101364 (2025). https://doi.org/10.1016/j.ssaho.2025.101364

Özdil, B.M., Debreli, E.: Exploring language teacher roles at a higher education context through the lens of critical pedagogy: Transmission or transformation? System. **130**, 103613 (2025). https://doi.org/10.1016/j.system.2025.103613

Pérez-Jorge, D., Olmos-Raya, E., Contreras, A.I.G., Pérez, I.P.: Technologies applied to education in the learning of English as a second language. Front. Educ. **10** (2025). https://doi.org/10.3389/feduc.2025.1481708

Phua, J.T.K., Neo, H.F., Teo, C.-C.: Evaluating the impact of artificial intelligence tools on enhancing student academic performance: Efficacy amidst security and privacy concerns. Big Data Cogn. Comput. **9**(5), 131 (2025). https://doi.org/10.3390/bdcc9050131

Pituxcoosuvarn, M., Tanimura, M., Murakami, Y., White, J.: Enhancing EFL speaking skills with AI-powered word guessing: A comparison of human and AI partners. Information. **16**(6), 427 (2025). https://doi.org/10.3390/info16060427

Proroković, J., Malenica, F.: Language corpora and first language acquisition—A case study of the ditransitive construction. Appl. Corpus Linguist. **3**(1), 100041 (2023). https://doi.org/10.1016/j.acorp.2023.100041

Qiao, J., Li, X., Gao, C., Wu, L., Feng, J., Wang, Z.: Improving multimodal fake news detection by leveraging cross-modal content correlation. Inf. Process. Manag. **62**(5), 104120 (2025). https://doi.org/10.1016/j.ipm.2025.104120

Rahimi, A.R., Sheyhkholeslami, M., Pour, A.M.: Uncovering personalized L2 motivation and self-regulation in ChatGPT-assisted language learning: A hybrid PLS-SEM-ANN approach. Comput. Hum. Behav. Rep. **17**, 100539 (2024). https://doi.org/10.1016/j.chbr.2024.100539

Rowland, C.F., Westermann, G., Theakston, A., Pine, J.M., Monaghan, P., Lieven, E.: Constructing language: a framework for explaining acquisition. Trends Cogn. Sci. **30**, 26–39 (2025). https://doi.org/10.1016/j.tics.2025.05.015

Shoval, D.H.: artificial intelligence in higher education: Bridging or widening the gap for diverse student populations? Educ. Sci. **15**(5), 637 (2025). https://doi.org/10.3390/educsci15050637

Sulis, G.: Exploring the dynamics of engagement in the language classroom: A critical examination of methodological approaches. Res. Methods Appl. Linguist. **3**(3), 100162 (2024). https://doi.org/10.1016/j.rmal.2024.100162

Sun, J., Wang, Y.: Fuzzy-set qualitative comparative analysis (fsQCA) in second language acquisition: An applied example of writing engagement. Res. Methods Appl. Linguist. **4**(1), 100193 (2025). https://doi.org/10.1016/j.rmal.2025.100193

Tafazoli, D.: Exploring the potential of generative AI in democratizing English language education. Comput. Educ. Artif. Intell. **7**, 100275 (2024). https://doi.org/10.1016/j.caeai.2024.100275

Taylor, L., Pill, J.: Language testing and assessment in society. Reference Module in Social Sciences Elsevier eBooks. (2025). https://doi.org/10.1016/b978-0-323-95504-1.00580-9

Tian, Z., Zhang, H., Wang, Y.: Personalised soft prompt tuning in pre-trained language models: Bridging multitask transfer learning and crowdsourcing learning. Knowl.-Based Syst. **305**, 112646 (2024). https://doi.org/10.1016/j.knosys.2024.112646

Tiwari, H.P.: Artificial intelligence in the classroom: revolutionizing English language teaching. J. Engl. Teach. Linguist. Stud. (JET Li). **6**(1), 42 (2024) https://doi.org/10.55215/jetli.v6i1.9757

Waheed, S., Pilotti, M., Abdelsalam, H.: Am I prepared for Calculus? An action-research study of female students emerging from patriarchy. Front. Educ. **9**, 1405571 (2024). https://doi.org/10.3389/feduc.2024.1405571

Wang, X., Lee, C.P., Mutlu, B.: LearnMate: Enhancing online education with LLM-powered personalized learning plans and support. **1** (2025). https://doi.org/10.1145/3706599.3719857

Wei, L.: Artificial intelligence in language instruction: impact on English learning achievement, L2 motivation, and self-regulated learning. Front. Psychol. **14**, 1261955 (2023). https://doi.org/10.3389/fpsyg.2023.1261955

Wiboolyasarin, W., Wiboolyasarin, K., Tiranant, P., Jinowat, N., Boonyakitanont, P.: AI-driven chatbots in second language education: A systematic review of their efficacy and pedagogical implications. Ampersand. **14**, 100224 (2025). https://doi.org/10.1016/j.amper.2025.100224

Xu, Q., Liu, Y., Li, X.: Unlocking student potential: How AI-driven personalized feedback shapes goal achievement, self-efficacy, and learning engagement through a self-determination lens. Learn. Motiv. **91**, 102138 (2025). https://doi.org/10.1016/j.lmot.2025.102138

Zou, Y.L., Kuek, F., Feng, W., Cheng, X.: Digital learning in the 21st century: Trends, challenges, and innovations in technology integration. Front. Educ. **10**, 1562391 (2025). https://doi.org/10.3389/feduc.2025.1562391

Author Index

© The Editor(s) (if applicable) and The Author(s) 2026
R. Sridaran and S. Priti (Eds.): AI-FCDAC 2025, CCIS 2866, pp. 191–192, 2026.
https://doi.org/10.1007/978-3-032-17300-3

MIX
Papier aus verantwortungsvollen Quellen
Paper from responsible sources
FSC® C105338

If you have any concerns about our products,
you can contact us on
ProductSafety@springernature.com

In case Publisher is established outside the EU,
the EU authorized representative is:
Springer Nature Customer Service Center GmbH
Europaplatz 3, 69115 Heidelberg, Germany

Printed by Libri Plureos GmbH
in Hamburg, Germany